MW01172618

The Bury My Bones Series:

Civil War Ghosts of Connecticut

Civil War Ghosts of Georgia: Volume 1

Civil War Ghosts of Georgia: Volume 2

Other Books by Courtney McInvale:

Haunted Mystic

Revolutionary War Ghosts of Connecticut

Courtney McInvale

First Edition:
First printing

Photos by Courtney McInvale unless otherwise indicated.

PUBLISHED BY HAUNTED ROAD MEDIA, LLC
www.hauntedroadmedia.com

Cleveland, Ohio
United States of America

First to my dad, John McInvale for instilling in me a love of history, a fascination with the Civil War and for helping to set me forward on this path. You taught me pride in my Southern culture, my Georgia ancestry and the importance of the Civil War. From the chess and war strategy and the history books as my bedtime stories, this seems a path that was set for me, directly under your influence. Thank you for impacting my life in such a way, and I could not think of a person that this book could be more aptly dedicated to. I love you and miss you.

To my Aunt, Jeanine McInvale who passed away just after I told her I would be working on this book but for years prior always stayed up late nights talking history, genealogy and traversing through cemeteries with me to keep the spirit of family history alive, I miss you and know you were on every step of this journey with me.

And to the Jeffers brothers of Macon, who came to make themselves known in Rose Hill Cemetery years ago and set me forward on a path to investigate the ghosts of Georgia in the War between the States while paying close attention to the brotherhoods that were a part of it, thank you for your service and your inspiration.

This book is for all of you and all whose legacy is shared within these pages

ACKNOWLEDGMENTS

A book filled with history and mystery would not be possible without the knowledge and support of historians, Civil War enthusiasts, park rangers, museum docents, paranormal investigators, family, friends, colleagues and more. To look at the stories of the lives of the Civil War men of Georgia, the battle-hardened grounds upon which they fought and to grasp as much information as possible from all of it is something that I had an incredible amount of support with. I was filled with knowledge because of other's people hard work and study that they shared with me.

I would like to acknowledge and thank first, my husband, Marty who traversed battlefields across the East Coast and across every corner of Georgia, from hidden burials to forts, from battlefield to museum, whether four hours from where we woke up in the morning or nine, he never complained about going to visit Civil War sites and often did the driving. His support of my rabbit hole into history is immeasurable and I couldn't have done it without him. Not to mention, he is always behind the scenes explaining battle lines and flanking maneuvers to me in language that somehow makes me fully grasp what I am looking at.

To my sister, Shelby McInvale who came to Georgia with me not just once, but twice hopping on a plane and open to being wherever I said we were off to next, you are a rockstar. Shelby went to every crazy remote site I could think of – even when it was none of her interest and taught me the importance of meals and snacks while traveling – especially for traveling with her Thank you, Shelby, for coming with me – it made everything more memorable. You are always my PeeWee.

To my sister Savannah and my mom, thank you for listening to my ongoing rants about trying to get all the information on to the page and having a nervous breakdown thinking I never would be able to get this book done in time – your support, belief and encouragement got me through to the end of this book and I am so eternally grateful that you did not allow me to give up on this journey.

Then, of course, I would like to thank my Georgia family. For this book, I went to my dad's home state and with him having passed and taken so much knowledge to the other side with him, I relied upon my family of aunts, uncles and cousins to host me and travel with me, ghost hunting on battlefields, cemeteries and more – and I must have the most amazing family in the world because – not a single one of them questioned it all and we made a family mission out of history and mystery on multiple visits. To my cousins, Ryan Watson, David Googe, Jennifer Flores, and TJ Jones, thank for exploring the craziness of the other side with me – I can't wait to have more adventures with you. To Ryan, your introduction to the Barnesville Train Crash opened the untold stories of this war in Georgia and I can't thank you enough for sharing it with me and walking those tracks to find the dead. To my Aunt and Uncle, Susan & Donnie Watson for opening your home to me as a home base as I traversed across Georgia, I can't thank you enough. It was truly my home away from home. To my Uncle Morton and Aunt Debra McInvale - thank you for answering my questions of history over family lunches and holiday parties – and being open to my Civil War deep dive at any time.

To my dad, who taught me all about the rebels as a young girl and started the seeds of inspiration when I was so young, thank you – I miss you always and hope you enjoy watching me traverse the history you valued so much as you watch from above. Your influence is felt every day. And sometimes, I'm quite confident, you're standing on those battlefields with me and the soldiers.

To my publisher and colleague, Mike Ricksecker – your patience and your support of this crazy dream of mine to follow soldiers through the Civil War in a series of books is a blessing. I cannot state how much, I appreciate the confidence that you have put in me to share the stories of the dead. It has truly been the greatest opportunity imaginable. I am very lucky to be working with such a professional, knowledgeable, and truly good person as you. It's an honor to be on this journey together with Haunted Road Media.

To Sierra Little, for holding down the fort at Seaside Shadows and making sure that tours run seamlessly while I'm immersed in 19th century warfare, I can't thank you enough. Not to mention, taking care of the fur babies while I was away – I could not have done a thing without your assistance.

As to the state of Georgia – I could not have asked for a more welcoming state than the Peach State – no matter where I went, I met the nicest and most accommodating people at every museum, park, battlefield, bookstore and more.

To Richard Pilcher, of the Longstreet Society, thank you for opening up the museum to me and sharing an entire day's worth of stories with me when you were otherwise closed. The information I learned about the Old War Horse was nothing I could have gotten from the history books – and the ghost stories are incomparable.

To Lee White, Park Ranger at Chickamauga & Chattanooga National Battlefield, thank you for telling me the truth about legends and lore, debunking myths, and sending me to the most fascinating sites on the battlefield for exploration, including a beautiful witness tree. And thank you for always being open to any crazy questions that came up later.

To Marie Maquar at the Chickamauga & Chattanooga NMP Park Store for introducing me to the Ambrose Bierce accounts and finding every first-hand account possible for me to comprehend the site, thank you.

To Teri Suber, Ranger and Park Guide at Andersonville National Park, thank you for speaking with me about the Georgia guards and the role of Georgia Reserves at the Prison camp, the conditions of their life and the lesser-known information about Andersonville. That perspective has been immensely helpful.

To all the State Park Rangers at Pickett's Mill Battlefield for opening up your library, your research room, and for talking with me for hours about the secrets of history and ensuring that this site remains protected, Thank you. A special shout out, especially to Ranger John who gave me more historic stories than my brain knew what to do with – I never felt fuller than when I left there!

To Tim Mosely, from Middle Georgia Haunted History for the long calls, late night texts and wealth of blog information about legends, lore and more. Your respect for history and embrace of the supernatural immediately stood out in our conversations – you are a professional and kindred spirit. I can't wait to work together more.

To the staff at the Marietta History Center, for opening up your archives to me and allowing me to read the original articles pertinent to the old hotel, the locomotive chase and the deserters and sharing your ghostly legends with me, thank you.

To John Hughes, of the Jefferson Davis Memorial Capture Site, thank you for opening your doors to the whole family and answering all of our questions – you are a wealth of information.

To the kind librarians at the Lafayette-Walker County Public Library for setting up shop for me in your history room and allowing me to talk with you all about the history of the region and go through your amazing collection – my favorite stories came from your archives, and I hope they get to stay there for many more generations to come.

To everyone at Fort McAllister, Fort James Jackson, Green-Meldrim House, Moon River Brewing Company and Marshall House – thank you for sharing the tales of Civil War Savannah with me – your stories are beyond incredible and the sites you host, ones I dream of visiting time and time and again.

To the people of the town of Andersonville, for opening up all your shops and museums to me and not batting an eye when I mentioned spirits – but instead sharing all your curious tales and photographs with me, thank you.

To Jacob Martz, Vice Mayor of Sharpsburg, thank you for sharing your local knowledge, historic gems and primary source documents – every time I think Antietam couldn't have more information hidden in her depths, I am wrong and you have done incredible research to paint an even broader picture for me.

To Mark Lemon, for sharing the portraits, stories and heart of your great-great Grandfather, Captain Lemon with me – your love for your ancestral home and those in your family who made such a change in the world is an inspiration for all of us – to care for our ancestors the way you care for yours. Thank you for your quick responses and your incredible insight.

To Audra Warren of Andersonville for her amazing stories, photographs and enthusiasm, your input made the spirit of Andersonville town come alive with stories.

To Vernon House, for sharing photos and stories of the 27th and your personal collection that touched my heart, thank you.

To my Airbnb hosts, who often made sure I had Civil War books and notes upon arrival at my sites and ensured I got everything I needed, thank you.

To the band, Whiskey Myers, thank you again for your songs of incredible influence and for having a song such as "*Bury My Bones*" to touch truly on the story of the soldiers and their need for peace and coming home. And a special thank you for the concerts I attended on my travels -- they were the brain break one needed after being immersed in such a historical period of conflict.

And most importantly, thank you to the soldiers, officers, and infantrymen alike for your service. Thank you for sharing your stories from the other side, for touching my heart, for inspiring me with your resilience of human spirit and allowing me to learn from your most profound lives. My life has always felt intertwined with those who came before me and I feel at this point, these incredible soldiers have become my spiritual family and I would be lost without them.

TABLE OF CONTENTS

PREFACE

A couple of years ago when I began my journey to write about the Civil War as it relates to my home state of Connecticut, I had to take an interesting step back to look at a state that had no battles take place on its land during the war between the states and decide how to address the spirits of those 55,000 Connecticut men who served during the war in an alternate way. The answer hit me like an epiphany – follow the soldiers, share THEIR stories from home to battlefield and what they endured. But how do you pick a soldier out of 55,000? It's simple, really. You don't. They pick you – they let you know in one way shape or form that their story must be shared. From Generals to Privates, I followed the stories of several men and regiments across the battlegrounds of the war to share their stories. Suffice to say, in this journey throughout Connecticut in the war, I realized I was only scratching the surface of the impact of the Civil War and the people within it. There were more sites and people who had to have their story shared and whose spirits yearned for it.

Connecticut is the state in which I was born and raised in a small, rural town in the "middle of nowhere." Connecticut was home to my mother's family since their arrival in the post-Civil War, post-Irish famine era. It is where I run a tour company, where I'm restoring a historic home with my husband and where I have posted my roots – as much as a Libra can have roots, for most years of my life. But – and this is a big but – my father was from Macon, Georgia, born and raised his whole life with his family having settled in the Deep South region in the mid-1700's. The rebel roots run deep in my bloodline and in the culture I was raised in with my father. Growing up, we had annual trips to Georgia and my dad made sure it was priority number one to educate me on the Deep South's history. Heck, I could even identify most Civil War generals at an early age by mere beard recognition due to his enthusiasm on the matter and the number of books he exposed me to on the topic.

So here I was, knowing that my journey through the Civil War had only just begun – I felt a strong calling to the battlefields and gravesites of the men who gave their lives for their home and I knew there was so much more to share so that their sacrifices would never be forgotten.

What would be the next best move? I wondered. Was this my calling? Had I gone right back to square one when I was little girl studying the war in my dad's books? Was my purpose to uncover the stories of these men to ensure their immortality in a way? That's a lot to consider. Nevertheless, I knew it was my passion and I felt my own sense of duty to these people of the 19th century. We often watch history get dismissed around us as insignificant or irrelevant to our modern-day life and it couldn't be more the opposite.

Looking at the history of America, the time period where most Americans died in war is unequivocally, the American Civil War – a four-year period where nearly three-quarters of a million casualties took place in our developing nation. Of course, they were all American, a war of brother vs. brother and a time period that influences our modern landscape every day.

To understand the war and its relevance, one must look at the people just as I had started doing before. And in order, to get the full picture one must look at the people on both sides and share the human stories of what brought them to war. So, I reflected on my past, on all of this and I said, okay, we're going to go through the war, through Union states, Confederate states and split states and share the stories of those from each and the places in each. And given, my own personal background and ancestry, the next state I would choose was obvious – the Peach State, the Goober State – Georgia.

And what of the spirits? The ghosts? I confess, my journey through these books has redefined my definition of a ghost, or a spirit as it were and what it means to encounter one. Have I stopped believing? No. Perhaps, I believe more than I ever did going in in the eternity of the human soul and their ability to share their stories from the next realm. But I believe what we define as a ghost or a spirit has to be more evolved. Those of us, who are interested in and believe in some sort of afterlife, often conclude that the afterlife is filled with the people who came before us and have passed on from their earthly vessel. Operating under this theory, that spirits are people like me or you, in their soul form, I believe we can connect with them in the most unique ways, especially when it comes to wartime in 19th century America. We can feel the impact of what they did, where they were, what they fought for coming from their stomping grounds, the battlefields, and their descendants. We can see their faces on those who have passionately dedicated their lives to their history. We can hear their echoes from the past not just figuratively, but literally as we step onto hallowed grounds. And we can appreciate the stories of their coming through to make themselves known in a traditional sense.

There are spectral stories to be included but also stories of heart, stories of truth – and looking at Civil War America, I encourage you to remember, nothing is more haunting than the truth.

This will be a historic and spiritual journey intertwined together throughout the 19th century in the heart of the Deep South. And due to the aforementioned influences, this journey into the Deep South will be a Confederate state that was inspired by my family roots. Georgia has become the home of *Bury my Bones, Volume 2.* Georgia is a change from the first book in the series, in that Georgia boasts home to several battlefields and the second largest battle in the entirety of the Civil War. This means that this has become a book of people *and* places together.

I look forward to bringing you, the reader on this adventure with me to meet the spirits of Civil War Georgia on our first series look into the rebels of the Confederacy and the stories they have left behind.

INTRODUCTION

The Bury My Bones Series & The Civil War Ghosts of Georgia

Welcome to the Peach State. In fact, one of the sweetest things to come from the Civil War was the fame and distribution of that delightful fruit. Civil War soldiers from other states would pick peaches while in encampments and near battle sites and fell in love with the flavor and wanted to be able to have some peaches at home as well. How divine! At the end of the war when the "New South" was being developed in absence of cotton plantations, the peach plantations took over! The Georgia Peach, a ripened peach, specifically is kind of a perfect metaphor for Georgia during the war – a place that was bittersweet. There were incredible soldiers and leaders, some of the best. There were beautiful mountains, flowing rivers, burgeoning rail lines, Southern belles and Southern gentlemen, farmers who worked hard and a landscape like no other – sweet, almost perfect. But under the surface there was poverty, fear and slavery that was seeping out and that would continue to affect a wrought involuntary, industrial Georgia in post-war America.

Georgia was considered part of the Deep South, the line starting at South Carolina and including their neighbors of Alabama, Mississippi, and Louisiana – today it still holds its title of being in the Deep South. Georgia would be the fifth state to declare their secession from Union, mere days after Alabama and Florida, just over a week after Mississippi and about a month after South Carolina. They would declare before six other Southern states and months before the attack of Fort Sumter in 1861. The attack on Fort Sumter prompted several more states to declare their secession for a total of 11. Part of the original seven states that seceded, Georgia was present at the creation of the Confederate States of America under the leadership of Jefferson Davis. (Of note, Jefferson Davis was elected President of the Confederate States, however, he did run without opposition.) Georgia was also part of the Western Theater as was anything south of Virginia during the American Civil War – which is a bit strange for some of us to imagine as it is definitively on the East Coast. The Peach State had approximately 120,000 soldiers fight for the Confederacy. One of 11 Confederate States, Georgia supplied nearly 20% of the men who fought for the Confederacy. It is estimated that near 21% of the 120,000 died during the war on a battlefield or in a hospital followed up by countless more in the years that would follow succumbing to their weakened state of wound or disease. Over two-dozen battles raged on Georgia soil during the war – 27 full-scale battles to be exact. However, there would be 550 battles and skirmishes recorded in total within the state. All these numbers include the second most major battle in Civil War history happening in Georgia – the Battle of Chickamauga occurring just months after Gettysburg in September of 1863.

The stories of thousands of people, hundreds of events and more run down the banks of the Chattahoochee River and up the slopes of Lookout Mountain, from the rural farmlands of South

Georgia to the sea of Savannah. From Ambrose Bierce's horrifying accounts in the Atlanta Campaign to the tales of Sherman's March to the Sea, Georgia is haunted across the state by its role in the Civil War. Defeats and Victories cover the Georgia landscape and the men of Georgia could be found at times fighting at home, or guarding the hell-hole of the south in the prison camp known as Andersonville, but more often than not if they weren't at home fighting, the Georgia rebel boys would be found up in the Eastern Theater in the bloody battles of Virginia.

Together, we will follow the men of Georgia through their home state and beyond. I have traveled to dozens of battle sites, graves and more across the coast and throughout Georgia to meet the spirits of the men who never made it home to their homes and families.

PART I

BATTLEFIELDS

Chickamauga

"River of Death"

How does one convey the gravity of what happened at Chickamauga – the death, the confusion, the landscape, the pivotal moment as the war raged on the borders to the Deep South? The Battle of Chickamauga is the deadliest battle in the entirety of the Western Theater of the Civil War and the second deadliest in the entire Civil War. To put this in perspective, the only casualty count that outnumbered Chickamauga was the casualty count at Gettysburg. Estimated casualties for the battle of Chickamauga are just under 35,000. The Confederate casualty count did outnumber the Union by a couple thousand despite their decisive victory. It should be noted, however, that Confederates were estimated to have about 65,000 troops present to the Union's 60,000 on those brisk September days of 1863.

Today, you can visit these hallowed grounds and experience the haunting history yourself. Just south of Chattanooga, this became the nation's first national military park in August of 1890, and dedicated in September 1895 with many veterans in attendance. Chickamauga's location in Northwest Georgia is still a national park and shares the immensely important stories of the lives that were lost here and the tale of the war between states making its way on to the border of America's heartland.

The Gateway to the Deep South was considered Chattanooga, the neighbor to Chickamauga, both settled upon the foot of the beautiful Lookout Mountain marking the border between Georgia and Tennessee. The region became rife with conflict as the Union tried to cut the Confederates off in their heartland and the Confederates worked to use a difficult landscape and terrain, they had familiarity with to gain the upper hand on the Yankees who would be out of their element.

Though a breathtaking landscape, it had long been associated with death even before the Civil War. Local legend states that in a regional dialect of the Cherokee tribe, Chickamauga translated directly to "River of Death." In fact, it is believed that the Cherokee found that when camping near the scenic creek, they would find themselves quite sick. The Trail of Tears ran right along Chickamauga creek causing the deaths of many Native Americans who would come to think of this area as cursed – the entrance of smallpox, the air of death would come around this wooded landscape that was not favorable for humans. Just 13 years after the conclusion of the Trail of Tears, the battle took place on these hallowed grounds and then the Spanish-American war took with a camp right on the Chickamauga creek years later and becoming an epicenter for typhoid fever and malaria.

Perhaps the spirit of Chickamauga has always been trying to warn people that this was a place doomed to be at the crosshairs of human's inevitable fate with death, time and time again. Admittedly, it's hard to believe such a thing to be true when you first walk through the beautiful cedar groves and tall oaks that line the battle region that anything too sinister could be behind them. You can watch the deer gallivant quietly and hear the birds singing in the distance, but even they, on occasion, grow somber, stare forward into the distance as they, too, know that something looms, an energy of sorts. There is a gloom there even on a sunny day with what comes in waves as an overpowering sense of sadness tinged with exhaustion and fear. Unshakeable is the sense of being watched. Centuries of legends and stories abound on these grounds. However, the fate of tens of thousands being decided on this land may be perhaps the most haunting of them all.

Georgia Monument at Chickamauga, 2022

After the Battle of Chickamauga, in fact, almost immediately after the war, locals and others began to tell tales of the battle they still heard raging on the site, of the moaning and cries for help they could hear echoing through the woods and fields that were once serving as a bloody carpet of remains. In fact, some accounts say for years after the battle, the blood ran from the trees every single September night, commemorating the anniversary month in a macabre reminder from beyond and creating an absolute horrific landscape. *The Macon News* reported in 1913 what was reported at the 1890 Confederate Reunion as well,

> "Down in north Georgia, below the battlefield of Chickamauga, many of the older generation of negroes, if not some whites, have no business that leads them through Chickamauga Park at night. An old negro man, formerly a slave in the family of Congressman Gordon Lee of Georgia, but who held on to his best friends until he died, used to declare during the month of September, "the trees drip blood" in Chickamauga Park and that ghosts walk there every night. He would drive five miles out of his way to escape a trip through the battlefield after dark."

The authors of this almost seem to imply that if the Black population reports it, maybe it's just superstition that they can't entertain – but why write it, repeat it – the authors and all those in region felt and believed the same. The truth was, they all knew what had happened at Chickamauga and everyone who went there couldn't help but feel that palpable energy. It's an overpowering sense that surrounds the Chickamauga battle sites. Confederate General John B. Gordon, he probably believed it too. You see, he had a near-death, and rather out of body experience at the Battle of Antietam in Sharpsburg, MD and that Georgia native was never the same after that. He reconciled in his memoirs that nothing challenged the Battle of Antietam's horrid deadliness more than the Battle of Chickamauga, writing graphically,

> "At Chickamauga, thousands fell on both sides fighting at close quarters, their faces at times burnt by the blazing powder at the very muzzles of their guns…"

But we'll get back to General Gordon in more detail to follow.

Woods of Chickamauga, 2022

Truly, the smell of death lingered for decades among the area, the smell of rotting corpses whose remains were left on site for varied amounts of time to decompose in the warm Georgia sun. That's an odor that came to stain the land and the memories forever after. They say senses are the most sensitive to memory – specifically the sense of smell. The smell of death can't leave a place – and such never can the memory. Even nature remembers – you'll find here and at the location of Andersonville Prison further south, locals will still tell you that the vultures come at the same time each year as if to still scavenge – their winged ancestors having passed on the message. Even, the wild hogs still come looking for something to eat. After the battle, even local hunters, would not eat or hunt the hogs because they knew they had been eating the dead and they could not fathom consuming the people themselves which, surely, they would by consuming a hog. The lumberyards rejected the trees from Chickamauga site, leaving the growth around them instead to hold the memories. They said the shell and shot stuck in the trees broke their machinery and still the blood and death on top of that was too much to bear. "Don't send us those trees from Chickamauga," they would heartily repeat.

One soldier recounted,

> "For years afterwards, the battleground of old Chickamauga shone like bright moonlight, even on the darkest night. The bones resembled piles of phosphorus or fox-fire that lighted the dark woods."

So, what on earth happened in that battle of mid-September of 1863 that would lead to the famous carpet of bodies referenced by so many? What led to the tales of the dead taking care of themselves as there were no burials as they became forever some part of the landscape?

At this time in the Civil War, is perhaps when we are seeing some of the most catastrophic of battles – the highest casualty counts, the carnage, bloodshed and violence paired with exhaustion, weariness, and trauma from having been in this war for years at this point and coming to the terms that there was no end in sight. Would the war end when there were no more people left to fight it? I'm sure this was something many soldiers came to ponder.

Confederate Veteran and Judge C.W. Heiskell of Memphis spoke to veterans of the Chattanooga Campaign on the battlefield in July of 1890 and set the scene for the hallowed ground in his reunion speech,

> "The ground upon which you stand is consecrated by the best blood of the South and of the Northwest. It is scarce a stretch of fancy to say that every sod beneath your feet is a soldier's sepulcher and that the

> grass above them is enriched by the blood of the brave and sanctified by the tears of their mothers and loved ones ... Upon this hallowed spot twenty-seven years ago was fought one of the greatest battles of all history, 120,000 men, sons of the South and of the North was a battle of giants and when it was done, over 30,000 killed and wounded attested its gigantic proportions."

By the early autumn of 1863, the Confederates were coming to terms with their losses in the Western Theater, quite recently at Vicksburg, and of course in the Eastern Theater at Gettysburg. Skirmishes and small battles had taken place in northwest Georgia prior to this and up into Tennessee at Chattanooga already – thus initiating what was known as the Chickamauga campaign which was ultimately defined by the penultimate battle of that name and location. *The Weekly Columbus Enquirer*, pled with the citizens of Georgia to let them know, that the war was coming to their doorstep however, it was anything but over.

> "The late serious disasters to our arms (Confederate) at Vicksburg and Port Hudson, together with General Bragg's retreat with his army to our very borders, while they are no cause of despair of our ultimate success, if we are true to ourselves and will place our trust in God, admonish us if we would protect our homes from the ravages of the enemy, it is time for every Georgia able to bear arms to unite himself without delay to a military organization, and hold himself in readiness at a moment's warning to strike for his home and the graves of his ancestors, with an unalterable determination to die free rather than live the slave of despotic power."

That call came out in late July of 1863, following the loss at Gettysburg.

Indeed, the war was coming into Georgia swiftly and by late summer of 1863, there was the aforementioned fighting around northwest Georgia. The Second Battle of Chattanooga on August 21, 1863, involved Union Light artillery shelling the town and sinking two steamers and upsetting the locals on a day of peace, in southeast Tennessee. A couple weeks later and just a week before The Battle of Chickamauga in northwest Georgia near Dade and Walker County, there was the Battle of Davis's Crossroads with 12,000 Confederates engaged and 8,000 Union, but the engagement did, luckily, come with minimal casualty counts. Union General Thomas was preparing to move into Lafayette, Georgia, to pursue General Bragg and his army located there.

Communication failures led Union General Rosecrans to think Bragg was in Dalton further south and when the Union went in separate directions, Bragg was open to attack. Bragg sent Generals Hindman and Cleburne forward, but they determined it was not suitable attack conditions as they had prepared. In sum, the battle was an aborted attempt at battle.

Movements for Chickamauga had begun. The Confederates wanted to consider any chance at resuming some of their victories early in the war and as such they had to be clever in their movements. Lincoln was looking to secure a quick end to the war and knew that the supply lines running through Chattanooga would be the beginning of the end for the secessionists if they could be cut off. General Rosecrans, who has been having successes of his own oversaw the initial Union maneuver to gain control and Confederate General Braxton Bragg was in charge of the Confederate Army in the neighboring Chickamauga and Chattanooga Campaigns. This came with some great hesitancy from Georgia's own General Longstreet ... a hesitancy which led to great division after the battle of Chickamauga. Though ultimately, it was a Confederate victory, the battle itself was disastrously deadly and filled with tactical mistakes. One thing that set Chickamauga apart is the proximity of the violence toward one another compared to any other battle in the war. For the majority of this battle, one day setting the scene and two days back and forth pushing lines across the now clear and well-traveled marker known as Lafayette Road, these men were as close as one can imagine to each other, engaging in hand-to-hand combat and taking part in the bloodiest and most haunting type of warfare imaginable.

Prior to the battle, Bragg's troops that had been sent to Vicksburg were returned to him – movements were being made by Bragg to go forward with his plan and gain troops in time for Chickamauga. The soldiers in the Eastern Theater Army of the Potomac were on an offensive break after defeat at Gettysburg and Chancellorsville. As such, the Confederates took advantage of their home base and General James Longstreet and over 12,000 men from the Army of Northern Virginia headed toward Georgia. It took them just over a week to arrive. Because of rail line blockages only about half (approximately 6,000) of Longstreet's men and Longstreet himself made it on their 550-mile journey to northwest Georgia. In the days and weeks prior to the battle, beginning in August, the Union had been begun stationing around Chattanooga and west of Lookout Mountain pushing the rebels to go south of Chattanooga to Lafayette, Georgia by the 8th of September that year. As such, Bragg thought it would be a good plan to fake them out and make them think that he was not going to stop at Chattanooga with his army but rather head to Atlanta. Rosecrans was delighted by this intelligence that was falsely planted and began to spread his armies in three different directions, swiftly and effectively taking over the region. Bragg, however, did not act swiftly enough on his plan. By waiting to move forward in the second part of enacting his agenda to push the Union north out of the valley with an advance reaching West Chickamauga, his plan that would have once been an easy victory for the Confederacy became increasingly headed toward conflict and possible disaster. Theoretically, his plan was solid and would have given good advantage to the Confederates if made in a timely manner whilst the troops were assembling on both sides. That was not the reality that would come to pass.

When the advance was made by Bragg's troops it was described as "sluggish." The troops he depended on were too far away to make it happen quickly and encountered Rosecrans's cavalry earlier than Bragg anticipated. By September 18, Confederate Generals Johnson and Forrest (Forrest equipped with his cavalry) crossed West Chickamauga Creek to attack the Union Line that were forming their left flank by Reed's Bridge. The Confederates were delayed by this. Accordingly, with need to gain forward momentum, General Forrest began a skirmish with Union troops just a mile from the bridge. This would be considered the official start of the Battle of Chickamauga. The fight went on from the early morning hours around 7:30 AM through until the early afternoon. Forrest was ruthless and bodies were likened to being stacked up like cordwood before the Union was pushed back to the bridge where the Union played defense and the Confederate, offense. The Union did their best to get reinforcements (armed with the deadly Spencer repeating rifle) but the reinforcements came from a struggle for the nearby Alexander's Bridge and coming weary, were unable to help their Union brethren in putting off the Confederate Cavalry. Forrest's men pushed the Union over the Bridge. Some Confederates under fire went with them however Forrest continued his attack with canister shot and Forrest's cavalry was able to ford the creek and the Union retreated. Why would canister shot be so decisive, you may wonder? It would cause absolute devastation upon close contact. One soldier, once likened a man hit by canister at close range as to becoming nothing more than

> "pink mist and a pair of shoes"

where he had once stood. Gruesome, grisly … hard to imagine. With that, day one of the battle had ended and this skirmish was a mere tip of the proverbial iceberg for the violence of Chickamauga.

By the end of September 17, the Confederate Generals had received their orders from Bragg for the next day and their skirmishes and movements on the 18th had gotten things in motion for the battle on the 19th. The bridge work and line pushes had begun on both sides. Generals Hill and Hood took control of the far sides of the Confederate line; Hill the left and Hood the right. Hood's Division was the only part of Longstreet's Corps who were present on the 19th. As Bragg tried to get his orders in place, seemingly sluggish in his delivery again, the Union took action. General Thomas attacked the Confederate right near Hood's division before Bragg's Army was ready and the battle plans changed. Forrest's cavalry was met early in the morning by General Thomas's troops and attacked on the road to Reed's Bridge. But Forrest was not alone; backed by two brigades of Confederate infantry. The Confederate and Union lines began their push back and forth, back and forth time and again. Making no gains, and also going back and forth near Reed's Bridge Union, General Baird took a moment to reset and rearrange only to be struck by 2,000 Confederates. It is said that the Union troops receded again

> "as a wave beaten back from the shore."

When they did recede back, the Confederates took over two pivotal batteries. Briefly, the Confederates under General Liddell were feeling victorious before they found themselves face to face with Baird's weary men who rallied and reassembled into a wall that looked impenetrable on the right. They also had more reinforcements and much like the Confederates, at the last minute, the Union Generals were assembling and strengthening forces. Liddell's Confederates came under fierce fire and retreated leaving behind any signs of conquest or victory from earlier. The time was just 11:00 AM when Liddell and his men had retreated. General Bragg tried to order reinforcements, but as seems to be the tale of Chickamauga, the reinforcements by way of General Cheatham were too late, and the Union troops under General Thomas were strengthened once more. Before reinforcement came for the Confederates, the Union was able to assail both flanks and push them back. Even with Cheatham's support, the Confederates were becoming quickly outnumbered, however that added support allowed them to regain their ground. When holes came up in the Confederate line, they were quickly filled. It's important to not leave a hole in the line, that's where the enemy would be set to win, whichever side your enemy may be, they would go for an opening in the line. As the lines fleshed out and hand-to-hand combat ensued, Bragg describes a fight that is "hotly engaged."

Suddenly, the Confederates noticed that anticipating an attack on the left, the Union moved extra troops to the right and changed the entire line. Bragg continued to issue orders to try and prevent this new Union line from getting the upper hand which was not easy.

Some of the deadliest fighting then took place as the day wore into night. The setting was described as one soldier put it

> "The country is mostly level, and is covered with dense forests of oak and pine, interspersed here and there with small cornfields."

But a few of those referenced trees remain for visitors to see today and are called witness trees, some of them just saplings but had witnessed the carnage occur around them.

Bragg stated of his lines,

> "Our right and center were heavily and almost constantly engaged."

Breakthroughs came for the Confederates and were repulsed, back and forth once more. Hood's division fought to drive back the Union all day into the nighttime hours. Hood was encountering Union General Wilder's brigade with the deadly seven-shot Spencer repeating rifle. They fired at each other in perfect line across the Lafayette Road and the adjoining Viniard Field. The Confederates had heavy casualties especially until they were finally repulsed by the Union on that side. When visiting the battlefield, this is perhaps the area with the most sadness, bleakness and energy felt. It's as if you can hear the moaning and cries beneath your feet, imagine the soldiers being left to die with horrifying injuries, still looking for help. Perhaps you get an air of the scent of the dead and dying around you – that would be believable as Sam Watkins of the 1st Tennessee described,

> "Men were lying where they fell, shot in every conceivable part of the body. Some with their entrails torn out and still hanging to them and piled up on the ground beside them, and they still alive. Some with their jaw torn off, and hanging by a fragment of their skin to their cheeks, with their tongues lolling from

> their mouth, and they trying to talk. Some with both eyes shot out, with one eye hanging down on their cheek…"

General Gordon described the scene,

> "The Lafayette Road along or near which the broken lines of each army were rallied and reformed, and across which the surging currents of fire had repeatedly rolled, became the "bloody lane" of Chickamauga."

Ambrose Bierce went on to write a historical fiction short story of Chickamauga inspired by this scene about a young, deaf and mute boy following in the footsteps of the soldiers around Chickamauga, throwing his wooden sword into a blazing fire as if imitating the men he witnessed whilst walking in their footsteps and walking around the men who appeared on the ground sleeping. Bierce then paints a bloody picture – the graphic witnessing of the boy's mother being the victim of the house fire he wandered upon and thew his sword into – and the house his own. A haunting story of the war coming into the home of each and every person in the South, whether they wanted it to or not and affecting them irreversibly so – a war that would leave every person in the country unchanged.

On the evening of the September 19, fighting continued for Cleburne's Division of Hill's Corps on the other side of the Confederate lines. Not quite as deadly as the side for Hood's Division, Cleburne's division was ending up a bit luckier and was able to have a great success with their drive to take the enemy by surprise pushing them nearly a mile out.

Bragg writes that they had intelligence from prisoners that they had seen the Union force by the time night fell. This gave added confidence to Bragg that despite the day's losses. He knew he had more reinforcements on the way and would be able to the thing that had held him back from further success on the 19th because he would have more of what he needed that next day: soldiers. Hood described having absolutely nothing –

> "Nor did my men have a single wagon or even ambulance in which to convey the wounded. They were destitute of almost anything."

The War in Georgia – Battle of Chickamauga, Sep.19 and 20, between Generals Rosecrans and Bragg, 1863 by J.F. Hillen (Library of Congress)

Due to Bragg's "sluggish" start and bridge blocking the uncoordinated efforts, the Confederate Army was pushed back from the Union more than they had anticipated on the 19th. To Bragg's dismay, they had not broken through a Union flank. They had, however, pushed back the line so this was verifying for Bragg, that with more people they could certainly change the battle next day to a clearer victory. Bragg grew even more confident, when Longstreet, himself, and two more brigades arrived. Though Longstreet and Bragg never expressed to be friends, Longstreet was a great tactician, respected by Lee and came with those extra soldiers. Bragg's decision upon receiving these extra troops was to have Confederate army split with a Longstreet and Polk wing accordingly to their army and flanks the next day. Longstreet spoke to General Hood after his arrival around 11:00 PM on the 19th, and looking upon the battle lines with Hood, asked questions. Hood had increasing confidence that they could finish routing the enemy out and despite the deadliness of the day, he was reassured that they had made significant gains in pushing the enemy back.

The night of September 19 grew cold for the injured of both the Union and Confederacy, who according to accounts, laid across Viniard Field where some of the fiercest fighting had taken place, leaving bodies strewn in a "bloody carpet" that could be walked from end to end without ever having touched the ground upon those field. The grounds were also filled with those trying to survive, and those not yet injured wondered how to survive the night in their positions. The two sides were encamped so closely to one another they could not light fires as to give away the position of their encampment and up near the mountains it was so cold, a frost was settling over the air and the ground. One soldier accounted just a week and a half after,

> "That was indeed a night of awful suspense which settled around us after the last gun had been fired on Saturday (the 19th). It was very chilly and cold, and much suffering amongst the wounded was occasioned thereby. Those who were still alive and well, although they were too exposed to the numbing cold, thought but little of their physical condition. True, no warm fires kept the influence of the frost from their limbs,

> for fires were strictly forbidden. No blazing light helped to cheer their minds and dispel gloomy images therefrom. But still as they sank down in the darkness upon the hard, cold ground, they entirely forgot their bodily privations as they strove to imagine what might be the result to themselves, the country and the cause of the gigantic struggle which mighty ensue on the morrow."

Viniard Field Chickamauga, 2022

He hauntingly continued,

> "No tongue can ever tell the yearning of the soldier's heart for friends and home as he lay on the ground that night grasping his musket. Nor pen nor pencil can picture the emotions of his soul as he thought of his mother, wife or children and expected that ere the

> setting of the morrow's sun thousands such as he and he himself, perhaps would have passed beyond the possibility of seeing these dear ones ever again on earth."

He went on to hope that there would be Sabbath on Sunday but history tells us there would not be for him or any others.

General Gordon described equal Confederate suffering,

> "Cleburnes Confederates had waded the river the water to their arm-pits. Their clothing was drenched and their bodies shivering in the chill north wind through the weary hours of the night. ....all over the field lay the unburied dead, their pale faces made ghastlier by streaks of blood and clotted hair, and black stains of powder left upon their lips when they tore off with their teeth the ends of deadly cartridges. Such was the night between the battles of the 19th and 20th of September at Chickamauga.

Once again, on September 20, the Confederates were off to a sluggish start due to a breakdown in communications among the Generals. Bragg claims to have met with all his men dividing assignments after Longstreet's arrival. Longstreet arrived at his line by daylight. Hill's men did not receive orders early enough and Polk and Hill pointed the fingers not at each other but rather at Braxton Bragg. Bragg said,

> "With increasing anxiety and disappointment, I waited until after sunrise without hearing a gun, and at length dispatched a staff officer to Lieutenant General Polk to ascertain the cause

> of the delay and urge him to a prompt and speedy movement."

The men weren't ready and fingers pointed at subordinates and officers alike.

Though at a delay, the Confederates attacked the far right of the Union capturing the Union Field Hospital on Thomas' side and then they met Thomas' Corps head on. They had suffered some losses on their right being repulsed during their time of unpreparedness. There was an hour of fierce and back forth on the Confederate left, the Union's right, before the Confederates were repulsed.

As luck would have it for the Confederates, the Union were mostly woefully uncoordinated early in the day as well and suffered an even bigger lapse in communications that would lead to a tactical failure from Rosecrans' order. In the morning assault, Rosecrans sorted out in his mind that there was a gap in his line, or at least he was convinced there was and ordered General Thomas Wood's division to fill that gap. A gap, as mentioned is a sign of weakness, that the enemy will look for. Wood knew there was no gap and that it would leave the Union vulnerable but wasn't able to defy his generals' orders having already gotten "in trouble" for not responding quickly enough to other orders. As such, he moved to Rosecrans' will and led the position toward a "division-wide" hole.

Longstreet noticed this quickly and with his men, they went to go through the gap. The Union men would state that this was the moment they knew the battle was lost for them and the battle's end had been decided. The Union confirmed they had become an army cut in two. The assault continued in hostility as the Confederates hammered through the woods.

Bragg described the assault as it reached 4:00 PM on the 20th,

Battle of Chickamauga, GA fought on 19th and 20th of September 1863, Library Company of Philadelphia (Wikimedia Commons)

> "The contest was severe, but the impetuous charge of our troops could not be resisted when they brought to bear in full force, even where the enemy possessed all the advantage of position and breastworks."

The Union agreed the aforementioned soldier spoke of the fierce repetition the Confederates brought on the 20th, the Sabbath,

> "Again and again, the rebel lines advanced from the cover of the woods into the open cornfields, charged with impetuous fury and terrific yells toward the breastworks of logs and rails, but each time the fiery blasts from our batteries and battalions swept over and around them, and their ranks were crumbled and swept away as a bank of loose clay washed by a

> rushing flood. But as fast as one line fell off, another appeared, rushing sternly on over the dead and bleeding bodies of their fallen comrades."

Rosecrans himself and his Union troops were pushed off the field, it was a seeming massacre. The Union soldier's account continued,

> "While I stood gazing upon the scene from the summit of the ridge, some rebel skirmishers appeared in the skirts of the woods opposite the gap I have mentioned, and firing perhaps a dozen musket balls into the field. Instantly men, animals, vehicles became a mass of struggling, cursing, frightened life. Everything and everybody appeared to dash headlong for the narrow gap and men, hoses, mules, ambulances, baggage wagons, ammunition wagons, artillery carriages and caissons were rolled and tumbled together in a confused, inextricable and finally motionless mass, completely blocking up the mouth of the gaps. Nearly all this booty subsequently fell into the hands of the enemy. Sickened and disgusted by the spectacle, I turned away to watch the operations of General Thomas' Corps upon which alone depended the safety of the army."

What he is referring to is this … the latter part of the day included a stand off from Major General George Thomas of the Union, who put troops on Horseshoe Ridge and Snodgrass Hill, refusing to leave. He put them in a defensive position, not retreating. The Confederates met a mighty force with the man who became known as "The Rock of Chickamauga" for his immoveable force. They were strong and firm and were able to repulse the rebels for a time despite their weakened ranks having deteriorated around them. But the rebels, as they had been continued to be relentless and the Confederate army assembled with Polk's Corps assisted by Georgia State troops. The Union men began to make peace with their inevitable death for a worthy cause as they watched the rebels gather in number. The violence was a new violence for the day and the advances back and forth continued, the Rock of Chickamauga and his men unwavering, but so were the desperate Confederates, wanting to beat the enemy Yankee out of their home and show they knew the land better. Only few fell back as night came upon them, the men for the union became described as heroes as the assault continued into darkness. Ultimately, even General Thomas and his men were forced to retreat toward Rossville and were able to make progress on their conquest of Chattanooga.

The day and the battle had come to an end on the evening of that Sunday, September 20, 1863.

General George H. Thomas, Union, "Rock of Chickamauga" (Wikimedia Commons)

Tallying up of the dead brought devastating information to both the victors (the Confederates) and those who had lost (the Union). The Union counted among their dead descendants of founding fathers, astrologers and thousands of others. The Confederates lost ten of their own Generals including Brigadier General Hardin Helm, brother-in-law of President Abraham Lincoln in the assault on September 20, near to the end of Longstreet's Corps position on the 19th. Beloved General, John

Bell Hood, lost his leg from injuries on September 20. His right femur fractured and his leg was amputated four inches below the hip. Assuming he would die, the leg was sent in the ambulance with him to be buried together. Legend states that leg and Hood were transported to the Clisby Austin House in Tunnel Hill, Georgia where Hood miraculously recovered and the leg was buried without him. (Descendants say they have records that prove this to be untrue – that he went from field hospital, spent one night in Tunnel Hill at a different house and likely not with his decomposing leg, took a train to Atlanta and then Richmond to continue his recovery) Locals, however, even say they know precisely where his leg is buried in Tunnel Hill. Hood did miraculously recover and was promoted to Lieutenant General at Longstreet's Assistance and went back into service in 1864 where the men would go on to refer to him as "Ol Peg Leg." At Chickamauga, General Hood's injury was one of thousands – and though showing the General's resistance who also had one useless arm by the end of the war, there was irreparable damage to many and local hospitals were filling up and trains were going to other hospitals to deal with the sheer number of catastrophic injuries.

Whilst, I was staying in Richmond once, I stayed an Airbnb that had recently been put on the historic registry for serving as a Civil War hospital during the war and during this time. I had stayed in such a place in Macon, Georgia a well. So many old homes served as makeshift hospitals. It was in Richmond, that I had the most profound spiritual experience, however. It was at this hospital they had proven that over 100 Confederates were buried in unmarked graves in the backyard and gardens. I, of course, went out there at night with my EMF detector and my spouse to see if we could sense anything. My husband was more focused on hoping a relic may pop out of the earth, having somehow not been previously discovered in garden planting and wandered off. I felt the soldiers around me, watching and curious if I were a nurse and wondering where I was from. I saw the spirits of what appeared to be a lot of young boys and some older men. When my husband wandered away, I started to talk to them and got flickers of light in affirmative responses to my question on occasion through the EMF detector, but it would always shut off when my spouse came near. I put on music and that seemed to really grab their attention, lighting up quite a bit. I felt … perhaps, they wanted to dance and have something of warmth or happiness once more – especially if they were haunting an old hospital. So, being the weird crazy ghost lady I am, I asked them if they wanted to dance. I felt a shuffle on the earth and then I felt this figure with more authority come over in my direction. I put on the “Ashokan Farewell,” an Irish instrumental that I always found touching and they might be familiar with. Not being a dancer myself I just extended my arms outward, one holding the EMF, the other my rather invisible dance partner, who strangely, I could almost see in my head as an officer, gruff looking but polite and showing the boys the ropes. Kind to me, the hand that held my EMF detector felt held, and the EMF detector lit up all five lights for the duration of our dance, thus confirming that feeling. I’m sure I looked a right nut to any proverbial flies on the wall, but I knew that officer was there, I could feel him in my hands. The EMF detector could feel his strength, and the spirit of familiar music catapulted us into each other’s realities – less of a ghost and more a trip back in time. I wonder sometimes who that officer was. When I found out about General Hood recovering well in Richmond, I wondered, could it have been someone so important? I learned later he did have affection for music. Perhaps, I’ll never know the identity, but I shall forever recall the night with my phantom dance partner. But alas, a nice memory long enough – back to the gruesome field of battle we go.

As for all our poor soldiers, privates and officers alike, at the Battle of Chickamauga, Confederate losses numbered around

20,000 and Union nearing 16,000 – it would be hard for a victory to be considered a great one with that type of loss and the Confederate army ultimately lost 20% of their remaining army at Chickamauga.

General Braxton Bragg, 1860-1870 (Library of Congress)

The Confederates were left wondering why they didn't capture the enemy, why they allowed their retreat and questioned the leadership of General Bragg. Some longed for the leadership of General Forrest who would have ensured that the Union would not be able to capture Chattanooga as they were in the days after. Forrest didn't understand the lack of pursuit and said,

> "Every hour was worth a thousand men."

He watched Chattanooga go to the Union and the future battles at Lookout Mountain and Missionary Ridge in the Chattanooga Campaign would have the writing on the wall. In fact, for the Chattanooga campaign, Georgia native, General Longstreet, begged Jefferson Davis to not put General Bragg in charge any further due to his multiple failures at Chickamauga. He said,

> "I am convinced that nothing but the hand of God can save us or help us as long as we have our present commander."

Jefferson Davis didn't listen; Ulysses S. Grant was then called in for the Union to the Chattanooga region as was William Tecumseh Sherman, and the losses for the Confederates were almost written in stone before they took place as Forrest so grimly predicted. Bragg had become one of the most controversial Confederate soldiers in Civil War history and failures at Chickamauga were a big reason why.

Ultimately, September 1863 was a time of death, and northwest Georgia a place to die that would become forever haunted by the activity those battle days. Chickamauga had earned its name as the River of Death once more. Death consumed Chickamauga in September of 1863 and became one with the landscape. One Tennessean soldier wrote,

> "The dying and the dead were scattered everywhere – some in heaps – shot in every conceivable manner. Dead and wounded horses as horribly mangled as the men. This is no imaginary picture, but a small part of the scenes that the battlefield presented that night. All night long that cold September night, the groans and dying shrieks were heard through the darkness. The night was spent caring for the wounded – the dead took care of themselves. They were never buried."

A Confederate Cavalry man wrote of his visit to the site after this had occurred and said,

> "The moon was far down the west and cast a ghostly light over the woods and fields. The stillness of the night was unbroken except for the sound of my horse's hooves and the hoot of some solitary owl. I had seen an old house near Jay's Mill filled with wounded and suffering men, and I had hardly started

> till I began to see dead soldiers yet unburied, lying in and near the road. I rode on, turning my horse first to the right and then to the left to avoid the thick-strewn bodies. In places I saw where great trees had been splintered by shells and riddled by bullets… Just before reaching the Brotherton house, I came upon a scene of death and destruction noteworthy even on that terrible field. I saw a piece of artillery, evidently a Federal piece, which had been knocked from the wheels by a direct hit from our guns, and apparently most all of the horses and men belonging to the gun had perished there for their bodies lay in grotesque heaps around their piece."

One reporter for *The Macon News* wrote in 1913,

> "Chickamauga has all of the quiet and melancholy interest that attaches to great battlefields. Men were killed there. Thousands of Confederate soldiers who surrendered their lives on that bloody field were buried in trenches where they fell. They sleep the last sleep on that last bloody field with none but nature and nature's God to keep them company. Their graves are humble, but their deeds are enshrined in the hearts of the people of the south forever."

Georgian Confederate General, John B. Gordon concluded,

> "Words, however, cannot convey an adequate picture of such scenes…unparalleled slaughter and agony."

Initially, there was not a mass body recovery and it was reported in the Abingdon, Virginia from a correspondent who "traveled over the field twenty days after the fight (a length about ten miles) and said,

> "It is but a vast cemetery. The bodies are buried mostly in groups of from two to twenty."

Local legend and ranger, Mark Thrash, a man living well over a century-long, was a former slave who by his own account was sent by a slave master to Chickamauga to look for a young man in the "master's" family." He once said to a visitor at his cabin in the park,

> "Miss-us, them ditches in the park are filled with dead soldiers that me and the other slaves put up there."

Mark Thrash, a Living Memorial
(Wikimedia Commons)

Many bodies were recovered, though admittedly not all would have been able to. Union troops would often send groups of men to come gather their dead as the government would pay for their removal to national cemeteries within short periods of time after battle or after the war. The Confederate dead had no such gathering as the government would not pay for their burials at a national cemetery commemorating the Union. Several southern women's aid groups gathered together to raise money and trips to gather their beloved Confederate dead from these fields and bring them to burials in Confederate cemeteries across the south. In fact, in 1866, a group of thirteen women from Resaca, Georgia, formed the Ladies Memorial Association for the purpose of having a Confederate Cemetery. The ladies turned to the state Georgia government for help and was granted $500 for a cemetery in Resaca and $3,500 for another cemetery to inter the dead from Chickamauga and the Atlanta Campaign. The ladies formed the Georgia Memorial Association with trustees and eventually the ladies formed the largest Confederate Cemetery to ever be established – the Marietta Confederate Cemetery, where you can visit today and walk through arrangements of stones by state and see statues of the ladies outside who invested themselves into the establishment of this cemetery. The population of Dalton, Georgia was eager to assist in bringing home their friends, loved ones and fellow rebels. Body removal efforts at Chickamauga began in 1867 and continued through 1869 with large movements of coffins being shipped and men and women to retrieve them. Close to a thousand Confederates were gathered from Chickamauga over this time. Of course, that would not account for all the dead. Nature would claim some, some may have been left on private properties, put in unmarked graves after spending time at nearby hospitals or homes. Ultimately, there's no way of knowing. The park rangers indicated that they know of a body, if not multiple bodies, on nearby private land, and those spots are protected. Most rangers and historians know that some soldiers will call the battlefield their final resting place for life.

Chickamauga is a hallowed ground and suffice to say that the decision to make it the first national military park in the country couldn't be more fitting due to the loss of life on both sides. However, sometimes, overshadowed by the battles of Eastern Theater in 1863, Chickamauga gets forgotten. Where was that? When was that? Only those immersed in Civil War history are as familiar with the word Chickamauga as they are Gettysburg. And that is, indeed, something to be changed.

When you drive down the Lafayette Road among the monuments and fields, looking through the groupings of trees it's hard not feel the spirit of Chickamauga, the River of Death around you. There's a gloominess and a chill in the air even on a warm day. You can almost still hear the fighting going around you. Some would call that a residual haunt. One of the Union soldiers, who had seen battle before remarked there was nothing quite like the sound at Chickamauga and said of the sound there …

> "The firing which had begun upon our left, swelled almost immediately into a dreadful roar, which filled even the souls of the bravest with awe. Nothing that I have yet listened to since the breaking out of the war, exceeded it in continuity and volume of sound. It was not a tumult which now rages and now subsides but one which for two long hours, rolled incessantly all along the lines of Thomas' seemingly devoted corps. So loud was the crash of musketry, that the repeated discharges of cannon following each other in quickly succession, could with difficulty be distinguished and seemed only like more emphatic passages in the grand diapason of thunderous harmony, which burst from

> the vast clouds of smoke and dust enveloping the contending hosts."

That is perhaps the most common battlefield haunting report – the sounds of gunfire, cannon fire, moaning and cries in the distance. And indeed, that can be said here but some of the spirits seem to be more active, as if almost re-living their dreadful cold night on September 19. As aforementioned about the battle, the soldiers reported not being allowed to have fires, having their first frost, laying there in the freezing cold thinking about their imminent demise. I had not realized when I started learning of the battle, that it would have been so cold on that evening. In fact, it never occurred to me that a battleground in Georgia in the late summer/early fall would be anything but rather warm or temperate at least. On one of my preliminary visits to Chickamauga with my husband, we rented a historic home located right on the railroad bordering the National Park and Battlefield. I love to be as close to the history and the spirits as humanly possible. On our first check-in to the home, we saw the lovely kitchen, dining area, living room, bedrooms all perfectly laid out, and since it was December, Christmas trees adorned the corners and lights were hung on the scenic porch. It was a wet couple of days spent in Chickamauga, the rain and clouds didn't want to let it up. That is not much of a deterrence either – gloominess leads to eeriness said my "paranormal" mind. Well, after check-in we did some initial visits to the museum and then came back to the house where we noticed one of the fireplaces was on. Strangely, the host had told us we could put the fireplace on if we needed, but we had not – it was a temperate day and there was no need to overheat the house. Once we noticed the flames going in one of the fireplaces in the living room, it quickly turned itself off. We even put our hands to the front to assure ourselves it was truly on. Indeed, the warmth emanated assuring us we had seen it. We agreed it was strange but continued with our night. We ordered some take-out and decided to bring out some of our "ghost-hunting toys." We turned on a SB-11 spirit box which sweeps through radio stations rapidly, generating white noise so as to allow spirits, theoretically, to manipulate the waves and communicate. A male voice kept coming through and repeating,

"I'm so cold."

I raised my eyebrows at my husband, Marty, who held the device. I said, "That's interesting." Marty responded. "How can he be cold? If he was a soldier – it was Georgia in September." "True," I continued. "Maybe he was dying and felt cold? It's hard to say." We turned off the devices to prepare for a day of walking the field the next day, watched some Netflix and got some sleep. I awoke suddenly in the middle of the night around 3:00 AM and looked toward the bedroom door. I saw an orange glow emanate around the borders of the door – it was indeed what had awakened me. I'm very light sensitive. I am a fan of near black-out conditions at sleep, so if there's a light, I will stir. Naturally, I did as any wife would do – elbowed my husband, and said, "Hey, there's a glowing light at the door. You should see what it is." He woke up, grumbled and looked at the door and said, "What is that?" – the delirious, yet annoyed, groan of a man awoken from his slumber whose brain had not turned all the way on yet. He opened the door into the dining room, and he said, "Courtney, look," and swung the door wide and showed me the alternate fireplace in the dining room was on – the flames roaring. I heard the voice on the spirit box again in my head … "I'm so cold." What on earth is going on? I wondered. My husband extinguished the flames and we resumed our sleep and woke up the next day, ready to start our adventure.

As we made our way down the Lafayette Road, where Georgia's 5th in Longstreet's Corps was assembled and where Georgia's 5th lost 55% of their regiment in battle – we visited the site where General Helm had been killed and walked through the eerie woods, gazing through the fog, with the continued feeling of not being alone.

Georgia 5th Infantry monument at Chickamauga, 2022

We then crossed the road to the Union Lines and an angle where much violence had occurred was marked by a plaque. The plaque was entitled "Hardship on the Union Line," and I began to read aloud, the third paragraph staring at me,

> "Cold and thirst plagued the Federals through the night. Their canteens ran dry and Confederates blocked their access to Chickamauga Creek and other water sources. It was unusually chilly for a September night, but with the enemy so near, campfires were prohibited. A Wisconsin soldier wrote, 'we had a slight frost. We lay on our arms without blankets or even coats, having thrown away everything but gun and ammunition.'"

My husband and I looked at each other – they had no fire; it was a frost … they were "so cold." True, we had come to communicate with as many Georgia men as possible as it was rare for them to fight so close to home and this book was about them, but the Union men, dehydrated and frigid, needed us to know they were there, they were cold and they wanted to start that fire. I knew that regardless of what legends and lore stated may be specific entities there, the spirit of Chickamauga was real and the spirits were the human soldiers.

Knowing we had experienced phantom fireplaces, that witnesses reported blood running down the trees and having experienced the feeling of being watched, I looked to see what legend and lore was passed down through the centuries – was any of it true? Or was it all a cheap horror story meant to spook others and thus leaving a bad taste in the mouths of historians everywhere. Well, it turns out a little bit of both. So, what's truth? What's fiction? What's undetermined?

One story caught my eye more than the others – and I know you're sitting there, saying, it's Ol' Green Eyes and to be honest – it's not, but we'll get back to him in a moment. The first story that got my attention was in an article that mentioned Ol' Green Eyes as it was in various other places across the worldwide web. In the *Rome News-Tribune* of northwest Georgia the article entitled "Legend of Green Eyes: a local Ghost Story" by Kevin Cumming, published on Halloween 2003, had a different spectral tale, corroborated by a podcast from a man named Lyle Russel in Tennessee in 2022 entitled "Tennessee Ghosts & Legends: Episode 4" on Haunted Battlefields. It was the kind of ghost tale one would almost welcome to happen to them on a battlefield – the kind an explorer and a historian would like. The article said that in 1998, a gentleman named David Lester, a Civil War re-enactor, had taken part in an encampment at the park as part of "Living History Days." The encampment was meant to show visitors what life was like for Civil War soldiers. Lester didn't specify where on the Lafayette Road or adjoining Snodgrass Hill he may have been but stated that while encamped one evening, he and his friends noticed a group of fellow soldiers setting up their tents. They decided to go over and make friends with their fellow Civil War enthusiasts and spent several hours chatting with them before going back to their own camp to sleep. Having found kindred spirits, Lester and his companions were excited about their newfound friends and decided in the morning to go say hello once more, perhaps they could enjoy a coffee together. But, when they looked around the field, they saw no one and they looked to the spot they had all been at and there was no sign of them having a campfire the night before or any evidence that humans had been there at all. Oooh, I get chills every time I think of it – to think – what did they speak of, did they stay in character all night thinking their comrades had as well? What did they learn from their friends in encampment that night – which side had they been fighting for? In retrospect and hindsight, if one knew they were talking to spirits it may have gone differently. But admittedly, I am envious of their experience.

A more popular and well-known legend about the battlefield is the Lady in White. The Lady in White can be seen strolling among the dead, peering from the trees looking for her lost love – a bride? A fiancée? Who was she to this man? No one knows for certain. It is one of the older tales told of the battlefield and occurs near the Wilder Tower which was near what was known as the Widow Glenn's house that burned down during the battle. It should be noted that Widow Glenn survived the battle and the ghost is not purported to be her looking for her lover as this ghost is said to do, as her husband was not fighting at Chickamauga. Widow Glenn was a young, 23-year-old woman and her former husband, John, a Confederate infantryman that died of disease in Mobile, Alabama prior to the Battle of Chickamauga. She remarried a few years later to W.B. Compton and lived the rest of her life as Eliza Compton rather than the widow Glenn the rest of her years. After her death, though, she seemed to resume the title. Some sightings place the famous lady in white at the adjacent Snodgrass Hill near the Snodgrass cabin. Legend states varying things but many claim that she is in white because it is her wedding gown that she wears and she is holding out a lantern as she is looking for her love among the dead. You may hear her walk, cry or see the glowing of her lantern among the trees. She is described as floating across the field, always looking down. Some can hear her crying (She has been seen for some time, even before there was a hospital set up near the Wilder Tower used to house the sick who were plagued with typhoid fever years later. Hundreds of men died there in 1898 and were later interred in nearby Chattanooga Cemetery.) A songwriting duo even once wrote a song called "Lanterns at Horseshoe Ridge," written from the perspective of the sad spectral woman that was used for the Civil War Trust in one of their projects. No one has debunked the Lady in White, nor have they have been able to properly identify which sad widow or lover she may be. The closest hint came from an encounter a group of teenagers had near the Wilder Tower with a ghostly man they believe may have been answering the cries of his lady. The teenagers saw a phantom torch in the tree line, a lantern, perhaps? And next to that glowing orb they saw a skeletal outline of a Confederate soldier upon his ghostly horse calling out for "Amy," before going into the brush and out of their vision. Are they connected? It's hard to say. Some say she was a wife – others say she was a fiancée looking for her soldier boy and continuing to look after even her death having never found him.

It was not uncommon for women to go to the battle sites down south to recover their beloveds or to look for them and the sorrow, grief and love they felt must have nowhere to go but back into the ethereal realm and bouncing back toward us. We can feel the weight of the lady's loss and the immensity of her love through each phantom sighting. It's hard to imagine what these women endured with worry during this violent time, the women holding together the homesteads, looking to start their lives and never expecting that their young husbands, some of them also young fathers would meet such an early and grisly demise.

The Lady in White's stomping grounds, Wilder Tower and Snodgrass Hill, have their own ghostly tales not inclusive of her, as well. Wilder Tower, marking the site of the widow Glenn's House was constructed in 1903 and marks the spot where that gap was left in the Union lines. A Union Colonel named John T. Wilder tried to hold back the Confederates with his men from this area and the tower is a marker to him. The same strange battle sounds of all haunted battlefields can be heard here but the strangest incident by far was one that happened in 1970. A Park Ranger named Charlie Fisher responded to a call and found a severely injured twenty-four-year-old man laying at the base of the tower, a man permanently paralyzed by whatever had happened. It came to light

Wilder Tower, Chickamauga, 2022

that the young man and his friends were out enjoying a few beers and feeling confident, the man looked at the tower and decided he could scale it utilizing the cable connected to the lightning rod. He did just that and went in through a gun slot window (admittedly he must have been thin) and he made his way to the observation deck cheered on by his friends. After his moment of glory, preparing to climb down and already out of the line sight of his companions, the young man screamed and threw himself out one of the windows, 25 feet above the ground. He was never able to say what it was that frightened him so, but his friends believed that it was something not of this world. There's been at least one death at the tower and tales of war souvenirs that were sealed into it going missing, never to be seen again. Some say spirits stand guard at the tower, to keep those at bay, perhaps trying to prevent all the abovementioned nonsense. "Don't tread here, you are not welcome," or so it would seem …

On Snodgrass Hill, young Julie Snodgrass, just six-years-old at the time of the battle remembered hearing a band strike up Southern tunes when they declared their victory on the battlefield – the fife and drums broke out in jubilation, and she heard women singing along joyously. It would appear the band still plays on Snodgrass Hill. A group of teenage Boy Scouts recalled their event vividly according to author, Georgiana Kotarski. They had been playing capture the flag by lantern light on top of Snodgrass Hill and their Scout Masters and another team were at the foot. The group on top of the hill heard music begin to play that sounded quite near to them. They could hear the rap of the snare drum distinctly. They began to race down to their companions, nervous about who the strangers were approaching. The scout masters tried to ease the boys' minds that it was probably pranksters in the dark, but they decided to call it a night for their game in any case. One of the scout masters decided he would go up to the hilltop after the boys were safe to see what he could assess. Sure enough, he heard the same ghostly music emanating from the woods. He watched the hair on his arms stand up and the goosebumps raise. He saw nothing that could be making the noise other than … the obvious. Just then the sky opened up, and it began to rain furiously, drowning out the sound of fife and drum into the distance. They were ready to get to their cabin and heard loud, furious bangs and the sound of thunderous running. But again, they saw nothing to match what they heard. They decided their time at Snodgrass Cabin had come to an end and they would enjoy the safety of their scout camp after that.

Snodgrass Hill, Chickamauga, 2022

To be clear, the boys were safe, and it was again another residual haunt or perhaps, young men seeing the other young men playing their game and wanting to take part. In any case, the music has been heard on several occasions. Once a tourist was so moved by the tunes he heard in the distance harkening him back to a long-ago time, he asked the ticketing office for directions to the fife and drum band only to find out that there was none. The tourist refusing to believe in ghosts took off looking for the band, but he was never able to find it.

Are there any other old tales of spirits at Chickamauga? Ghostly music, a lady in white, soldiers in camp or in the woods would seem to be plenty. Let us not forget, the "fire spirits," as I like to call them but there are indeed more. Another spectral image, nearly quite as popular as the music or sounds of fire is the tale of the headless horseman. To be transparent, no pun intended, being beheaded by a cannon or grapeshot, was not unheard of and as you read from the soldier's accounts. And sadly, many of the horses were just as mangled and suffering as the men on the field. So perhaps, it's no strange thing that a man missing his horse or his companion, would hear them in the distance coming toward him. In the days, months and then years following the battle tales were told of the clap of hooves against the earth coming in at a rapid gallop, a feeling of the horse growing so close upon you, it may indeed tread on you if you don't move. One responds as expected – throw yourself out of the way before the horse runs you over. But as the individual rolls or throws their body, they look up to see the culprit. And thereupon they see, a horse with a rider galloping quickly, and the horse looks like an officer's horse, some say a stallion and the rider, has no head. The headless horseman has been reported wearing both blue and gray. He has also been erroneously identified as Lt. Colonel Julius Garesche of the Union, who did indeed die a gruesome death where his head was squashed by a stampede of horses who trotted it along with them several yards. His men his discovered his trunk after the incident and of course, that tale was legendary. However, Lt. Colonel Garesche died at the Battle of Stones River in Murfreesboro, Tennessee, and is likely not the headless horseman of Chickamauga.

Now, many of these legends and folklore are as good as the person who tells them, and over the years these tales become a game of telephone sometimes, everchanging and perhaps a way for those who suffered such loss to try and establish sort of peace with the afterlife and the continuing on of the eternal soul. I do also believe that when an event this large takes place, it's impossible for that energy not to stay within it.

However, one tale of Chickamauga is one I am not dedicating much time to despite it being the one that most people are afraid to dispel of due to the fact it is quite popular and that is the tale of Ol' Green Eyes. There are an abundance tales of Ol' Green Eyes – he has been described as everything from a cryptid to a ghost. He is always watching in the woods, waiting for his next victim. Sometimes he is tiger-like and animal. Others say he is just lost a soul looking for his head like the horseman. Others say he inhabits the animals of the wilderness with his green eyes glowing. I have read too that he is rather scraggly looking man walking down the Glen Kelly Road of the battlefield looking for your attention with a maniacal joker-like grin. I've read that he is a demon who stole the souls of the dead and became some spiritual monster empowered by loss. Some say the bigfoot-like creature has spooked people so much so he's caused car accidents and some Native Americans insist that he is much more ancient than a lost battlefield soldier possessed and something that came with the land at the River of Death. I confess, it is a good story, and If I'm going to look for Civil War Ghosts in Georgia, Ol' Green Eyes – ooof, that's a standout one right there at Chickamauga. However, the reality is, he was made up, a conglomerate of other legends from other towns and regions melded together and told so often that people spooked themselves into believing it true. You see, decades ago, a park ranger named Edward Tinney, wanted to make sure that reckless youths didn't break into the battlefield at night and get up to trouble or cause vandalism, etcetera. So, he thought of his time in World War II and a region he visited in Germany that had a green-eyed phantom figure. And he told the tale of a soldier with green eyes, somewhat monstrous and intimidating enough to keep the youths at bay. But the legend he created took off like wildfire to the point it's almost impossible to get people to say that it isn't true. However, I am here to tell you I have spent hours, days upon the field of Chickamauga including the Snodgrass Hill where Ol' Green Eyes is supposed to lay, and I have not met him, felt him, seen him or anything demonic or half-human. I felt history, I felt people, I felt loss and I felt spirit. And I encourage you, rather than look for a cheap thrill you can buy at a haunted house attraction every October, to encounter real spirit instead. And to that, you can go to a battlefield in search of the stories and the humans who made their sacrifice on those grounds for the people and the land they held dear.

Deer at Viniard Field, 2022

If you ask me where to go and feel the spirit of Chickamauga, I would guide you toward the Viniard Field, where the Witness tree remains, where the deer gather in large number and watch from the wood line representative of the soldiers themselves watching. It seems to me every time, I visit a battlefield, I am led to the spirits by way of a young buck. A young buck representative of the young men whose lives were cut short. And as they look back with wonder and fear at me as I look at them, I know they are them, and I nod, give a small curtsy and say, "Thank you. You are remembered."

*Note, if you are looking for the men of Georgia at Chickamauga and any other notable sites that relate to the locals –

the Georgia Memorials marks a large line where several men were stationed. They are on the Lafayette Road but further down from the Viniard Field and were not, for the most part, in the heat of battle. But Georgia's 5th on the opposite site near General Helm were there much more engaged in the violence and the feeling of their spirit there – so close, yet so far from home is deeply felt. And, if you are looking for local folklore, not of the spooky kind but of the remarkable kind, you can visit the site where the gentleman named Mark Thrash, formerly enslaved, once lived on the battlefield (after the battle). Having been sent there by a slaveholder to look for his son, he went with his twin brother and looked among the battlefield for him and his own son who was enslaved to that man. No record states if they were found and Mark's brother seemed to go on elsewhere, but Mark stayed in Chickamauga, helped to bury the dead, retired from the Parks service at age 101 and lived to be 123 years old – or so the story goes. He had memories he'd share and even a jacket from President and General Ulysses S. Grant that he would boastfully wear. A small plaque marks his homesite on the battlefield.

Viniard Field at Dawn, 2022

Lookout Mountain, Missionary Ridge & Orchard Knob

"The Battle Above the Clouds"

Lookout Mountain sits in three states centered around the far Northwest corner of Georgia, just far enough on the edge of the Eastern Time Zone to the Central Time Zone that your phone or watch may get a little confused based on the proximity. Just south of Chattanooga, the mountains are a natural paradise. On a clear day, you can see across the majestic mountainous landscape for miles – and if you look closely enough, you'll be able to see seven states from its summit, or so they say. The birds soaring above the valleys and ravines below captivate the soul and the lights on the sides of the mountain from the other homes are the only signs of human life as you breathe in that fresh mountain air and feel a little bit of a chill no matter the season. The streets are named as if in fairy tales as you make your way up the mountain and it's true you end up so high, you can almost touch the clouds. "The Battle Above the Clouds," is what they called the Battle at Lookout Mountain in late November 1863. It added a mysticism to it and soldiers were even distracted by the breathtaking views surrounding their battlefield.

Geographically speaking, Lookout Mountain is located half in Georgia and only three miles are located in Tennessee, while the rest of the mountain extends into Alabama. The Battle of Lookout

Lookout Mountain Scenic View, 2022

Mountain, about a month and half or so after the Battle at Chickamauga was a defining time for the Chattanooga Campaign and changed the tale of victory for the Confederacy pretty quickly after their win on the fields of northwest Georgia. Lookout Mountain and the nearby battle at Missionary Ridge were held within a day of each other and the Battle of Orchard Knob overlapped on the day of battle at Missionary Ridge. All said, these battles took place just north of Georgia in the bordering vicinity of Chattanooga, the gateway to the Deep South. They preceded the final battle in campaign on November 27 in nearby Ringgold, Georgia, the Battle of Ringgold Gap – so their connection to our beloved Peach State cannot be overlooked.

By the end of Chickamauga's battle, General Bragg felt strongly that he could starve out the Union forces from Chattanooga and force them into surrender by siege. You may recall, the Confederate Generals did not agree with Bragg's plans

Battle of Lookout Mountain, 1863, Kursz & Allison (Wikimedia Commons)

moving forward, let alone his leadership. However, Confederate President Jefferson Davis was not swayed. On the flip side for the Union, they were refusing to lose again and with the horrors of Chickamauga, Abraham Lincoln took the position under consideration and moved out General Rosecrans and made way instead for General Ulysses S. Grant who was put in command of the full Western Theater and replaced Rosecrans' immediate position with The Rock of Chickamauga, Maj. Gen. George H Thomas. Then, with Grant's approval of General William Smith's, plan the Union was able to secure provisions to feed their men thus thwarting Bragg's tactics of starving them out and giving them leverage in the Chattanooga Campaign. The next three one-day battles would be an end for the Chattanooga Campaign in Union favor, thus a complete turnaround from the Confederate victory at Chickamauga.

Suffice to say, the men of Georgia were on the borders of their home state, so close, yet so far from home much like those in the northwest of bordering Chickamauga just months before. However, feeling confident since Chickamauga and having the advantage of being at home, the Confederates didn't really see what a danger to their position the Union assemblage was becoming with their change in leadership. Having the higher ground around Chattanooga, they felt their geography would still prove to be advantageous in preventing supplies and more. It had been working for near a month before conflict escalated. General Grant came in listening to General Smith's ideas to float supplies into his soldiers that had been taken siege nearby the Tennessee River and establish a bridge head. Bragg, Longstreet and others tries to block these motions but weren't able to because there was still no agreement between them. This allowed the Union to restrengthen physically and mentally.

Under Grant's orders in November, Union Generals dispersed to the regions where Confederates had their defense – General Hooker toward the left and Lookout Mountain, General Sherman toward the right and Missionary Ridge. Having gotten lost in the fog, Sherman ends up off his immediate spot, and General Thomas is sent toward the middle grouping and Orchard Knob. They were probably some of the strongest assemblages of leaders and soldiers that could have arrived for this campaign on the Union side. And furthermore, when the Battle of Lookout Mountain had ended, Hooker's men would go on to join their brethren at Missionary Ridge, the last Confederate stronghold.

As far as Georgia's presence at battles in their home state, it's important to remember that most Georgia boys were fighting in the Eastern Theater, however, there were two Georgia batteries that were of great importance in the Chattanooga Campaign. The Cherokee Georgia Artillery completed time at Vicksburg before coming over to Lookout Mountain and Missionary Ridge with their 12-pounder Napoleons. They served in the same Division as Rowan's Georgia Battery and in Stevenson's Division including Cumming's Brigade with the 34th, 36th, 39th and 56th Georgia. Also at Lookout Mountain were men from Cheatham's Division including in Jackson's Brigade the 1st, 5th, 47th and 65th Georgia as well as 2nd Battalion Georgia Sharpshooters. Casualties at Lookout Mountain for the battle on November 24, 1863, totaled approximately 671 for the Union and 1,251 for the Confederates. The Confederates had, in total, about 8,700 stationed in defense of Lookout Mountain and the Union under Hooker's command came in with about 10,000 to 12,000. Georgia men would also find themselves at Orchard Knob, Missionary Ridge and Ringgold Gap and men from Anderson's Brigade in Hood's Division from the 7th, 8th, 9th, 11th and 59th Georgia would see battle as well. Then, there was the well-known Wofford's Brigade, led by a prominent Georgia man himself with the 16th, 18th, and 24th Georgia as well as Cobb's Legion and the 3rd Georgia Battalion Sharpshooters. In Walker's Division, Gist's Brigade came with the 46th Georgia and 8th Georgia Battalion while Wilson's came with the 25th, 29th, and 30th Georgia as well as 26th Battalion and 1st Georgia Battalion Sharpshooters.

Ultimately, the Union was able to push back the Confederates at all three strongholds with their plan and the total casualties of the preceding Orchard Knob, were totaled around 1,700 (1,100 Union and 600 Confederate) and the devastating Missionary Ridge casualty count was 5,824 for the Union and 6,667 for the Confederacy, out of approximately 100,00 men assembled between both sides. Some of the Confederate officers felt as if their men had lost their stamina and fight by the Battle of Missionary Ridge and were acting cowardly and defeated in the face of their enemy. Though history tells us, that it was the leadership and miscommunication among those leaders that led to the men being woefully unprepared for the Union's movements and thus leading them to be rightfully, frightened.

Lookout Mountain Monument, 2022

As stated, the men of the South had almost completely reversed their victory at Chickamauga into total loss of Chattanooga. They had one last hope and that was an Irish-born immigrant to the Deep South, a General named Patrick Cleburne who was going to usher and protect them back in the Deep South of Georgia in a town called Ringgold. The Confederates were retreating south after their heavy losses and they were headed to Dalton. To allow for safe passage, General Bragg sent Cleburne to defend their area. This was their only hope to stave off further loss and see if there was any chance at regrouping. So, off Cleburne and his unit of 4,157 men went, prepared to defend themselves from the victorious Union forces.

But before, we get to Ringgold, we must mention at least a few phantoms of the mountain. If you find yourself in northwest Georgia, it is worth visiting the abovementioned sites and walking around the trails of Lookout Mountain. You can see where the boats brought supplies to the Union. You can sit where the soldiers posed for scenic photos while there – on the rocks high above the town. You can imagine the volatility of fighting on a mountainous landscape, above the clouds. The battle site is part of the National Parks and is located at Point Park. Orchard Knob is part of the parks service as well and is in a bit more of urban landscape on the outskirts of the battle sites. Missionary Ridge cannot be visited as a protected site and is completely residential at this time. Believe me, we tried! You can drive the roads of Missionary Ridge however to see the steep and overwhelming landscape that the soldiers faced, leading it to be such a deadly event. When visiting the Lookout Mountain region and enjoying the scenic beauty, there is still a very haunting feeling to know that battles and death that overcame the mountains around you. Perhaps, it's more eerie because you feel that much closer to heaven and the men themselves.

Ghost stories abound in any mountain community – in fact, I often think of the rolling hills of Ireland and Scotland and the amount of supernatural tales that occur from that setting and Lookout Mountain reminds me of that. Adding a battle to a spooky landscape only helps to enhance the ghostly stories that come from such a place and increase in the number of spirits that may be wandering. Many tales of so-called "hauntings" on Lookout Mountain are related to the men who died there … or got lost there. One tale states that a group of young, Union soldiers got

Point Park Gate Lookout Mountain, 2022

disoriented after hiding in some local caverns. They had been cut off by their regiment near battle. The book, *Ghosts of Lookout Mountain* by Larry Hillhouse states this battle was near somewhere called Adamsburg. Perhaps, the name has changed since then, but regardless, they ended up lost on Lookout Mountain and totally out of their element. Scared and wounded, trying to find their comrades, they instead continually ran into Confederate sympathizers or better yet, the Confederates themselves. Some died or went off on their own and eventually, only a grouping of seven men was left. They continued to wander in circles, three times one night headed southwest toward sinkholes and cliffs. They never found the path and the seven were never seen again. However, shortly after the war, people began to hear men talking in the woods and marching and then crying or yelling before a brief stop. The voices resume and then fade away slowly. And sometimes people have even discovered footprints near to where

Lookout Mountain Scenic View, 2022

the voices were heard, walking across a field from in the middle. The locals refer to them as the ghosts of the "lost regiment," and are used to their coming by the area.

Another soldier ghost is a Confederate, origin, unknown, perhaps from Georgia. In what is now a scenic overlook near Cloudland, high on the mountain, Confederates had an advantageous view of the major Union routes and could remain more or less, completely hidden while monitoring their movements. Southern locals who sympathized with the Confederates gave them this intelligence and the Confederates posted men there regularly. In fact, Confederates felt so safe there, that even when the Union was encamped around, they could still sleep knowing they wouldn't be found. And they could then send secret signals via mirror reflection to their counterparts below. The Union would disregard thinking it was not anything to do with them. Legend states that one Confederate rebel at the hidden site

Lookout Mountain Rock Formation over River, 2022

when the Union came in had gotten trapped within for several weeks as the Union didn't leave. Unfortunately, what was to be an easy post became life or death – the man assigned was already weak from previous wounds and quickly running out of food and water. Eventually, unable to move due to risk, he starved to death and he is said to still be haunting Lookout Mountain, conducting his spy work and sending his signals. Local lore says you can see flashing lights throughout the day and smoke signals day or night from the rebel soldier in his hiding spot, not ever having realized he had died.

It can be said that the people of the area are quite comfortable living with their ghosts – as they speak of them as no more than neighbors – a neighbor dead though they may be, they learn to co-exist just like they do with the living. This next story involves a spirit quite familiar to the people of the mountain, a young, Georgia boy who did mail drops during the war. He had been

Lookout Mountain Battlefield Rock Formation, 2022

retrieving mail at the nearby postal facility near Sulphur Springs, Alabama, and was running back with his messages in tow when he came upon some Union men who were arriving from Ohio. One of them was so spooked by the sight of the running Rebel boy in the evening, that he fired his rifle at him and cut the 14-year-old's life tragically short. The shooter was immediately scolded by his superior officer who then had to fly a white peace flag as he took the remains of the boy and his accompanying letters to the Southern soldiers and expressed apology. It would be expected that gentlemen of war would handle such things with dignity toward each other. Lookout Mountain never forgot their tragic young boy and, though the post office and general store was replaced with a saloon and later a motel, people still remember. Regardless of what building adorns the modern landscape, people still hear horse hooves coming down the road and see a small, young man running down their street in the shadows before vanishing into the air. They sigh, turn around and know it's just the "Rebel boy from Georgia making a mail run."

Lookout Mountain possesses the visitor with the dichotomous feeling of awe and horror when thinking of what happened there. When I was visiting the park, myself, I was drawn into a small area of rock formation that overlooked Union supply lines. I hopped down there having felt watched from underneath it. Later when I read of the hidden spot, I couldn't help but wonder if the rebel spy was who I felt beneath my feet. I had even sworn I'd seen flashing lights from my lodgings on the mountain the night prior. In sum, it's always best to let the spirits of Lookout Mountain guide you to their presence, whether they fly upon the wings of the birds or sit beneath the stones, awaiting their release to the next life, the soldiers' presence can be felt day or night.

But alas, we've ventured to Tennessee long enough. Let's follow our Georgia boys back down to Georgia, shall we? And let's see how Patrick Cleburne, the Stonewall Jackson of the West, made out in protecting his Confederate comrades in retreat.

Ringgold Gap

Patrick Cleburne: "The Stonewall Jackson of the West""

Irish-born, from County Cork, and proud Southern Immigrant to Arkansas, Patrick Cleburne almost sounds mythical the way other Confederates described him. Robert E. Lee likened him to a

> "Meteor shooting from a clouded sky."

He was referred to by most as the "The Stonewall Jackson of the West," and if you're familiar with lore and history on Stonewall Jackson, which is something that comes with the highest of praise. Cleburne could hold ground when others failed and foil his enemy in doing so which was similar to Jackson and earned him the nickname Stonewall in the first place. The men of war all became legends in their own right but Cleburne was still different – set apart from the crowd. When Patrick Cleburne first joined the Confederate Army as a Captain it was of the "Yell Rifles," even harkening to that rebel yell and showing the heart behind what he did. Cleburne stated that he did not join the cause for slavery as he did not care about it, but rather joined the Confederate cause because the Southern people adopted him as their own after he migrated over to Arkansas. By the end of 1863 when he sensed a Confederate loss in morale, he even proposed that the enslaved

General Patrick Cleburne, CSA

folks be freed and the South pursue their independence with the former slaves as their companions and equals in making this happen, also as soldiers. Cleburne was well respected but that idea was met with a resounding silence.

Going back to his military history, initially his brigade, The Yell Rifles were part of the 1st Arkansas Infantry. Cleburne had served under William Hardee, served in Missouri and then crossed the Mississippi toward Kentucky. His regiment merged into the 15th Arkansas before the end of the first year of the war, and just a few months later in 1862, Cleburne was promoted to Brigadier General. By this time in 1863, he had been promoted to Major General after the Battle of Stones River. He had been at Chickamauga and had also been in Shiloh. This was not his first rodeo. But this was the end of the Chattanooga Campaign – what happened next would mean something. And truly, the story of Ringgold Gap is the story of Patrick Cleburne and his comrades. In fact they would go on to receive a form thank you from the Confederate Congress for their work on the campaign. Under Bragg's leadership, they made the best out of a dire situation. They were up against a formidable enemy and fighting against problems on their own side among leadership.

And so, Ringgold Gap, was in the hands of Cleburne. If anyone could do this, it was he. Promotion from a private to Major General in just 18 months was the mark of a superior soldier. After initial skirmishes on November 26 including engagement with Union

General Sherman's column, Cleburne and his 4,000 men camped near the West Chickamauga Creek near Ringgold Gap and before sunrise, Cleburne received his orders to hold the gap at all costs. Cleburne's Division was made mostly up with men from Arkansas (Cleburne's new home state) and Alabama, Texas and Louisiana. Many of the Alabama regiments included men from the bordering Northwest Georgia. After Cleburne and his men received orders, Captain Kennard with the 10th Texas recalled,

> "We were ordered up to stop and prepare for wading the river which was soon accomplished. After the river had been crossed, the men redressed and the morning being very cold, were formed in line and arms stacked and fires built to warm by. About break of day, we were ordered to fall in and commenced the march through the town of Ringgold."

Cleburne sent his men to high ground on White Oak Mountain and Taylor's Ridge, keeping artillery out of sight of the Union forces. They covered cannons with brush and waited. Union General, Hooker and his men, estimating about 12,000 in force came into town soliciting information from the locals and enslaved people about the Confederates but received none. A Union group from Missouri advanced toward the depot at White Oak Mountain and encountered some of the Texas men. Cleburne's Texans forced the Missouri Union boys back after capturing 60 to 100 of them. Meanwhile, a group of Union men from Illinois casually occupied the local Jobe house in good spirits sensing nothing terribly wrong. Cleburne watched and waited for them to be comfortable, just as they were, before he would hold artillery fire. And when he was ready, he shouted in brogue,

> "Now then boys, give it to 'em boys."

Battle of Ringgold Gap (Georgia Public Broadcasting)

The Confederates saw the Union troops fall to the ground with their hats and weapons flying in the air. The privates of the Confederacy then got overconfident thinking they killed them all before Cleburne reminded them there would be plenty enough left to kill them too and squashed their excitement.

Sure enough, it seemed initially like success after a very weary couple days for the Confederates. They had held White Oak Mountain and Ringgold Gap until the trains were away and they received orders to withdraw. They had held position for five hours before Bragg had notified to retreat. They retreated around 2:00 PM and burned a bridge on the way out. But before Bragg and Cleburne knew it, Union Major General Ulysses S. Grant had arrived in Ringgold with his staff. Grant also feeling casual ordered remaining Confederates to leave the gap but no one to pursue them. For five hours the forces had gone back and forth throughout the day, the Union being repulsed from White Oak until Cleburne's forces left. Ultimately, though the battle was considered a Confederate victory, however the Union was able to successfully settle in around the Ringgold area and though initially many moved back toward Chattanooga, finding nothing in Ringgold, many would also go on to camp there for the winter. Upon leaving the Union burned everything they didn't take. The once bustling town of businesses and homes became a desolate collection of chimneys according to the locals, who frowned up the "Yankees" with disdain. Sherman's March to the Sea was being foreboded from Ringgold. Georgia had no idea that the Atlanta Campaign was yet to take siege of their soon-to-be capital city.

They wanted to rejoice in the moment – Cleburne had done it. He brought the Confederates at least one victory in the Chattanooga Campaign. He suffered twenty of his own men being killed according to the initial report and 201 wounded. Union casualties far surpassed his and topped over 500 killed and wounded. Cleburne and his men's award from Confederate Congress seemed quite deserved, but it would not be enough to save the South or the ultimate conclusion of the Chattanooga Campaign despite their best hopes. Ultimately, despite rebel victory under Cleburne, the Union were the victors of the Chattanooga Campaign still.

Visiting Ringgold Gap battlefield today is only mildly possible. A small carve out of land with a statue of Patrick Cleburne (Circa 2009) remains at a portion of the battle site in Northwest Georgia. The small roadside park on Route 41 is not far from the Western and Atlantic Depot which still shows evidence of the artillery fire. The site was not added to the National Register of Historic Places until 2011 but now there are markers in the region marking the event – something similar for most of the "smaller" battles in Georgia.

Patrick Cleburne Statue at Ringgold Gap (Wikimedia Commons)

Ringgold Gap's day of violence in late November of 1863 has left plentiful haunting stories of the region but perhaps one of the most haunted locations that you can find yourself visiting in

Ringgold is the Whitman-Anderson House constructed not long before the war in 1858. The home served as Union Headquarters at the conclusion of the Battle of Ringgold Gap and for Ulysses S. Grant upon his arrival after the battle. The Whitman family had been in upheaval since the war found it's home in Northwest Georgia. William Whitman had gone into partnership with the Lee family and built a dry goods store in the 1850s in Ringgold and became quite known in the area for his store and eventually became first treasurer of the county. He was able to buy additional land on Tennessee Street in 1858 and construct the home that he moved into with his family. His first wife was Cordelia and they had two young daughters – one who passed away in infancy and another who married a business partner of the Whitmans. Whitman's wife Cordelia died in 1857 and as such she would not see the house that he would go on to live in with his second wife, Margaret (sister of Cordelia) and with whom he had nine children. By the Fall of 1863, the Whitmans had been growing their family and watching the war rage on in the country for over two years. They saw Bragg's failures at Chickamauga and feared Grant's arrival as bad news for the Confederacy. The Whitmans were in Ringgold as Cleburne's troops served as rear guard and fought back the attacking Union on White Oak Mountain in notably bad weather. This was less than a quarter-mile from their home and the family watched anxiously what was happening through the front windows. It is said the family watched violent hand-to-hand combat for over two hours before the Union artillery arrived. Then suddenly, as the day drew to a close, there was a knock on their door and they were told that their home would serve as the Headquarters for the Major-General of the U.S. (Union) troops. Whitman, a Confederate sympathizer who was forced into retirement by the destruction of his store due to Union soldiers was devastated. Nevertheless, General Grant tried to develop a friendship and kindness with the family, offering dolls to

Whitman's three-year-old and eleven-year-old daughters as a token of peace. The younger girl happily accepted her doll while the elder daughter refused the doll in anger at the General's presence. Grant offered money for his stay that night – $50 in U.S. money – but the Whitmans would only accept a Confederate bill which he provided. Grant feeling soft for the family even left a soldier at the house to guard them until the wars end. When Sherman's soldiers were ordered to destroy Ringgold, the Whitman house was saved due Grant's insistence. The house remained in descendants' hands until 1902 when it was sold into the Smith-Anderson family.

Local legend states that the home has had no shortage of supernatural occurrences. There is a soldier that is referred to by the title "Captain" – many assume a Union soldier due to the headquarters and the man stationed there. They say "Captain" watches guests in the bedroom but he does not just show up unannounced. He is a phantom of manners. It is said he knocks on the front door first and then waits by the bed. They say he waits with patience and many have wondered if he's waiting for a letter to come from his long-deceased sister-in-law but it is not clear why this letter would be of such importance to wait for. The home is a private residence at this time.

Some locals may tell legend of the haunted depot in town and some young Ringgold boys who have a storied history leading to a haunting. The tale centers upon a pair of brothers in which one named Clem fought for the Confederacy having run off from home despite being too young. Eventually, Clem served under General Patrick Cleburne in the legend and fought at Chickamauga and Missionary Ridge after fighting in Kentucky earlier in the war. The story goes that while Clem was gone in Kentucky, his brother Will fell in love with Clem's friend, Sarah Johnson and they married before Will too enlisted inspired by Cleburne. Will and Clem were both able to come together, brothers in arms under Cleburne's command. Legend says they both fought in the battle of Ringgold

Gap and tragically, both brothers met their death there. Sarah waited at the train for her husband and her friend and when they did not return, she too did not want to live without them and snuck into the depot and hanged herself. The story went on that Sarah roamed as a restless ghost until Will and Clem found her at the depot that they all now supposedly haunt together. It's a remarkable story, right? Spooky, tragic … but entirely made up by the city for a Halloween event. Don't worry, these things happen and it's important we strip real legends from fictional ones. The Whitman house story is real by all accounts, never embellished. And it's too bad about the depot – just like with green eyes, we put the bombastic away in search for the authentic.

As for rebel hero, Major General Patrick Cleburne, he would go on to lead men through the Civil War for about another year, when on November 30 he would meet his tragic end on a battlefield In Franklin, Tennessee. No tales of his haunting survive Ringgold Gap though a few think he may have lingered in Tennessee where he died. He was buried nearby before being moved home to Arkansas and some sense him there as well. The most haunting tragedy of Cleburne's death is that he spoke out against the assault in that battle, thinking it would go wrong but was outnumbered in opposing opinion and met his end having been proven right. An Irishman, Cleburne always shared his opinions, even in opposition to his own men, but ultimately his loyalty to his home and his family would always propel him forward, past any opinion he may have held. And for that alone, he is an Irish and Confederate legend.

Atlanta Campaign

Resaca

The sheer massive nature of the Atlanta Campaign defines the history of Georgia to this day. Precisely, how many battles comprised the Atlanta Campaign? At how many sites in the Atlanta region? Historians and battle experts can sometimes disagree on their definitions of battles, engagements and skirmishes. Some say there were seven to nine "battles," while others claim it was more likely that seventeen to nineteen constituted "battles," and that the rest were skirmishes, engagements and operations. The entire Atlanta campaign lasted for about four straight months from May 7 to September 2, 1864 and was in direct follow-up to the Chattanooga Campaign in the Deep South.

Though Chickamauga had been an end to Union offensive, the war raged on over a year later and Grant, newly arrived to the theater and promoted to General in Chief of all Union armies, had appointed his friend and comrade, General William Tecumseh Sherman to take over his old position of Commanding General of the Department of the Mississippi. This command was in charge of Union Forces west of the Appalachians (most of Western Theater). The two Union men devised a plan to bring an end to the Civil War once and for all. Though, overall, the war had turned into Union favor on the battlefield, it was anything but won or lost by either side. The war was dragging on longer than anyone had anticipated and the Confederates may have been greatly affected in number but not in passion for the Confederacy and they were not planning on giving up. Lee and the Southern generals intended on carrying forward. The Presidential election of 1864 was leaning toward a George McClellan presidency and that would end with negotiations with the Confederacy and legitimize their cause thus perpetuating slavery which the Union still adamantly opposed.

The best plan Grant and Sherman came up with was to completely devastate the south, blocking supply lines and destroying the armies both physically and mentally. In March of 1864, the Union duo of Grant and Sherman met in their home state of Ohio and came up with the plan that ultimately Grant would take on Lee and the Eastern Theater and Sherman would take on General Joseph Johnston in the West and Sherman had his eyes on and heart set on the road to Atlanta, the hub of rail line and provision supply lines for the south. Atlanta would be a halfway point for the Confederacy and cutting them off, would split them in half. It would have theoretically kept the soldiers in that theater from leaving and kept supplies and transportation routes from the Deep South running simultaneously. Sherman said of the Grant's and his plan,

> "We finally settled on a plan. He was to go for Lee, and I was to go for Joe Johnston. That was his plan. No routes prescribed. It was the beginning of the end as Grant and I foresaw it here."

Grant was on his way to Virginia to cut off Richmond and Sherman to Georgia to cut off Atlanta – the next offensive was just weeks after their meeting. Sherman was equipped with the Army of the Tennessee (primarily, the Army of Ohio and Army of the

Cumberland to assemble the Military Division of the Mississippi.) Sherman started off with approximately 99,000 troops compared to the Confederacy's 50,000 under Johnston. Suddenly, some of Sherman's troops were furloughed, lessening his forces temporarily while the Confederates bolstered up to 65,000 with reinforcements from Alabama. However, a month into the campaign, Sherman restrengthened, and the Union was back to higher numbers, in fact, well over 100,000 soldiers. The Confederates were comprised primarily of the Army of the Tennessee and came with commanders Hardee, Hood, Polk and Wheeler.

War historians immediately pinpoint an issue in command difference between these two armies. Sherman was a known aggressive combatant and strategist, and did not fear violence or extreme action as would be shown even after following the Atlanta Campaign with his March to the Sea. Johnston was never confrontational which admittedly is strange for a General, and he had a reputation of withdrawing his troops before things escalated to assaults. This would not be possible in Georgia, where they had to present a strong defense against their invaders. Johnston focused on strong entrenchments and Sherman focused on outmaneuvering defense and coming in on the flanks.

Following up on the close of the Chattanooga Campaign, the Atlanta Campaign conflict erupted slightly to the southeast of Chickamauga and Ringgold in the Dalton region, known as Resaca. The battle of Rocky Face Ridge took place around May 7, 1864. Battle may even be a strong word for this event; however, it was the escalation of the campaign and the rather unofficial beginning. The Confederates were entrenched on the Rocky Face Ridge Mountain between the Western & Atlantic Railroad and Dalton. Sherman approached against the position and sent men from the Cumberland Ohio to the North and the Tennessee to Snake Creek Gap at Resaca cutting retreat and supply routes. The next day the Battle at Buzzard's Roost also known as Mill Creek Gap began and continued until May 9. On May 9, the Georgia Military Institute Cadets became engaged in the skirmish before the battle. They became unspoken heroes for the people of Georgia for their service in the Atlanta Campaign and in trying to impede Sherman's March to the Sea that followed. In many ways, they were considered just as successful as the famous students from Virginia Military Institute at New Market. By the time troop movement was happening that May in Northwest Georgia, the *Atlanta Constitution* in 1890 reported,

> "Military enthusiasm was at its height in the battalion of boys and conversation was aglow with eager yearning for the fray. The armies were moving from Dalton on to Resaca…In almost the twinkling of an eye, the brave boys sprang from their beds, donned their uniforms and assembled in front of the building for roll call…Orders were given to march to the depot in Marietta and take a train to go to their front which was then about Resaca. When they reached the seat of war, they were placed in lines and the Battle of Resaca is where the boys first saw fight."

The 9th Illinois wrote of their encounter with the Cadets and described them almost as mythical creatures, who had

> "come out from the woods at Resaca and formed their line behind a rail fence. After a volley from the cadets, which killed several of our men, our regiment charged them. Thus it is shown and acknowledged by one of our opponents that the cadets were intrepid and effective in their very first engagement…In the charge upon them at Resaca, the cadets acted with

> remarkable coolness and discretion as though they were veterans and were complimented and praised by their officers. Though it is acknowledged that they killed several of the federals, no one of the cadets was hurt in that charge."

The boys were forced to give up their position on that spot on the 9th but celebrated their first combat. This would not be the end of their time in the war … but for the Atlanta Campaign, they continued provost duty and monitored as the troops came closer to their school and they inched closer to leaving home. I bring up the young boys, because it is the Georgia youth that gets caught up in the Atlanta Campaign much of the time, having come of age in the height of war and known nothing more than an adulthood of fighting for one's home. It is their spirit that is felt deeply within the regions around Atlanta.

The Union troops continued movements after the aforementioned skirmishes and engagements to and around Resaca led them to where they found entrenched Confederates in defense. Many of these battles overlapped in the engagements leading up to the more wildly known start of the Atlanta Campaign, in the nearby town of Resaca, at the Battle of Resaca om May 13. It should be noted that the Battle of Resaca is thought to encompass all of the above engagements as well.

On May 13, the Union arrived under fire from Confederate cavalry just in front of Resaca, however the Union troops under McPherson quickly moved the cavalry back toward town and captured Bald Hill and sent those men back to the aforementioned Snake Creek Gap. Sherman did not feel like this was tactically sound and insisted that McPherson "dig in," while he brought the rest of the Union army through the gap. By the next morning on May 14, Johnston who still been fulfilling his rather meek attitude on the battlefield, had his rebels positioned north and west of

Resaca for about four miles. The large Camp Creek became the obstacle between the two armies and giving the Confederates slight advantage in their defense position. Sherman used diversion tactics and smaller attacks while a Union division traveled downstream to cut off the railroads. Union troops tried desperately to cross the Camp Creek and with little knowledge of the ground and the muddy banks and shifting earth, they were consistently thrown into poor positions allowing the Confederate line to fire their musket and cannon efficiently upon them. The incoming attack was ultimately, well repelled by the rebels under Cleburne and Hindman though Bate's division suffered the most casualties at this time.

Battle of Resaca (Library of Congress)

Eventually the Union assault ended around 3 after causing nothing but death and injury and the Union decided to bombard the Confederate works instead. The violence continued the 15th. The Confederates under Hood planned to position a battery where they could put their Napoleon cannon and fire upon the Union, however before they could connect the earthen works to their rifle pits, the Union attacked. Most were repulsed but some from Union General Ward's brigade continued to storm the Confederate earthworks and in close contact bayoneted the rebel gunners who

> "defiantly stood by their guns til struck down."

Heavy attack continued from the rest of the Confederates upon the Union, attempting to repulse them. However, at the end, neither side fully retreated and neither claimed the battery. The Confederates called out,

> "Come on- take those guns,"

while they wanted to attack and the Union guys responded,

> "Come on and take 'em yourselves."

In nightfall, after all the taunting had ended, the Union snuck into the earthworks and grabbed the four guns for themselves. By the night of May 15, Johnston ordered his Confederate troops to withdraw because they had been flanked. They tried to burn bridges on their way out – (gives new meaning to burning bridges of contact, does it not? This is where it comes from!) but the bridges were quickly repaired by the Union. The Confederates and Union each suffered approximately 2,800 casualties in the Battle of Resaca and there was no victor. The Confederates continued to move toward Adairsville and the Union was following right behind them.

Part of the battle site is protected today, and the first Confederate Cemetery established by the Ladies' Memorial Association in an effort to bring home deceased loved ones was indeed in Resaca where the Resaca Confederate Cemetery remains today in that honor. Some claim this to be one of the most haunted cemeteries in all of Georgia containing the graves of more than 450 Confederates killed in the fighting of that region. The battlefield is preserved by several nonprofits and Gordon County. There are about 500 acres along the Camp Creek that can be seen. Part of the battlefield was destroyed by the construction of Interstate 75. The cemetery and battle site are on opposite sides of the interstate.

Most soldiers were not scared of death, so much as they were frightened of being forgotten or worse yet, left behind on the battlefield and never brought home. Death was inevitable, but did it to have ring true that the earthly vessels in which they had died, must remain on that cold, dark battlefield forever cursed to live in that moment of violence? Of course, that doesn't seem fair, and it doesn't allow a spirit to rest peacefully. The song that influenced the name of our series, *Bury my Bones*, likens the graves of those brought back home after an untimely death as a request of theirs,

> "Bring me back to Anderson County. Drive real slow and take the long way home."

They described being buried,

> "Under the tallest pine; dig it real deep where the roots touch mine,"

And though, that song was written in 2019, it shows that as humans we want nothing more than to be brought home, peacefully for our souls to rest among the land and people we love.

Two years after the Battle of Resaca and a year after the end of the war, the Jackson family of Griffin, Georgia grieved their young son who died in the battle of Resaca on the Western and Atlantic

Railroad. He was not one of the cadets, but he very well could have been with his youthful teen looks, no facial hair and his desire to fight for home. Private Jackson was buried, according to his comrades, in an old pine box constructed of planks from a nearby bridge. Instructions were sent to his parents directing them to where they could find their son's remains as they had expressed interest in returning him home to Griffin. His father followed instruction with friends and family but after a thorough search was unable to find his son. He returned home to deliver the sad news to his wife, desperately mourning her son. A few nights later, Mr. Jackson awoke in the night after having the most vivid dream of communication with his deceased son. In the dream, his son smiled and stood by his bedside as he told him precisely where his remains could be found. Mr. Jackson reported that his son spoke the words,

> "Father, I am buried under a mound which was thrown up by the Yankees after I was killed. You will know the mound when you see it by the pokeberry bushes growing upon it. Go and take me up and carry me home to Mother."

He knew what his dad had no way of knowing, that the Yankees were rebuilding bridges and as such, this happened in their wake. But the only way to know, if this was truly his son's spirit speaking was to follow his instruction. Mr. Jackson went back to the battlefield with one of the soldiers who had fought with his son and quickly they found a mound with a pokeberry bush. They dug furiously and found the pine box just inches below the surface of the ground. Inside was a deceased Confederate soldier. Legend differs here on what happened next. Some say, Mr. Jackson immediately recognized the remains of his son. Others say that the remains were so decomposed they were beyond recognition, however, he noted that the soldier's shoes were the same pair he had gifted his son shortly before he went away to fight. He had found his son. He gathered his sons remains, put them in a "fine casket," and brought him home to mother. He is now buried in the Oak Hill Cemetery in Griffin, Georgia. The ghost – nay, the spirit, spoke directly to his family, to find his way home.

In nearby Tunnel Hill, Georgia, between Chickamauga and south of Ringgold, others swear that ever since that battle at Chickamauga and Chattanooga took place and then amplified by the beginnings of the Atlanta Campaign, hauntings have flooded the area. In Tunnel Hill they report lights that look like fires at a campsite or explosions on a battlefield and the horrid stench of decay filling their entire town. And yes, Tunnel Hill is the same town that's rumored to have the General Hood's leg buried somewhere in town though historians say … it would have been far too decomposed to make it there and is likely by a field hospital in Chickamauga instead. Tunnel Hill residents do boast that there is a one-legged ghost that walks around the gravestone for General Hood's leg that may nor may not be there as well but they are no stranger to other ghostly sightings in town.

Tunnel Hill, Georgia, embraces their ghosts be they from Missionary Ridge or perhaps from the nearby battle at Ringgold Gap, that spirit emerged from or even the Battle of Resaca which too was not far. One profound tale states that there were reenactors preparing for their time to re-play the battle of Missionary Ridge and were encamped in Tunnel Hill, Georgia, on the preceding night when they saw mysterious campfire start to emerge. They exchanged dialogue with each other about how nonsensical it was and thought better of wandering off to investigate unprotected and grabbed their rifles. They tiptoed around their fellow Confederate reenactors as the wind began to howl and the mysterious fires raged fitfully as if being tended to. When they made it there, they discovered no one in sight. But suddenly, they witnessed hands emerge from darkness over the flame and saw two boots standing by the fire. Someone was trying to warm their hands and was rubbing them together. They noticed he had a uniform like theirs – made of gray and felt some comfort in that. The men remarked that he looked more like a painting of man staring into the flames than an actual man himself and his skin was pale and sick. Suddenly, the specter looked at them and they felt unable to move as they made eye contact. Then just as quickly as he appeared, the man and the fire vanished, and the two friends ran back to their campsite. They had just made eye contact with a real Confederate officer, and they would never forget that moment. His identity or where he fought to arrive in Tunnel Hill – we do not know, but perhaps the men preparing for Missionary Ridge's reenactment brought one of the officers with them.

At Resaca Confederate Cemetery, there is a sense of reverence and not feeling quite alone. Mary Green who helped in establishing more cemeteries told tale that her and a former slave recovered soldier's remains after the battle of Resaca when they saw them where they fell or in a shallow grave. She and her sister were so upset, they came up with the plan to retrieve them all and give them proper graves. Her father gave them two-and-a-half cares of land to use as a cemetery which was the unofficial start of the Resaca Confederate Cemetery before the Association moved forward. It is local lore that the ghosts of souls buried in the cemetery are still somewhat restless – perhaps, despite their community of comrades, some of them still long to be closer to home but it just wasn't as possible. I take heart in that, they were brought to a place of peaceful rest and not left on the grounds of the hostility, however, it is still not quite home for some. Tales of orbs, strange sound and more have been reported by paranormal investigators throughout the years. I like to think that perhaps it is the young women continuing to check on the souls' they tried so desperately to bring peace to.

Adairsville

The spirits of Resaca would have undoubtedly wanted to see how their brethren made out in the rest of the campaign -- so let's journey down to Adairsville. On May 17, 1864, the next engagement came on the heels of Resaca. Sherman and the northern soldiers followed Johnston's retreat South. Johnston decided to set up a defense around Adairsville while the Confederate cavalry sent Sherman away from Atlanta. Predicting a large engagement in Confederate favor, Johnston was disappointed to find that Sherman had divided his forces in three columns and skirmishes happened along the routes. The skirmishes continued until Johnston, not able to make his location at Adairsville work had to withdraw. Johnston thought while doing so, that they could perhaps have the opportunity to attack one Confederate column and he sent troops to Kingston while he and the rest of the army fell back toward Cassville, Georgia. As predicted, Sherman took the bait and figured that most of them had gone to Kingston and the group of Confederates at Kingston were charged with holding the Union back while Hood and Polk destroyed the last column in

Cassville. The plan was working fairly well; however, Hood ran into a Union brigade in the east that gave the Union a favorable position and though they did skirmish, ultimately the Confederates fell back as Johnston's timing had missed a window of opportunity. Though they had all gathered back toward Cassville assuming attack on May 20 that they could repulse, that did not happen. Overnight, they Confederates withdrew, feeling they had lost strong positions in Dalton, Resaca, Calhoun, and Adairsville, keeping with the defense modus operandi of General Johnston. Morale was dwindling and so was faith in General Johnston. There were approximately two hundred casualties for the Union in the Battle of Adairsville and an unknown amount for the Confederacy. Both armies were approximated to be between four and five thousand in number at that time of the battle.

One poor cursed Southern family that lived in Adairsville and had some spooky occurrences during and after the war were the Barnsley's. In fact, fitting their curse, they seemed to suffer ill luck for decades prior to the war. However, it was during the war in the battle near to their house in Adairsville, when General McPherson – the Union General himself, was impressed with their stately gardens and ordered soldiers not to destroy it and instead, to march around them. Now, prior to McPherson's arrival in 1864, a Confederate Colonel went straight to the Barnsley's to warn them of the Union approach and was shot dead by a Union soldier while doing so. Perhaps, it was this warning that helped Barnsley think on his feet for the upcoming army approach and make sure he had a certain flag upon his house. He was lucky McPherson liked his gardens but then McPherson also noticed the British flag flown at the house when he arrived there – at that time in war, a sign of supposed neutrality was evidenced by the British flag. This could save his house from flames. Of course, the neutrality wasn't true; the Barnsley's had Confederate bonds in a safe and two sons enlisted in the war, in the Confederate Army. And when that was eventually discovered, the Union ransacked their storage buildings. The tale gets stranger yet. Family patriarch, Godfrey Barnsley tried to recoup what he could after the war and lived in "genteel poverty." He went to New Orleans to revive his cotton business and make money again but died there unsuccessful in 1873. He wrote a letter to his daughter, Julia at home in Adairsville telling her, he would join her mother in the spirit world. Julia had his body returned home after he did just that and buried at home where vandals dug up his grave and severed his right hand from his corpse. Legend states that the grave robbers used his hand for voodoo rituals. Julia's ghost is still seen near the gardens, Godfrey's ghost walking the estate and the ghost of the killed Confederate is still seen running up to the house to try and help the family from the intruders. The family has had Cherokee Chiefs come to the property to rid them of their long curse after the war … but the ghosts tell the tale, that the curse is never ending and that they will still haunt those old grounds in the Woodlands at Adairsville.

The best place to encounter more of the history of the Adairsville engagement would be at the Adairsville Depot History Museum which also features their role in the Great Locomotive Chase … which believe me, there's more to say about that. Please see the Chapter 27, Part V, regarding the Southern Locomotive Museum and the Great Locomotive Chase for more. Additionally, in the Adairsville Cemetery, there are plaques suggesting that the cemetery, hauntingly enough was established where part of the battle took place.

New Hope Church, Pickett's Mill & Dallas

New Hope Church

A week after the engagements around Cassville and Adairsville, the Atlanta Campaign gradually proceeded southward and battles broke out over a period of just a couple days in three different areas – New Hope Church, Dallas and Pickett's Mill. Johnston and his men, who had retreated to Allatoona Pass were trying to decipher the next point of Union attack. And though, Sherman considered Allatoona Pass, he felt that it would be too deadly and history tells us that battle there would wait until a different campaign months later. Johnston figured out what Sherman's next move would be and that was to head toward Dallas, a crossroads town just 30 miles from Atlanta. Johnston felt that he could block the Union at New Hope Church. Sherman believed this was a token force aka a force not to be taken seriously and ordered Hooker's Corps to attach on May 25. The terrain was rough. The rebels had the coverage of a well-wooded area and had made strong earthworks. The Union soldiers could barely see the earthworks especially as darkness settled. It was coming to be evening time and they found themselves at New Hope in the "Hell Hole." The Confederates had set up around a ravine and almost creating a second ravine with their earthworks.

This ravine was a death trap. For three hours the troops became entrenched in fighting hand-to-hand in the woods. The battle only came to an end under a vicious thunderstorm – one that the survivors of the battle reported was nothing like they had ever seen. The scene described Union men trying to crawl through the rain into the neighboring ravine outside the trenches to escape the death. The moans of the dying mimicked the sound of the thunder thus assuring in the everlasting name, "Hell Hole." Hooker reported losing nearly 1,700 people and the Confederates about 300 to 400. The Confederates under Stewart had sixteen cannons and though they had had only 4,000 Confederates at New Hope to the Union's 16,000, their guns and cannon gave them an immense upper hand. Ultimately, the Battle of New Hope Church on May 25 to May 26, 1864 was a Confederate victory. After an inconclusive battle at Resaca, a loss at Adairsville, and the looming loss of the Chattanooga Campaign, this small victory was a morale boost for the Confederacy even if the Hell Hole became a memory that they would never want to re-live. It was hardly a battle of glory. The brutality and filthiness of it is something that's hard for us to imagine. New Hope had mostly men from Georgia, Alabama and Louisiana fighting in the Confederacy and one of the major Brigades was Stovall's Brigade with the 40th, 41st, 42, 43 and 52nd Georgia Regiments present.

When I arrived at the site of New Hope Church with my family, darkness had set in on the early December evening I was visiting, and I hadn't yet read any ghost stories. In fact, I didn't really fathom the importance of this battle or the violence of it, the brutality of it until I was there and could see it in the dark and in the quiet. For me, it seemed a rather small battle site tucked in at a small crossroads by the New Hope Church near Dallas. The church had been there at the time of battle as had the cemetery across the path where much fighting occurred. If you park in the church lot, you can see the big obelisk commemorating the forces – Union and

Confederate who fought and other small memorials. Then you'll see a sign that says Confederate Trenches and you'll see the dugout area that is clearly left from 1864. On the right-hand side as you face this, you see the wooded ravine area and if you follow the trenches and woods, it goes deeper with residential area on the left-hand side. Suffice to say, there's definitely a good chance that a home or multiple homes could be haunted abutting the battlefield that way. It was a clear night when we arrived after dinner and attempted to investigate and walk the premises.

Hell Hole at New Hope Church (Emerging Civil War)

Immediately, I was drawn to the trenches and the area deemed to be the "Hell-Hole," and as the darkness was setting, I swore that I saw a man standing among the trees watching, seeing who we were. Not sure in the darkness, if we had trod upon another explorer, my cousin walked down to where the shadow figure was to see who was about. Quickly, a local police officer had come to check on us but after allowing our exploration, had left the lot and the shadow figured remained lurking in the woods. In many ways, we were hoping there wasn't someone sinister lurking in the woods. My cousin got down to the area where the shadow figure had been and where we then confirmed my cousin's presence and the spectral presence with a thermal camera. My cousin saw no one as I did, or the camera reflected, and eyes were still set upon the mysterious man when the thermal camera showed him walking to the side of my cousin into the trees as if to give him space. When my cousin left, the figure resumed his initial standing place.

We were starting to feel a little on edge. It was if we heard limbs cracking from heavy steps rather than squirrels and almost a distant hum or moan in the air. Our equipment was lighting up furiously at its seat around the monument and then suddenly, the sky opened up with torrential rain and thunder – out of nowhere. We checked the weather radars on our phones, and it showed nothing – clear skies, clear forecast but there we were standing in the torrential rain. Everyone ran back to their car but I felt compelled to get one more photo and there standing in the rain was the shadow figure of a man coming through the rain toward us. Truth be told, the hell hole, ranked high on eeriness for me, but what about for others? Was this just a fluke evening?

Well, according to Civil War forums, some of the eeriness relates to the fact that the 40th Georgia was fighting in their home county, perhaps on the graves of their ancestors and hiding behind headstones from the Union – could this lead to an energetic vortex, I wondered? Other locals have written legends about the moaning coming from the woods, the sentry that stands watch (a lot like our shadow figure) and some have even captured images. What legend seems to always state, however, is that when visiting the Hell-Hole, there *always* seems to be a thunderstorm that rages above after a visit, and a specific stir especially when close to the anniversary of the battle. I got chills, myself, when discovering this – we had that fluke storm too, could it be that this is an example of

Shadow in the Rain at New Hope Church, 2022

a time slip haunting, where upon those grounds, the veil between our worlds is so thin, it could actually affect the weather over the century a later. For a moment, were we not in the time we're so familiar with? Collectively transported to the past? It seemed as such. What perhaps was the strangest discovery about the location of New Hope Church was that over a century after the battle there was a fatal plane crash right next to the location. A thunderstorm, out of nowhere, came over head on April 4, 1977 and the Southern Airlines DC-9 plane crashed while attempting an emergency landing on the main road resulting in the death of 72 plane passengers and nine people in town; a terrible tragedy to be sure. Suffice to say, to say, to me the time slip theory could ring true – after such death in that area, perhaps something in the woods that we can't see with the naked eye is there like a vortex. It is a looming hole where storms and figures of the past can coexist among us, if only for a second. And if you visit around May 26 take extra care not to get caught yourself into the throes of a historic battle.

Confederate Trenches at Battle of New Hope Church, 2022

*Please note, though there is a story written about a New Hope Haunting with elements of true accounts, the story of the relic hunter that can be found on the internet is a story of fiction unlike the accounts above. There are continued reports that are synonymous with this historic fiction tale – smells of decaying flesh, hearing of screams and some ghostly apparitions match some encounters though not specific to that tale. A group of Sons of Confederate Veterans actually reported in the 1980s that a ghostly figure showed up by the monument on camera and for a little while, the photo was even on display at the nearby Pickett's Mill Battlefield.

Pickett's Mill

New Hope was the left flank of General Johnston's Corps and on the right was a location called Pickett's Mill. Just 24 hours after the attack on New Hope Church, Pickett's Mill would come under fire. Pickett's Mill was a couple dozen miles northwest of Atlanta and was located at a Creekside gristmill owned by the Widow Pickett whose husband of the 1st Georgia Cavalry had been killed at Chickamauga just eight months prior to the battle coming to her doorstep and bringing more untimely death. On May 27, 1864, in Paulding Country one of the worst massacres that some consider a war crime, took place under General Sherman's orders. When visiting battle sites in Georgia, it is Pickett's Mill that summons one back time and again – it's not the largest, nor the highest casualty count in the Civil War, but it is the most brutal and the one where the orders were made with some of the greatest mistakes. Some say the orders that day for the Union were careless and showed extreme lack of judgment.

Pickett's Mill is a beautiful state park now, that continues to share the story of what happened and aid in the training of current military cadets and privates in what not to do, or how to maintain effective battle strategy in certain terrains. The walking paths behind the visitor center divert through the woods around the area but the area surrounding the visitors center and just a short walk down the path was the site of the worst of the battle.

Pickett's Mill Battlefield, 2022

Coming up to Pickett's Mill surrounded by the Georgia pines, it's easy to find yourself in multiple parts of the protected state park, however for the Civil War site, you'll want to go directly to the visitor's center. I've gone in different times of year and found the energy to be the same regardless of whether the trees and plants are in full bloom for spring and entering summer, or in the stark, "bleak, midwinter," the same quiet and need for reverence is felt. It's not a place where one jumps and plays, and though you could walk your dog on a nice, wooded path, you'd still feel the energy.

One of the park rangers and I had a long discussion regarding the ethereal as it relates to several sites, but especially, Pickett's Mill. The ranger and I discussed his near-death experience and his changing view of the afterlife when that happened and how that has affected his views of haunted locations. It turns out we both had a similar belief in energy. He explained how energy is what lives on after our human bodies don't and that is what we become however the energy we output while in our bodies can still stay somewhere. That begged the theory then, that in a site where nothing short of a massacre of Union troops occurred, that fear, pain and whatever else would have overcome the men would stay in that area and could be felt. And in my opinion that, death agony, is absolutely still in the earth at Pickett's Mill as are some of the people's human vessels themselves.

What on earth happened in this battle, that set it apart from so many others in the Atlanta Campaign or the Civil War as a whole? To be honest, it's still being studied. The death and casualty count is still in question. If anything, experts say, the reality is that there more dead than they could have ever imagined. Most modern understanding and interpretation of the battle comes from author and Union soldier, Ambrose Bierce. Ambrose was also a military cartographer and he recalled that due to hastiness and lack of time, he wasn't even able to go scout out the site properly (reconnaissance) to help ensure troop movements were what they needed to be. He confessed that this was the only time that that had happened to him in battle and that missing reconnaissance alone was almost a precursor for what was to come in mistaken judgments. Bierce even starts his work entitled, *The Crime at Pickett's Mill*, by stating

> "The civilian reader must not suppose when he reads accounts of military operations in which relative position of the forces are defined, as in the foregoing

> passages, that these were matters of general knowledge to those engaged."

What was supposed to happen even remains murkily known in the best situations because officers on the battlefield were questioning orders (specifically on the Union side) as they were coming down and when the battle was in effect. The Confederates were equally questioning why the Union was effectively making such a suicide mission of the matter. Ambrose Bierce's account is haunting and distressing to read – how did this failure come about? Why so much catastrophe at Pickett's Mill?

For the Union, the General Sherman was again, trying to "circumvent," General Johnston's Confederates and Pickett's Mill, on the other flank from New Hope, was sent with Union General Olive Howard. It took about five hours for the men to arrive in rugged terrain before encountering Confederate troops at Pickett's Mill. The next day, Howard wanted to go on the offensive of the Confederate works manned by none other than the Stonewall of the West, Irishman Major General, Patrick Cleburne. The attack began just around 5:00 PM and continued into the evening. The error in judgment happened in those mid-afternoon hours. When those Confederates were discovered digging trenches at Pickett's Mill, Union officers, Howard and Wood, who had discovered them noted that the entrenchments did not extend left. So, Howard ordered Generals Johnson and Wood to swing to the right and McLean would make a

> "False attack that would take away from a real one led by Wood. Though Wood prepared, Johnson and Mclean didn't. Howard, unsure of what was going on with his men told his superior, Thomas, that he was "turning the enemy's right flank, I think."

Thomas's reply was to go ahead art 4:00 PM. Howard, looked at the trenches, terrains, lack of movement and saw what was to be a pit of death at the bottom of the ridge, and asked again with hesitancy and palpable,

> "Are the orders still to attack?"

The orders were still to attack. Sadly, McLean and Howard's personal lack of favor for one another since the Battle of Chancellorsville about a year prior was part of what led to the breakdown in communication that day. One historian, Albert Castel said of McLean,

> "Of all the brigade commanders in Sherman's army, a worse one to assist in Howard's attack could not have been found."

Howard's influence from Chancellorsville came from an upset where General Stonewall Jackson had maneuvered in attacking from the rear briefly to crush line into confusion and have supporting attack in front. Howard wanted to enact this same measure upon the Confederacy and General Sherman knew this in placing Howard in position here, at least according to Ambrose Bierce. They were prepared to attack in column of brigades but though their march coming on the day was less than a mile, they were delayed by three hours as the aforementioned slow-moving nature implies. This gave the Confederates an enormous advantage to be able to see what the Union was doing – and perhaps that led Thomas to assure Howard in his moment of despair to go forward, not seeing himself, what Howard was seeing.

At Pickett's Mill, when this order was given to carry forward, rather than an assault with full support from the Union Army, Howard decided to send out one small brigade of only 1,500 men to attack the full Confederate force of 14,000. General Hazen was with the brigade that was sent forward. Ambrose Bierce described Hazen as

> "The best hated man that I ever knew."

Hazen had resentments toward all his superiors and was consistently charged with stealing and cowardice. He was however loyal to his men. Hazen saw Wood's order to Howard that he go in and see if he had success. He knew it would be a suicide mission to go up against a well-entrenched, ridge filled with the Confederate Army but did not challenge his orders and waited for the order to go. Ambrose stated,

> "Only by a look which I knew how to read did he betray his sense of the criminal blunder."

It was apparent, that the Confederates at the time of Thomas' orders had seven hours to prepare. The Union entrenchments were not rapidly to the left. So, the Confederates moved Cleburne's division to the right to meet them and Hood had this move assist Major-General Wheeler's cavalry who was engaging in the Union.

The 1,500 troops under Hazen waited for their orders to march a quarter-mile uphill

> "Through almost impassable tangles of underwood, along and across precipitous ravines and attack breastworks constructed at leisure and manned with two divisions of troops as good as themselves."

Bierce reported where he had heard the audible murmurs of the Confederates to his officers as he was the topographical engineer, but from Union lines, the Confederates could not be heard. Men from Ohio and Kentucky lined up amid jokes being made, lightening the mood, from what was becoming increasingly known to the men – they were in a dire, extremely dangerous situation – they were about to die. Bierce's account paints the picture as they come to the fork of the ravine, the split of formation begins among the men – color bearers at the front, flags being torn to rags, horses in the rear and an intent to reform upon arrival. But there would be no further arrival for that ravine became the pit upon which the Confederates had their line stationed.

> "Suddenly, there came a ringing rattle of musketry, the familiar hissing of bullets and before us the interspaces of the forest were all blue with smoke. Hoarse, fierce yells broke out of a thousand throats. The forward fringe of the brave and hardy assailants was arrested in its mutable extensions…The uproar was deafening; the air was sibilant with streams and sheets of missiles. In the steady, unvarying roar of small-arms, the frequent shock of the cannon was rather felt than heard, but the gusts of grape which they blew into that populous wood were audible enough, screaming among the trees and cracking their stems and branches. We, of course had no artillery to reply,"

explained Bierce. He explained the flags going up and down changing hand throughout. Bierce, a journalist, even interviewed his enemy following the battle, and they obliged as a gentleman and officer would and answered Bierce's questions. In his documentation, he often explains their accounts. Confederate General Johnston explained from his perspective much of the same.

Pickett's Mill Ravine, 2022

> "The federal troops approached within a few yards of the Confederates, but at last were forced to give way by their storm of well-directed bullets, and fell back to the shelter of a hollow near and behind them."

He hauntingly continued,

> "They left hundreds of corpses within twenty paces of the Confederate line. When the US troops paused in their advance within fifteen paces of the Texas front rank, one of their color-bearers planted his colors eight or ten feet in front of his regiment and was instantly shot dead,"

Johnston continued even further to talk about each Union man, perhaps realizing his destiny right then and there, running forward into fire,

> "Received death as speedily as his predecessors."

By some accounts the Confederate soldiers began to feel guilt-stricken as if they were assassins not soldiers in war. One said,

> "Though they had been my enemies, my heart bled at the sickening scene."

Why do they keep coming, they wondered? Why not retreat? This makes no sense. Ambrose described a dead-line that if crossed was certain death and they all knew exactly where it was because it became lined by corpses and eventually stacked by corpses by which the Confederacy could even have hidden their location if they wanted to. The dead-line was described as a group of men shot in the head, with their,

> "Skulls busted open and their brains running out."

All that horror and never making it to the enemy line.

If you visit Pickett's Mill, you can look at the ravine and the hill/precipice upon which the Union ran up and almost see them lined up body by body like cordwood as described and stretching out the line. Only a third of the men were ever within fifteen paces of the Confederates, and none within ten. Unlike the bayonet and hand-to-hand fighting at New Hope, the bullets and rifles were the true cause of death at Pickett's Mill. No command was given to the Union men to fall back, and they followed their orders valiantly. Bierce was fascinated with this dedication and loyalty, this allegiance to the cause and the willingness to die.

Man after man approached the dead-line, and as the line began to fall apart and move back, they were flanked by the Confederates from Arkansas. But the Union in their last gasp, for whatever heart they had left in them, and an instinctual desire to survive, formed a line and fired. They used the woods to their advantage. It stopped that group of Confederates briefly enough so that they could continue to make their way back. They passed neighboring brigades including Gibson's … who Bierce accounts, had not been five minutes behind them. Fourty-five minutes had elapsed without relief on their brigade. Gibson's brigade didn't make it within one hundred yards of the Confederates, their lines broken within a minute and suffering considerable losses. That day Bierce estimated Union casualties to be about 1,400 with at least half being from Hazen's men. General Johnson counted 700, but Bierce said he knew the numbers were different. Bierce wrote,

> "I remember that we were all astonished at the uncommonly large proportion of dead to wounded—a consequence of the uncommonly close range at which most fighting was done."

When Howard received orders to end the Union attack, at long last just after 6:00 PM, Howard had to prepare to protect his flank and get up to Acworth evading Johnston. Whilst debating what to do, a shell fragment ripped off part of his boot. He began to cry,

> "I am afraid to look down!"

repeatedly – as he had already lost an arm in battle before. The shell had somehow ripped off the bottom of the General's boot and only bruised his foot giving Howard a limp. It's said Howard directed the lines of the maimed whilst focusing on his foot and sent one last wave of men to recover the Union wounded as much as they were able. The Confederacy released a volley to those that were ordered forward and then the Union had to wait until nighttime to gather their dead. But Confederate Generals prepared at night to launch one more attack. They let out their rebel cry within the close ear shot of the Union scaring the Union men out of the way after they fired one volley.

Texans in Granbury's Brigade pour deadly volley into advancing Union at Pickett's Mill

Confederate General Granbury's men, seemed increasingly cruel, operating in an all is fair in war mentality when they caught stragglers in the woods, and killed them all as they pled for their lives.

Howard spoke of his men that night and witnessing them,

> "Faint fires here and there revealed men wounded, armless, legless, or eyeless; some with heads bound up with cotton strips, some standing and walking nervously around, some sitting with bended forms, and some prone upon the earth,"

wrote Howard.

> "A few men, in despair, had resorted to drink for relief. The sad sounds of those in pain were mingled with the oaths of the drunken and the more heartless. That night will always be a sort of nightmare to me."

At the end, it was estimated that the Union casualty count would sort to around 1,600 men compared to the Confederates, 500. Seven hundred of the Union deaths had occurred outright. As stated though, most were dead within hours or days after the battle if not killed outright. Studies are taking place to find out, if perhaps, the fatality number could be almost double. Not all bodies were recovered from the site, especially in regard to the Union. And the site remained vacant for a near century after the war, left mostly to the dead with the locals preventing access to the land. When the dead Union were removed, it would be only head and torso they would take and it is said on the park grounds, in an undisclosed location, there remains that limb pit filled with all the post-mortem and injured limbs – many who did their own amputations that day on-site or had them done by anyone of any skill. Bodies were arguably left behind in full as well, though at such close capacity, it's not certain how many of their remains would be left.

I tell you all this about Pickett's Mill – the gruesome, bloody nature of it all because that is the energy that is left behind. Sherman would not even write about Pickett's Mill and acted as if he had to move on and as if it was a negligible loss. Ambrose Bierce suggested that Sherman and others be held accountable and charged with war crimes for sentencing their mean to death with a haphazard plan that never had to take place. No charges were brought forward and for Sherman, who believed more than any other Union general, "all was fair in love and war." Plus, he had

Woods at Pickett's Mill Battlefield, 2022

Lincoln's unwavering support in his decisions. It's a harrowing story and people feel as if the surface has just been scratched at Pickett's Mill. Bierce is the utmost source on the issue those studies are in progress as of the writing this to find out if about the increased casualty count and also exactly who was fighting that day. Some say even Georgia men were there and that is under study as well. History does not always reveal itself so quickly.

History places the Battle of Pickett's Mill on the smaller side of battle – and in scale, it is but in horror, it tops the list. If energy can be felt, the scent of blood smelled distant in the air, the somber quiet hush upon the woods, over a 160 years later, then it is evident something historically grave happened there.

The park rangers are no stranger to stories from visitors of voices, cannon fire, phantom musketry, and such at Pickett's Mill. They've even met descendants of soldier who died there and who have reported feelings of their ancestors standing with them at the spot where they met their end. But they go on to say, there's nothing to be scared of Pickett's Mill and if anything, we should give our empathy to any spirit who may find themselves left behind in such a place as this.

In the 1990s, at Pickett's Mill a security officer reported that he came upon a man who appeared to be a Confederate officer on horseback by the creek. She called out to the potential reenactor and upon not receiving a response, quickly made way to the office to discover there were no reenactors present. Years later in 2016, a family returning from church in the vicinity also reported a Confederate soldier with a rifle cross in front of them and disappear to the side of the road. They got out of the car but couldn't find him.

When you visit Pickett's Mill, it's important to mentally prepare yourself – not for the sighting of an apparition but for the experience of walking into a place that inhabited terror, sacrifice and the martyred, yet oft forgotten, death of thousands.

Dallas

Though this site is not protected due to urban development, there are plenty of signs around the Dallas region in Paulding County regarding the battle that took place. This rounds out the trifecta in a sense of battles the New Hope and Pickett's Battles in the days prior. The Confederate right had been attacked in Pickett's Mill and as such, the Confederates probed Union defense on Sherman's right in Dallas. What started as a skirmish escalated into fighting among the thousands gathered. By the Battle of Dallas and among the battles of New Hope and Dallas together – it was estimated there were over 80,000 Union troops and 40,000 Confederate. In Dallas alone – the numbers of engaged were estimated to be about 11,500 for Union and 10,000 for Confederate. The heavy fighting that escalated led to casualties of up to 1,200 for the Confederate army and about 379 for the Union. The fighting continued from May 28 until eventually the Confederates were repulsed and retreated on June 1. This led the engagement down to Marietta, closer and closer to Atlanta.

The Marietta Operations:

Pine Mountain, Gilgal Church & Latimer's Farm

The Marietta Operations and action at Pine Mountain dominated the early half of June 1864 in the Atlanta Campaign. A series of battles between June 10 and June 19 occurred from Lost Mountain to Pine Mountain following the previous trifecta at the end of May. The Confederates had withdrawn to a new defense line and caused Sherman to rearrange his forces. The Union left 2,000 men to garrison Rome, Georgia, 1,500 men to garrison Allatoona and arrived in Acworth, Georgia with 9,000 veterans. Their aim was to take position on the railroad, rebuild the bridges and assure Sherman's access to advance. Johnston estimated that he was gravely outnumbered two to one and though outnumbered it was more three to two in actuality. Johnston going between Lost Mountain and Gilgal Church decided to also focus on the railroad. On June 10, Sherman advanced and occupied "Big Shanty," and found the Confederates holding an area known as Brushy Mountain. The Union army deployed themselves in columns, left, center and right toward Newton's Mill, Pine Mountain and Gilgal Church accordingly. On June 10, the Union ran into the Confederate skirmishers near Pine Mountain. Though a skirmish ensued, the Union only had orders to dig entrenchments not fight as Johnston had hoped would have been the case. The weather was rainy and treacherous throughout the days leading up to this part of the campaign but the railroad for the Union had been fixed and Sherman was using locomotive whistles to taunt the Confederates. The rain continued until June 14, and Sherman took a closer look at Pine Mountain.

Sherman asked his men to fire three salvos – which is a simultaneous discharge of artillery. To overwhelm, distract and often intimidate, a salvo would be useful. Several Confederates on Pine Mountain witnessed this artillery and started to disperse after the first salvo. But as the second and third salvos took place, Confederate General Polk was found struck in the side by a 3-inch ordnance rifle that had gone through his chest, ripped out his heart and mangled both arms. The remaining Generals reluctantly had to leave the scene. Eventually, the 30th Illinois captured the ridge that overlooked Hood's men and the Confederates withdrew again. This led Johnston to focus on the other end – Gilgal Church.

It was a smart focus because Sherman believed all Confederates had retreated after Pine Mountain and Sherman focused on flanking Kennesaw Mountain and seizing Gilgal Church. The Union had a few small successes enroute to Gilgal and Hooker's Corps overran front Confederate outworks however were repulsed east of Gilgal. The Union troops could not break through the Confederate main line despite several desperate hours of fighting in the east. What they could not get through were Cleburne's men at Gilgal Church the night of June 15 to 16. Many Alabama, Arkansas and Texas men recounted their time tearing down the church before fighting commenced so the Union could not take it. There were an estimated 650 Union casualties and 250 Confederate for the action at Gilgal. For the most part the Confederates had the upper hand that day and the Union a little bit of success on the eastern flank. Sherman still hoped for Johnston's retreat and ordered to push ahead. Thomas ignored orders and instead attacked Confederates. Polk's nephew was brutally injured in the withdrawal in the night of the Confederates and had to have his leg amputated after the crossfire. Cleburne's lined had been shelled from three different directions and fire had broken out in the area. Sherman and the Confederates like Cleburne had lost some control and pivoted toward a location known as Latimer's Farm.

On June 17, Thomas ordered another attack on the Confederates however equipped with Wood's Division who had been mercilessly slaughtered at Pickett's Mill, they moved slowly, timidly and hesitantly forward with their limited number. This angered Sherman who gave no pity for what they had endured. Their slowness allowed Johnston to figure out what was going on and prepare a new defense line for the Confederacy and then the rain returned. Heavy skirmish lines emerged, and fifty Confederates were captured. The Union captured the farm area and considered it a victory with a resulting 200 Confederate casualties. Today, you can visit the Battle of Gilgal Church battlefield and see a reconstruction of the Confederate earthworks and visit the neighboring Pine Mountain and imagine the confusion, the skirmish and hear the salvos in the distance.

Kolb's Farm

But as the fighting continues … the more haunted territory awaits to welcome the inhabitants of its new landscape on Kennesaw Mountain. Just days before the battle at Kennesaw, another farm would become the site of a bloody battle and that was the Kolb Farm near to Marietta and advancing toward the Kennesaw Mountain line. The Kolb Farm site is part of the Kennesaw Mountain National Battlefield today and the original house for the Kolb family still exists on the site. The Kolb's had left the area upon Union approach and came back to ultimate destruction after the battle on June 22, 1864. The Union Army had set themselves up on a low ridge and awaited Confederate arrival with nearly 40 cannon and outnumbering Confederates by 3,000 men. They opened their batteries with shell and canister fire when the Confederates arrived just 500 yards away. The Confederate troops panicked, and confusion came under a sky of smoke and artillery fire. Men fled into the ravine or into the tree line, but the Union continued to fire down on the ravine with "plunging shot," and the Confederates were massacred. It's estimated that General

Hood lost 1,500 men and two-thirds from one division while the Union only suffered 250 casualties.

Not too many ghostly sightings have been reported at the family farmhouse, but the property was divided up between the National Parks Service and housing developments later on. A development known as Kolb Ridge Court built on part of the battle land has several modern residents who claim Civil War soldiers walk through homes and one home claims the ghost of a soldier even lives in their guest room! A family known as the Tatums had an encounter with a ghostly spirit in their house on the development. Mr. Tatum went to the bedroom bathroom one night and Mrs. Tatum to the hallway one. Mrs. Tatum saw a shadowy figure of a man walk by her bedroom door donning a hat and an overcoat. He looked like he was moving hastily judging by the swing in his arm and he headed downstairs. Assuming, it was her husband, she paid him no mind and went back to her bedroom only to discover her husband in bed. Though this shocked her, she shrugged it off until about a month later when she was reading in bed after dinner while her husband was fastening some boards in the hallway. Her husband stepped away from the project and she heard the drill turn on and off repeatedly. Confused once more, she went out to discover that the drill was cold and not moving at all. The Tatums also were no stranger to popping noises, tugs on their clothes, cold spots and more. Their decorative bells sometimes ring on their own and items continue to spill and move as if the soldiers are making themselves quite at home in the houses built upon the land on which they died! Some swear Kolb's farm is also a hot spot for spirit photography and capturing evidence on camera – so paranormal investigators may find themselves wanting to pay a visit to check it out!

Lafayette

As bloody horror was about to overcome the beautiful mountain landscape of Kennesaw Mountain near Atlanta in an unimaginable way, back up in Northwest Georgia, one of the long-forgotten events of the Atlanta Campaign took place on the outskirts of many other battles in north Georgia. On June 24, there was the Battle of LaFayette up near Chickamauga region. It was a peculiar battle between a force of Confederates and a force of Southern Unionists. Union Colonel Watkins of the 3rd Brigade, 1st Cavalry had occupied Lafayette also known as Chatooga with 450 men from Kentucky Cavalry and headquartered in the town Court house on June 18. On June 24, controversial Confederate General Pillow, once fired by Confederate President, Jefferson Davis and one of General Bragg's only defenders, was assigned with disrupting Sherman's communications between Chattanooga and Atlanta and that brought him to the small town occupied by Southern Unionists. Upon their arrival around 3:00 AM into town they intended to burn railroad bridges over Chickamauga Creek and generally harass those lines. Watkin's Southern Unionists were taken a bit by surprise and quickly barricaded their quarters and fought back but barricaded in for safety, they found themselves running out of provisions for weapons and nourishment. By 8:30 AM, a Union picket had gotten out for help and found the 4th Kentucky Mounted Infantry under Union General Croxton. Croxton quickly engaged Pillow's men and stampeded their horses. Pillow eventually abandoned and withdrew with a loss of 23 killed and 78 captured. The Union suffered only seven killed and 53 captured in comparison.

Several Confederate horses were lost as well. The local historic Marsh House Museum that had been built in the 1830s has had curious paranormal investigators look into the local hauntings and capture what they believe to be photographic evidence of a Civil War soldier wandering – perhaps from this battle? More on that can be found in the chapter about the house. The house did not specify uniform but the town of Lafayette named after the Revolutionary War hero, with its proximity to Chickamauga and Chattanooga most certainly boasts home to any number of spirits from the surrounding battles and skirmishes.

Kennesaw Mountain

Just days after the fighting at Kolb's Farm, the Confederate and Union armies found themselves at the Battle of Kennesaw Mountain on June 27, 1864. Sherman had realized after Kolb's Farm that the Confederate Army was stretched thin in their seven-mile defense line taking place in a half-moon around Kennesaw Mountain. Typically, Sherman avoided pitched battles at fortified positions like Kennesaw and Johnston knew that. Fortifying around Kennesaw gave a distinct advantage to the Confederates. The Mountain, 1,800 feet in elevation was intimidating, especially for those unfamiliar with it. But Union confidence was bolstered, especially after Kolb's farm and as such, Sherman formed a full-frontal attack. It would be the very first frontal attack the Union ordered during the Atlanta Campaign which, as you may have noted, had been a series of flanking maneuvers up until that point. Sherman's attack orders were issued on June 24 to assault Confederate right and center and utilize the Army of Ohio to divert the Confederate left. If they could do this, the gateway to Atlanta and the Union destination at long last would be had for the U.S.

Confederates Dragging Guns up Kennesaw Mountain, 1888 – Buel & Johnson – Battles & Leaders of the Civil War

Army. And the Confederacy would have to give up the gateway to the Deep South in a much more definitive way than they already had at Chattanooga Campaign. Though the armies numbered in the tens of thousands in total at this time, the strength of the Union at this battle was about 16,225 and the Confederates 17,733. The battle scene erupted on the morning of June 27 and quickly made

Kennesaw Mountain one of the most dreadful battlefields in Georgia, some would say, second only to Chickamauga. Because of geography, Chickamauga and Kennesaw were both Confederate victories, the scale of the battle was simply different.

At 8 in the morning Union troops with more than 50 cannon came up to the region and skirmished with Confederates to prevent movement to nearby locations known as Little Kennesaw and Pigeon Hill. The rifle pits were entrenched all around and, when visiting Kennesaw, you can see some earthworks that remain where the Union marched into the well-fortified Confederate works but due to incline, rain, flush trees, and low visibility, they would absolutely fall unawares to the Confederate cannon that could and would fire back upon them. The Union backed off the Confederate artillery and instead focused upon the center of the Union line only 400 yards away from the Confederacy. Union Lt. Colonel Joseph Fullerton remarked of the scene,

> "Kennesaw smoked and blazed with fire, a volcano as grand as Etna."

The Confederates knew the Union was making more demonstrations than assaults and were secure in their entrenchments while the Union was exposed to steep slopes and thickets in the bad weather. One Union General removed his men from their original attempt to break through the line when he found them being uselessly slain. It was two miles to the south, near the center line that the main attack began at 9:00 AM in an area known today as Cheatham Hill. This was where the Union was once more up against the well-entrenched divisions of Confederate Generals Cheatham and Cleburne. The Union was again unable to break through the fierce firing and the terrain.

One Union division under Davis formed column formation with the orders to take the Confederate works and give a signal to reserve to move forward to secure the railroad and cut Confederate troops in two. Union Colonel McCook's Brigade embarked forward to do this crossing a large wheat field to attend the Cheatham Hill. But they came underneath the Confederate works at a large advantage and incline to them. The Confederates were able to essentially, fire down upon the Union at close range. McCook was killed on the Confederate parapet shouting,

"Surrender, you traitors!"

Battle of Kennesaw Mountain, On the line of the Western & Atlantic Railroad, near Marietta, Ga., June 27, 1864.

Hand-to-hand combat ensued until 10:45 AM. The Union brigade lost two commanders, almost all officers and a third of its men at Cheatham Hill which would become better known as The Dead Angle. Sam Watkins of the 1st Tennessee described the carnage at the Dead Angle,

Tunnel Kennesaw Mountain, 2022

"My pen is unable to describe the scene of carnage and death that ensued in the next two hours...talk about other battles, victories, shouts, cheers, and triumphs, but in comparison with this day's fight, all other dwarf into insignificance."

It was evident by noon on June 27, that the Union attack had failed. However, two Union Colonels started discussing during the retreat that they needed to lessen the bloodshed under heavy fire and to do so, they would dig into the brow of the hill near the Dead Angle which would cover them from the heavy fire about 30 yards away. Half of the Union troops fired toward the earthworks with the Confederates and the other half dug trenches with tin cups and bayonets. At night, the Union brought up tools and dug two lines of entrenchments and then a standoff of sorts would ensue.

For six days, sniper fire was exchanged between the Confederates and the remaining Union troops with both sides expecting an attack from their opponent at any moment. On June 29, there was a brief truce to bury the dead. The Union intended to blow up the Confederate earthworks on the Fourth of July after that and began constructing a tunnel in which to do so, part of which remains today. But on July 2, the Confederates left the area and retreated into a flanking maneuver from Sherman's men. The tunnel entrance was marked with a stone arch in 1914.

Kennesaw Mountain near to the Dead Angle and the Tunnel marked by a monument to the Illinois men who lost so many that day, has become known as one of the most haunted locations in all of Georgia and for Civil War sites as a whole. A journalist for the *Daily Enquirer Sun* out of Columbus, Georgia wrote of Kennesaw's prominence and the haunted history it held decades ago,

> "A grander old veteran of the war stands not today on Georgia's soil. From base to summit, he is battle scarred. It is said that nearly every tree and rock upon him bears the marks of having been torn and cut by the missiles of war and twenty years of agriculture not served to obliterate traces of the rifle pits and

> breastworks that seamed and furrowed his sides, but he has long ago put off his bloody garments."

He describes seeing it from the train and almost seeing the battle taking place,

> "In imagination, see the great battle fought o'er again; then an abrupt turn in the track suddenly shuts the scene from our sight."

And in that brief statement, the journalist gathers the full sentiment of those who look upon a battle-stricken site such as Kennesaw – a landscape, no matter, how beautiful that remains forever changed and nature forever changed by its grapple with death. The Union casualties of 3,000 and the Confederates of 1,000 have their spirits, their souls felt all over the mountainous battle site.

When I first visited Kennesaw Mountain and stood near to the tunnel, imagining the fear and desperation that dominated the US and Confederate armies in their time there, my cousin inquired of me of if I had heard of a song entitled, "Sticks that Made Thunder," by an Americana group known as The Steeldrivers. I informed him that I had not and he went on to explain that it told the tale of a Civil War battle from the perspective of a tree, giving a whole new meaning of course to witness trees. We played it was we stood there by the Illinois monument and listened as we looked upon the battlefield. Tears seemed to well up in my eyes as I could picture the battle to the words and feel the sadness of nature witnessing such grievous loss and the brutality of war.

Now, when I hear that song, I think of standing upon Kennesaw Mountain and what the trees would have seen.

> "Some wear the color of the sky in the winter
> Some, were as blue as the night

They came like a storm with the light of the morn
And they fell through the whole day and night
Colors flew high and they danced in the sky
As I watched them come over the hill
Then to my wonder, sticks that made thunder
Such a great number lay still."

The song continues in haunting imagery and I still think of how I listened that day on top of Kennesaw Mountain. I could hear the roar of the gunfire, the screams of agony, and see the march forward of the Union and the hiding in the breastworks of the Confederates. I could feel the death and the eternity of Mother Nature's memory forever emblazoned onto that landscape. I truly could see the battle happening as if in real time and hear the cannons roar through the trees. It was if I, like the trees were a first-hand witness who could do nothing. And that is the best way I can think of to describe sensation that best describes the spirit of Kennesaw Mountain.

Battlefield Kennesaw Mountain, 2022

Much like at Chickamauga, my favorite ghost story of Kennesaw Mountain comes from a reenactor. He recalled in 2000, being part of the 28th Georgia infantry reenactment group. He was spending the weekend with his comrades of the 28th not because the 28th had fought in that battle but because they were hired to do living history. (To be fair, the Confederate order of battle at Kennesaw Mountain did include a fair amount of Georgians, untypical for many battles in Georgia, but included the 37th Georgia, 4th GA Sharpshooters under General Smith the 1st, 54th, 57th and 63rd GA under General Mercer, the 8th Georgia Battalion and 46th Georgia under General Gist, the 47th, 65th, and the 1st and 2nd Georgia Sharpshooters under General John Jackson, the 1st Georgia Confederate and the 25th, 29th, 30th and 66 Georgia regiments under General Stevens, the Cumming's Georgia Brigade including the 34th, 36th, 39th and 56th Georgia regiments and the 2nd Georgia State Line, the Stovall's Georgia Brigade including the 40th, 41st, 42nd, 43rd, and 52nd Gorgia regiments and the 1st Georgia State Line, Howell's Georgia Battery, Anderson's Georgia Battery, Havis' Georgia Battery, Corput's Cherokee Georgia Battery, Rowan's Georgia Light Battery, Croft's Columbus Georgia Battery and one section of Davis's Georgia Battery. and several Georgia cavalries in Iverson's brigade including the 1st, 2nd, 3rd, 4th and 6th and the 5th Georgia cavalry under Anderson as well.) Perhaps, the inclusion of so many Georgia boys so close to home leads to such a haunting element on the smaller battlefield as well – what stress to feel the battle at your doorstep and to be so close to home but unable to visit. Several soldiers would recount such a sentiment and not being able to say goodbye to their family or get one last visit, oftentimes before they perished.

Nevertheless, let's go back to the 28th and their living history group demonstrating encampments of 19th century lifestyle in the war. It was in late June just before the anniversary of the battle when the group of reenactors, young, old and every age in between were gathered there preparing their camp for the night. They utilized lanterns and candles to light their paths as they trudged through the woods. They described even the smell of death that they likened to the rotting corpse of an animal as they made their way to Cheatham Hill … home of the angle and the tunnel. One of the adult reenactors accompanied by a young boy walked around the Illinois monument toward the angle and began to remark about hair on the arm standing on end for them as they reached the trench. The boy dismissed the sensation and continued their walk on the trail toward the grave of an unknown human soldier buried within feet of the Confederate trenches. (A spot that is now often reported to have much energy and where I always am sure to pay my respects upon visiting.) Their energy of fun had quickly changed to a somber mood and they began to hear sounds all around them accompanying the crickets and cicadas. They heard footsteps, voices and scraping sounds though they were alone. They returned to the monument and split off with their companions in two groups. The adult reenactor's group returned back the way they had come utilizing just one lantern and staying close. A small group of four included the boy, who began to whisper,

> "We gotta get outta here! I don't wanna die!"

The adult eased the boy telling him ghost couldn't hurt him but they boy continued to cry that he was going to die. Finally, they asked the boy what had him so frightened of death and he described his vision in the woods, a

> "Union soldier in a tattered uniform with his left arm all torn up. The soldier walked by, turned his head, and looked at me and walked into the woods."

The boy then looked above the trench line and saw four more soldiers watching the reenactors. The adults claim they didn't see this vision in the dark but wondered if as they stood near the unknown tomb, if what he saw didn't go directly with the sounds of voices and footsteps they heard. It did.

Now, it's generally not allowed to go into the battlefield at night unless you're an employee however Kennesaw Mountain is also heavily developed in many areas abutting the protected battle area and as such roads go all around the populated Atlanta suburb. One local claimed that it was in the evening when he and his teenage son were driving through the Battlefield roads in the early fall and something tried to cross the road right in front of their car. The gentlemen looked out the window, mouth agape as they slowed down to stop for the rider of a horse, a man in a Union cavalry uniform with a saber in hand. He stopped his vehicle with an abrupt push on the brake as the horse and rider came in front of the vehicle and then crossed straight through a fence on the opposite side of the road before vanishing into air. The nervous duo was panic-stricken as they drove home.

The phantoms of Kennesaw Mountain seem to often make themselves known in the most visible way. Some say it's merely a residual haunting reliving itself while others are certain the souls of the deceased still see the living. Both vivid story examples suggest that indeed both theories could be true. The reliving sensation as seen from the 19th century journalist from the train matches the story of the cavalry with the saber. In fact, it even matches a bit what that boy saw except for that one look that was exchanged between the two for a moment. It's that look that makes one wonder, are we standing on a time slip between two worlds, two eras when we go to a battlefield (as we mentioned at New Hope Church).

To be sure, I often feel as if I have one foot in reality and one not upon such a place. And for me, in Georgia, those places are undoubtedly, Chickamauga, Kennesaw (both mountainous landscapes), New Hope Church and the tragic scene of Pickett's Mill.

As for our soldiers in 1864, with the Confederacy having a decisive win at Kennesaw, it gave them a sense of renewed hope. So weary from their losses in the war up to that point losing men by the thousands Kennesaw led them to believe that with some success at one's home, maybe they could actually protect it from its northern invaders. And so, the Atlanta campaign forged on. This time the collective armies were finally going to arrive and face off in Atlanta.

Pace's Ferry & Peachtree Creek

It was just around Independence Day when Sherman's and Johnston's armies found themselves in a region known as Pace's Ferry Road in "old" Atlanta, now in an area close to Northside Drive near to Howell Mill Road. They were headed toward Peachtree Creek when they came upon each other, and a skirmish erupted. Sherman had been continuing to flank Confederate position and sent Howard's IV Corps to pursue retreating Confederates on the railroad. Despite loss at Kennesaw, Sherman's forward momentum toward Atlanta was met with little resistance until they arrived near Vining's Station and crossed over the Chattahoochee River toward Pace's Ferry. The Confederate pontoon bridge over the river was located there and at Pace's Ferry there was a brigade of dismounted Confederate Cavalry. The Confederates desperately tried to get rid of their bridge before the Union gained control, however Union General Thomas was able to push back the Confederates with his men by outnumbering them and thus, preserved the greater part of the bridge. The Union troops, having pushed back the Confederates awaited their Union pontoons and on July 10 moved north and outflanked the Confederates once more. On July 11, the US Army followed orders and the Union secured the heights south of Chattahoochee and the skirmishing at Pace's Ferry had ended. The Union crossed the Chattahoochee River and the last barrier between them, and Atlanta was out of their way.

Confederate General Johnston decided to withdraw across Peachtree Creek north of Atlanta and plan to attack. At long last, instead of running and being defensive, he was ready for the offensive. But his motivation came too little, too late. Confederate President Jefferson Davis was tired of his lack of aggressiveness and assertiveness and replaced him with General Hood, a known, battle-hardened, and brave General, not afraid to be aggressive. You may recall his leg amputation at Chickamauga and that didn't put a stop to him, one bit! The orders switching command came on July 17. The switch took place on July 18 with Hood launching a counter-offensive and, immediately thereafter on July 19, Hood suddenly learned that Sherman had split armies coming in for a swift attack on multiple directions. Union General Thomas' men were headed toward Atlanta while the other Union generals headed towards Decatur to cut supply lines. Thomas had to cross Peachtree Creek before he could construct breastworks with his Union men and during that time, he would be vulnerable. Hood determined this made it the perfect time to attack. Hood intended to wreck half of Sherman's force before reinforcements could arrive and they could only do so if they struck hard and with full force.

Confederates were outnumbered by just over a thousand with the Union Army of the Cumberland at an estimated 21,655 engaged and the Confederate Army of Tennessee with 20,250. As soon as Hood planned his attacks, a Union force threatened the Confederate right east of Atlanta and he had to split up his force to react and shift his line. This led to a 90-minute lag time in shifting. You may recall in Chickamauga, that this lag time can be detrimental to an army and incredibly deadly. Because of this lag time, the Union Army crossed Peachtree Creek in the opportunity gap and began entrenching.

Confederate General Hardee advanced in the later afternoon against the Union men and the Union was ready to respond accordingly with musketry and cannon fire which would go back and forth for hours from about 3:30 to 6:00 PM. The Confederates were never able to break through the Union line. For a brief time, there was overlap but never a break. Hardee's attacks failed. Then a division of General Stewart under General Loring tried to attack near to Tanyard Creek and though they did briefly overrun Union lines, it was not maintained. Going to the other flank, Confederate General Walthall's men broke through the Union flank but were quickly repulsed. In fact, it got incredibly violent and eventually the Union counterattacked and pushed back the Confederates. The fighting on this flank also ended around 6:00 PM and the Battle of Peach Tree Creek ended in a decisive Union victory. Hood had too late of notice, in some strategist's opinions to come up with a proper plan. Perhaps Johnston should have been removed earlier, just like Bragg if they had wanted a chance. The Union and Confederacy had devastating casualty counts at Peachtree Creek with the Union losing 1,750 men to death and injury and the Confederacy losing 2,500 to the same. There is no battlefield you can visit to mark Peachtree Creek which has been developed over in the Atlanta region by commercial and residential buildings making a city landscape. Nevertheless, the battle hauntings continue.

In 1998, ABC News affiliate, WSB-TV moved into its new studios built atop trenches used in the battle on West Peachtree Street and soon thereafter, began to hear suspicious noises, noticed items moving and loud inexplicable activity in one big empty space at the offices. A sales executive claimed that something quietly came up behind her and flipped her hair playfully only for her to turn around and see no one there. An HR employee consistently heard papers shuffling and furniture moving when no one else was there and no machines were on. The staff, affectionately and fearfully named their ghost, "The General" and kept an area of their offices unpopulated, including a full cubicle where they claim he lives. They dare not visit him. They understood they built upon his ground and were giving him, at least some of his space. Residents along the area have long claimed that the spirits of soldiers can be felt when walking along the creek itself – and perhaps, in an urban landscape, the sense of what has come before is what the intuitive can sense most deeply. A marker of nature through the city would certainly bring back the memory of an earlier time, especially a time of conflict.

Though the area is developed, the people of Atlanta had wanted to protect it for decades after the war and in 1899 petitioned for it to be a national park. They claimed that they were still retrieving rudimentary made coffins and bodies from its land. Perhaps the hastiness of 20th Century development ruined that objective and that's what left the spirits restless in Atlanta, wandering for a place to rest peacefully? Maybe they have come to travel among their artifacts at the Atlanta History Center just two miles from the battlefield or in the resting place of so many Confederate dead – the widely known and haunted, Oakland Cemetery on the other side of the city. Nevertheless, Peachtree Creek was not where Atlanta's brush with war would end – in fact, it was only the beginning.

The Civil War and Atlanta had a much more deadly relationship that would take over in the sweltering summer heat, a Confederate's last effort to win, almost a desperate plea. Hood wasn't willing to give up and neither was the South. And two days later on July 22, 1864, the stage was set for the Battle of Atlanta.

Atlanta

On July 22, 1864, in the sweltering summer heat, exhausted troops numbering over 75,000 in force between Confederate and Union armies converged in Atlanta. The Union army continued to remain divided around the city on July 21, 1864. General McPherson's Army had it's left flank in the air and they were near the railroad. This seemed the best place for Confederate General Hood to launch a Stonewall Jackson-Chancellorsville inspired flank attack on the Union. The ghost of Stonewall Jackson remained with the Confederacy throughout the war and remains with many Southerners till modern day, sort of a human demi-god of military strategy and swiftness. Hood planned to send General Hardee to drop back from lines north of the city in a fortified perimeter overnight and then would have the remaining Generals and their brigades follow accordingly. Hardee would go through the city with Wheeler's cavalry and hit Union General McPherson's left rear while Wheeler attacked wagon trains. The plan was good in theory, but in practice it required an ambitious 15-mile march through the night by Hardee's troops with an attack upon arrival at dawn. That is a lot to ask of battle-weary men. Nevertheless, this is what they had to do. Due to the long march, the Confederate troops arrived late and exhausted. The night was hot, and the men were feeling sluggish when their assault divisions arrived not in the wrong place, but not in the right place either. They weren't far enough into the Union rear area when Hardee deployed them on a rough terrain. At this point, in the day, it was high noon. This was problematic because it was not dawn when engagement would have been easier. And adding to complications, Confederate General is Walker was killed during the placement.

General Sherman at Federal Fort No. 7 in Atlanta, 1864-1865

The Union under Sherman had opportunity for better luck once again. They were in the prefect position to meet the opening assault from the Confederates and the Confederates met seasoned Union men who were not overweary and who were ready to fight. However, the Confederates had Irishman, Patrick Cleburne's division which had notoriously been one of the most hard-hitting of the Confederacy throughout this campaign and they struck down the Union's Seventeenth corps as their reputation did not disappoint.

After this strike, was when Union General McPherson himself came from the Sherman headquarters to check on his men's contention with the Confederates. Part of the rebel army in Cleburne's division were on the wagon road when McPherson made his way down that passage. McPherson received the welcome one might expect from the rebels in such a circumstance. The Confederates were surprised but not unprepared for this encounter. They signaled for McPherson to surrender, and McPherson saluted in response and then quickly turned and dashed off in a gallop. Confederate Captain Richard Beard accounts,

> "Corporal Coleman, standing near me, was ordered to fire, and it was his shot that brought General McPherson down."

Some of McPherson's officers and soldiers ran away at the moment McPherson was brought down and the time of death was marked as 2:02 PM on the pocket watch that was smashed at that time McPherson fell. The young Union General's death left a shadow on the Battle of Atlanta for both sides. Why didn't he surrender? That was what the rebels wondered. It was said the rebels retrieved his watch, his sword belt and a book with private papers as he lay there dying. Private George Reynolds of the 17th Corps reported that he tried to assist his mortally wounded General before he took his last breath and placed his head on a blanket while offering him water. The General was unable to speak. The stolen items were later recovered with the watch as exception from some captured rebel soldiers.

McPherson's body was recovered and brought to the door of

Sherman's headquarters where Sherman reacted with deep emotion and reportedly wept at the sight. McPherson was young, relatively speaking, he was only 36 and had even attended West Point with the opposing General Hood. McPherson was the second-highest ranking Union officer killed in action during the war. His fiancée, Emily Hoffman had a whole life planned out with her beloved James (McPherson.) And perhaps that's the tale of all those, officer or not, that haunts the war the most. Someone at home loved them, waited for them, wanted a life without war to experience together. It was said Emily never recovered after hearing the news and locked herself away for weeks. It was then that she received Sherman's letter,

> "My Dear Young Lady, A letter from your Mother to General Barry on my Staff reminds me that I owe you heartfelt sympathy and a sacred duty of recording the fame of one of our Country's brightest and most glorious characters. I yield to none on Earth but yourself the right to excel me in lamentations for our Dead Hero. Why should death's darts reach the young and brilliant instead of older men who could better have been spared."

His letter confirmed the worst -- the death of her beloved and recalled several battle tales of the men together. One also must wonder; did Sherman feel guilty? McPherson had recently requested leave to marry his beloved Emily and Sherman had told him it would have to wait until the end of the war. Grief, guilt, friendship, division – that's the tragedy of it all – the loss of friend, comrade and lover was a loss women and men in households across the North and South felt daily during the War between the States.

Even school companion and Confederate opponent General

Hood was devastated by the loss of his classmate,

> "I will record the death of my classmate and boyhood friend, General James B. McPherson, the announcement of which caused me sincere sorrow. Since we had graduated in 1853, and had each been ordered off on duty in different directions, it has not been our fortune to meet. Neither the years nor the difference of sentiment that had led us to range ourselves on opposite sides in the war had lessened my friendship; indeed the attachment formed in early youth was strengthened by my admiration and gratitude for his conduct toward our people in the vicinity of Vicksburg. His considerate and kind treatment of them stood in bright contrast to the course pursued by many Federal officers."

One can visit the site of McPherson's death today, the site still marked and feel the sadness and tragedy almost overwhelming so even in the urban landscape. You can find this site at the intersection of Monument and McPherson in Atlanta – just off Glenwood.

After the death of McPherson and their initial success in coming on to McPherson's men, Cleburne's men were, at least, feeling a battlefield sense of hope, though one always hesitates to rejoice in death, this was still war. And they wondered, if perhaps there was a chance for their side. It seemed even more possible when hen they overran the Union line, captured two guns and several hundred prisoners. Cleburne again had his men in position of an upper hand, but they quickly encountered Union infantry and artillery who had higher ground on a hilltop under Union General Leggett's division and their successes were stopped.

Site of McPherson's Death, Atlanta by George Barnard, 1864

(Library of Congress)

Though Confederates added another division to their side with Cleburne they were completely fired upon in a bloody massacre. By 3:00 PM, just about one hour after McPherson's death, Hood orders another effort for Cheatham's corps in the east. It was a fierce assault against the Union's 15th Corps, briefly successful as was Cleburne's in running over the Union line and capturing artillery. The counterattack, once more, was more powerful and ultimately the Confederates all had to retreat back to their initial positions.

Atlanta, Georgia, Confederate works in front by George N. Barnard (Wikimedia Commons)

The Union had yet another victory and the bloodbath and carnage surrounded Atlanta. Over 9,000 casualties took place in just a few short hours, 3,722 Union soldiers and over 5,500 Confederate. The armies had no time to recover. Sherman wanted to attack the Macon & Western Railroad which was all the Georgia men had left to preserve and they gathered their weary armies and shifted west toward Ezra Church where they put their feet down and a month-long siege began.

The Battle of Atlanta, historically, would remain, the bloodiest and deadliest battle of the Atlanta campaign and once again cannot be visited in a typical sense as the battlefield was not preserved. Cannons mark the death sites of Generals McPherson and Walker (the Confederate general whose death was lost in the chaos of recordings and has had conflicting accounts) and the best place to get a full grasp of the Battle of Atlanta is to visit the Atlanta History Center that houses the original Cyclorama done over time and again throughout the centuries depending on its owner but brought back to an original presentation (or close to). The Cyclorama presentation gives the visitor a full idea of what Atlanta looked like and how the battle took place. Many of the Confederate casualties would come to rest Oakland Cemetery in Atlanta for their final slumbers. And, in fact, the Oakland Cemetery has become best known as the most haunted place in Atlanta and, definitely, the most haunted place as it relates to the Battle of Atlanta. Author Jim Miles has referred to it as "Bivouac of the Dead," as have many others, inspired by a poem of the same name about war heroes. The spookiest story of Oakland cemetery comes from a man who heard the roll call of soldiers being called out in the section saved for unknown burials and who suddenly heard his own name at the end … but we'll get more into that when we speak of the site of Oakland Cemetery later on.

Author, Jim Miles reported that another ghost of a Confederate soldier from the Battle of Atlanta seems to roam, sometimes homeless, along the underground tracks where the Western & Atlantic Railroad once stood and where the Georgia Railroad Freight depot was developed in Atlanta. The ghost named Colonel C.J. by witnesses has not been known to interact with any witnesses. Many believe that the ghost of General McPherson is one of the many specters of Atlanta as well.

Atlanta was never the same as it was before the summer of 1864. Atlanta's Oakland Cemetery is home to the interment of one Margaret Mitchell who immortalized the Battle of Atlanta in her novel that was transformed into a feature film known to all as *Gone with the Wind.* It is her description that some say depicts the fear of Atlanta that summer and I've heard folks say that it is the most historically accurate depiction in the artistic vision of all of *Gone with the Wind.* The fear and terror for the people of Atlanta as the Union army came into the city, the chaos, the running, the city of civilians losing heart in their home and in the war was all real. And worse yet, was the worry, were they, the residents of the

South next? (The answer was yes, but not for just a bit longer.) The truth was Sherman's arrival was an omen of things to come for soldiers and civilians.

Fires Blaze while Union destroys railroad in "scorched earth" policy at Atlanta (Britannica.com)

As for local Georgia men in the order of Battle for Atlanta, there are many Georgia regiments to list here – many of which were also at Kennesaw Mountain. The regiments included the 37th Georgia, 4th Georgia Sharpshooters, 46th Georgia, 8th Georgia Battalion, 15st Georgia Volunteers, 54th, 57th, and 63rd Georgia, the 1st, 25th, 29th, 30th, and 66th Georgia, and the 1st Georgia Sharpshooters Battalion all in Hardee's Corps but not in Cleburne's Division. There were also the 2nd Georgia State Troops, the 34th, 36th, 39th and 56th Georgia as well as the 1st Georgia State Line with the 40th, 41st, 42nd, 43rd and 52nd Georgia in Hood's Corps. The Confederacy was also backed up by the 1st Division of the Georgia State Militia with reserve soldiers – who were generally older or extremely young under the leadership of Gustavus Smith. Additionally in Wheeler's Cavalry Corps, they had Iverson's Brigade of Georgia Cavalry including the 1st, 2nd, 3rd, 4th, and 6th as were at Kennesaw. More men seeing their home torn apart by war and destruction while being so close yet so far from their family in the scene and heat of battle.

Though the city of Atlanta, is not a battlefield where one can listen in the quiet nature, there's still a sense that in brief moments the city fades away and the old dirt and cobble stone streets emerged covered in earthworks, gunfire and smoke as the Union versus Confederacy fight ever on in eternity.

But let's go forward with those who survived this battle as they were make their way to Ezra Church.

Ezra Church

As Sherman focused on the railroads running southwest from the city and arranged his armies accordingly whilst protecting the city of Atlanta in Union hands, and protecting the position north of the city with the Army of the Ohio and Army of Cumberland respectively, Sherman took the Army of the Tennessee, (now with General Howard in charge replacing his protégé, McPherson) toward the railroads. On July 27, Howard's men embarked outward but Confederate cavalry was ready and watching.

Hood received news of their movement within just a few hours of their departure. Howard's men filled in the Union line toward the railroad throughout the day of July 27 and once in position on July 28, they dug in and put their artillery on Howard's line. Union General Logan extended the extreme right of the army with his divisions and brought forth more ammunition. Perhaps, it was the loss of McPherson or perhaps it was their frustration at the continuance of this war but the Union Army was ready to end these rebel soldiers however they could on that warm summer day. Hood knew they would extend their line toward Lick Skillet Road, or at least assumed so and as such, sent 30-year-old General Stephen Lee to go along the road and take position at Ezra Church (the church much like New Hope marked a key crossroads). The Confederates goal was to "stop the Yankees," as they maneuvered south down the road. Confederate General Stewart was going to take his men and attack in the rear of the enemy as they made their way down the road, and this was to lessen the blow that would come upon Lee and his men.

It was a good strategy for Hood to have this assault come on to both sides of the Union. What the Confederates could not know was that the Union was already there at Ezra Church. Oblivious to this, the rebels moved according to plan and not according to reality. As the men began their march, the cavalry members reported the Union at the front, and they realized there was no hope of defensive position. Young General Lee decided to attack straightway on the morning of July 28 with this news and waste no time. The first division was sent in around high noon once more through unfriendly wooded terrain. The Union was ready, they had log and stone built works and a cruel motive in their hearts to take down as many as they could that day. Something was different about that day at Ezra Church. The Confederates watched their men "driven with great slaughter." The lack of coordination in the face of this unexpected death march, similar to the death march of the Union at Pickett's Hill took over the Confederate army.

The Union was strengthening as the rebel army fell apart. The Union had reinforcements upon reinforcements until finally Confederate General Clayton waited for orders before he continued in an useless fight. Lee's Corps was done but Stewart's came in as fast as they could. Lee provided the intelligence that the Union couldn't have been there that long which was not true. He didn't realize what an upper hand they had had being there overnight. So, when the reinforcements came, the "slaughter continued." Confederate soldiers dropped by the hundreds and began to hide, screaming, yelling for help – not their fierce rebel cry, but a cry of horror and fear as they desperately sought shelter to survive. The blows continued until nightfall when the Confederates withdrew their surviving members as best they could.

The Confederates lost nearly 3,000 men – possibly more that day and the Union fewer than 650. It was a massacre and the siege of Atlanta had only just begun. And as for the battle-weary men…searching for answers, they were about to have their own paranormal experiences that were no fugue state of Georgia heat could cause. They were caused only by the reality of death surrounding them making itself known in a way no one other than they could imagine.

Stoneman's Raids (1864 & 1865) Dunlap Hill & Sunshine Church Macon; King's Tanyard – Winder

Though Sherman had much of his army surrounding Atlanta and the war raged on all around the Southern City, the Union men imprisoned in the hell known as Andersonville Prison south of Macon, were waiting on "Uncle Billy," to send someone to the rescue. They knew their comrades were in Georgia and felt like their companions must in some way, be there for them to be saviors. What they couldn't or wouldn't want to realize was that it was too risky according to Grant and Sherman to have a big rescue mission of prisoners and it would not be a good use of valuable resources.

However, General George Stoneman convinced Sherman to allow him to attempt a cavalry raid to free the men held at Camp Sumter in Andersonville and, also, Camp Oglethorpe in Macon. Sherman's conditions to Stoneman were to proceed with caution and only make movements if conditions were favorable after breaking a rail line between Macon and Atlanta. That was still Sherman's and the Union's priority in the midst of warfare. They had plans to stick to. Thus, Stoneman and 2,104 men proceeded into the hot, middle Georgia terrain on July 27, 1864, going down the railroad, trying to damage the rail lines as much as possible, tearing up tracks and also according to many southerners terrorizing them along the way – looting houses, stealing livestock, burning barns, etcetera. Perhaps, Stoneman was acting in advance of what Sherman would come to do just months later in similar destructive, "scorched earth," etiquette.

Upon reaching the area known as Dunlap Hill near Macon, on July 30, 1864, skirmishing had gotten intense and seemingly was going to turn into a battle. Stoneman ran into a heavy line of skirmishers three miles out from Macon at the Dunlap location who fell back into their earthwork fortifications around the city. The Confederates also had a battery of field artillery at the Macon location of Fort Hawkins, having existed there since 1808. They had a lookout post to assist them and were able to fire heavily upon the Union lines. Because of their advantage and having local Georgia men in the militia ready to protect their home fiercely, Stoneman's troops weren't able to respond right away. Later, the 23rd Indiana Battery fired one of its 3-inch rifle guns on the city of Macon, itself creating total destruction of anything in its path, and disturbingly, they acknowledged the intent of civilian death. In fact, the cannonball house in Macon still contains a cannonball in the walls from that very event. Women, children and enslaved people were almost equal targets for this group of Northerners.

Ultimately, despite these attempts, the Union wasn't able to break through Confederate lines and capture the railroad bridge they wanted and they withdrew. Stoneman's raid was not over, however, nor was the war's presence in Central Georgia by Dunlap Farm/Dunlap Hill. However, first, when Stoneman failed to defeat the Georgia militia at Dunlap Hill, he needed to find a way to cross the Ocmulgee River if he was going to make it further south to Andersonville. And he figured out that the Confederate cavalry was moving location to follow him. So, his move south was looking increasingly unlikely and dangerous. Stoneman decided to turn around and bring his men back to Sherman's lines in Atlanta swiftly so that the followers could not catch up. Stoneman and his men reached an area known as Sunshine Church, named after a church like many other battle sites. It was here, he discovered several Confederate soldiers were dug into a ridge waiting for him. These men were under the command of seasoned veteran, Confederate General Iverson's and were his Georgia cavalry. Iverson was a local man who had lost much of his men in defeat at Gettysburg and was sent by Lee to go run the cavalry in Georgia. He was familiar with the territory he grew up near and battle-hardened.

Iverson blocked the retreat route and as such Stoneman ordered 2,100 of his men to attack and the Battle of Sunshine Church officially began. This was fight was vicious; the locals wanted to defend their home and the Union troops were desperate to get out. The fighting took place in a rough, wooded countryside. The Union was stalled long enough for the Confederate reinforcements to make their way up from Macon and attack the rear. Stoneman quickly realized he was surrounded and started grasping at straws. His last-ditch effort was that he would stay behind with part of his command waging battle while two of his brigades tried to escape. Perhaps, he could save some, if not all. The two officers bringing their men back to Sherman's lines were Colonel Capron and Lieutenant Colonel Adams; most of Adam's men made it.

Capron's, however, were attacked in Gwinnett County at the Battle of King's Tanyard. Adams and Capron had thought that they could attack Athens on their way out and took different roads. Capron's road led him to Jug Tavern where a number of enslaved people began to follow him. By August 3, the Confederacy brigade from Kentucky known as the Orphan Brigade surprised the Union of Capron's cavalry in their sleep and overran them with pickets. Many of the cavalry was unarmed because of Sunshine Church and a sort of moving battle took placed between escaped slaves, Union cavalry and the CSA Orphan Brigade. Only Capron and six of his men made it back to Sherman.

Meanwhile, back in the July 31, Battle at Sunshine Church, Stoneman surrendered. His "black guide" was hanged by the Confederates, and they prepared to do the same to the General himself to hold him accountable for his destruction. Stoneman was captured by the Southerners and taken to one of the very prisons he had wanted to emancipate – Camp Oglethorpe. Stoneman was considered the highest-ranking Union officer to ever be captured in the war. The Confederates then built a u-shaped earthwork in front of the Dunlap House to protect the railroad trestle at Walnut Creek from future attacks which would come again just months later in November. The earthworks can still be seen at the site today.

Stoneman's raid in 1864 was ultimately unsuccessful but he would make his way out of Oglethorpe via a prisoner exchange and he was relieved from duty until Major General Schofield of the Union army persuaded Grant to put him back in the game, so to speak. Immediately, Stoneman proposed another raid and stated that he had an ax to grind with the Confederacy. Stoneman said,

> "I owe the Southern Confederacy a debt I am anxious to liquidate and this appears a propitious occasion."

Stoneman's Raid in 1865 throughout the South was authorized by General George Thomas, the Rock of Chickamauga. Stoneman, was this time to free the prisoners from Salisbury Prison in North Carolina and run in to South Carolina to destroy railroads and supplies as the war came to an end. Thomas' instructions were that Stoneman could

> "Destroy but not fight battles."

When it was evident that Sherman had already entered South Carolina, Thomas' orders to Stoneman were revised to go from

Kentucky and Tennessee to Virginia and cutoff escape routes for General Lee.

Ultimately the Stoneman raid with nine Union cavalry regiments started in Morristown, Tennessee through North Carolina and up to Virginia in early April 1865. They destroyed 150 miles of railroad track, burned half the town of Abingdon and then went back to North Carolina where they entered Salisbury. They evacuated the prison there and set fire to it. They moved on to destroy more rail lines and went west through North Carolina before going back into Tennessee accompanied by hundreds of freed slaves.

The 600-mile raid ended April 26, 1865, when oddly, Confederate General Johnston was also surrendering to Sherman in North Carolina. Stoneman felt vindicated but the South was haunted by his final raid at the end of the war. Already suffering from Sherman's March to the Sea in Georgia – more destruction and loss was the last thing the Southerners needed. The famed song, "The Night They Drove Old Dixie Down," written by Robbie Robertson for The Band was written about Stoneman's Raid – the man who had once been captured in Macon, Georgia but came back and assisted in putting one of the last nails in the Confederate coffin inspired the song. They primarily refer to the destruction of rail lines in Danville, Virginia. Lyrics such as,

"Virgil Kane is the name
And I served on the Danville train
Till Stoneman's cavalry came
And tore up the tracks again
In the winter of '65
We were hungry, just barely alive
By May the 10th, Richmond had fell
It's a time I remember, oh so well
The night they drove old Dixie down

And the bells were ringing
The night they drove old Dixie down
And the people were singing
They went, "Na, na, la, na, na, la"
Back with my wife in Tennessee
When one day she called to me,
"Virgil, quick, come see
There goes Robert E. Lee!"

Even, I who have heard the song so many times never seemed to process what the song was about which was the end of a Confederate dream and perhaps, I underestimated its importance. It is the locals of Macon, Georgia who remember that they had once captured General Stoneman, the man who came back with a vengeance and who inspired that song, that still so many in the South feel in their hearts. A song of an end, of destruction, of loss in war. But their capture of Stoneman will forever be part of their proud history.

If you'd like to visit Dunlap Hill, where Stoneman's first 1864 failed raid began, it's actually part of a State Park in Georgia for the Ocmulgee Mounds – Native American mounds that have been preserved for centuries that the fighting actually occurred around. The mounds have their own native and indigenous spiritual energy and many "spirit animals" have been seen around the mounds, but the folks there are no strangers to war ghosts either. On one occasion, visitors to the mounds reported seeing a reenactor in Confederate uniform. They figured it was a tour guide waiting for their group to arrive or a reenactment that was going to take place. When they inquired about the program to see if they could sign up, they were told no staff had been wearing a Confederate uniform and no one at the visitor's center was aware of anyone there who was wearing one.

Deer at Dunlap Hill Battlefield, 2022

When I visited Dunlap Hill, it was a rainy, dreary day. There was still something magical about it, though, and when I got to the area of the battle slightly set apart from the mounds, a group of deer arrived to us quite close – looking at us unblinking and it may sound strange, but perhaps not, as you, gentle reader, are likely a paranormal enthusiast like me, but as I mentioned at Chickamauga, every time a deer, in particular, a young buck arrives on my journeys through battlefields and cemeteries, they almost always, without fail lead me to the spirits of young soldiers. At my lodgings in Chickamauga, the young bucks ran nightly in the rain in the back. On the battlefield they traversed the bloodiest area of the Viniard Field watching me do the same. When I looked for my three-times great-grandfather of the Macon area who died in Virginia in the war and was buried in an unknown, a young buck pointed me in the direction of his burial. So needless to say when I saw the deer at the Mounds by the battle area across from the path to the earthworks, I knew it was once more, the soldiers looking back at me and I, at them. Yes, the spirits of the mounds would be present too, but it was an overwhelming sense that I knew who was sending the deer at that time and it was the men of the war.

Paranormal Historian and Founder of Middle Georgia Haunted History, Tim Mosely has spent much time by the Ocmulgee Mounds and Dunlap Hill. Interestingly enough, he's also learned many local tales about Fort Hawkins – the watch tower that would be used twice in the battles that ran through Macon. Most state that a soldier still stands guard there and people often see him, but differing accounts make it hard to know if it's a Revolutionary style soldier from the War of 1812, a Civil War Confederate from the militia or someone entirely different since the tower has been rebuilt. Regardless, the tower is deeply connected to the dead in Macon. In fact, the stone and walls around Fort Hawkins, when dissembled were used to build the walls of Rose Hill Cemetery, housing famed dead and locals, and thousands of soldiers for their final rest. The story of soldiers and Macon will always be carried on by Mother Earth and somehow connect to Dunlap Hill and that moment in time that lives on in the "Heart of Georgia."

The Battle of Sunshine Church is not a preserved battlefield or park and ultimately was the pinnacle battle in Stoneman's failed 1864 raid, however, a state historical marker stands on the west side of Georgia Highway 11 – North of Gray and much can be seen of the site from the highway. The marker is located in the center of the battlefield between the lines. The modern Sunshine Church, sort of the mascot of the site, for lack of a better word and the namesake is only a short distance away on Highway 11. This site, not as easy to visit doesn't seem to have as many tales of hauntings but that is perhaps because people aren't visiting as much because of what it reminds them of – a defense of home only to have retaliation come from Sherman and later Stoneman again throughout the South – making their victory so short-lived and making matters worse on civilians. I have no doubts that there are spirits at Sunshine Church – Confederates still on defense and Union men sent on a terrible mission that resulted in their death.

(You may also find yourself wanting to visit King's Tanyard where the Union men of Capron's brigade were more or less slaughtered, injured or imprisoned. Sadly, with development not so much is left of the site. The Bartow County Museum in Winder, Georgia, has an old marker for the site and references that there is a new historical marker about the battle on the front lawn on the courthouse in Winder. The battle site can be approximated to the intersection of Georgia 211 and County Line-Auburn Road.)

For more on the Second Battle of Dunlap Hill – please Part I, Chapter 5, March to the Sea.

Brown's Mill

At the same time as Stoneman's first raid was the rather small Battle of Brown's Mill. In late July 1864, General Sherman sent General McCook with his First Division of Cavalry to sever railroads southwest of Atlanta and then link with Stoneman to seize the Andersonville prison camp and free the prisoners. They crossed the Chattahoochee on a pontoon bridge and reached Palmetto where McCook's troops did effectively cut the Atlanta & West Point Railroad and captured 1,000 Confederate supply wagons that they burned on July 28. They also destroyed civilian property. When his raiders reached Lovejoy's Station and began wrecking the railroad, McCook called off the raid and turned across the river because Stoneman failed to appear and they tried to return to the rest of the army, McCook's division was attacked at Brown's Mill near Newnan by Wheeler's Confederate Cavalry. McCook let his officers lead their battalions separately in lieu of surrendering and were woefully defeated losing 1,285 men to casualties, 1,200 horses, ambulances, artillery and more. Wheeler also was able to free 300 Confederate prisoners that McCook had captured.

Battle two miles west of Atlanta, July 29th, 1864 (Possibly Brown's Mill) (WikiMedia Commons)

A Confederate nurse, Fannie Beers described the disturbing scene,

> "The dead lay around us on every side, singly and in groups and piles; men and horses – in some cases, apparently inextricably mingled."

.One Confederate soldier described it as,

> "The greatest slaughter I ever saw in front of a cavalry line."

Wheeler's casualties were incomparably small to the Union – just 50. Brown's Mill Battlefield can be visited in Newnan, Georgia in Coweta County, a state park. Most of the Union men who died there were subsequently buried in the National Cemetery at Marietta, in graves marked unknown. Some believe the battle site to be haunted … and due to the sheer amount of carnage in such a short time, it likely is indescribably eerie.

But the most popular ghost story of the battle comes about from a Confederate who was injured in the battle. The Confederate named John Griffen was wounded but felt he could recover and leaving the site bypassed the Confederate hospital and continued his ride 35 miles on horseback to find his sister who attended school at the LaGrange Female Academy. He arrived at Smith Hall to find her and received medical attention but ended up succumbing to blood loss. Former College President Waights Henry, Jr. wrote that many people have since felt Griffen's spirit and remarked,

> "When darkness descends upon the spot where the building stands, certain inexplicable happenings occur that have made the persons involved wary about entering again after sundown."

Students have been shoved, tripped, or had freezing cold spots. One woman even reported to work alone in Smith Hall when she tripped and fell in the otherwise empty hallway. She collected herself after discovering she tripped over nothing and explained to her friend how it felt like it was someone's leg she had tripped over. Many self-proclaimed psychics have also claimed to pick up on the energy as well. So perhaps a visit to the college will introduce you to at least one spirit from Brown's Mill named John Griffen!

Utoy Creek

Meanwhile, as the majority of the Union and Confederate troops circled around Atlanta and as July slid into August, the armies found themselves at Utoy Creek, just west of Atlanta with much of the armies still circling the supply lines at the Southern city. The Union was determined to win their siege of Atlanta and hit the railroad points. Sherman's Generals were sent along the North bank of Utoy Creek which they crossed in tandem, some on August 2 and some on August 4, accordingly. The Union attacked Confederates in the young Lee's Corps with no success as they were backed by a brigade of cavalry. The U.S. Army men continued in their efforts with brief moments of success for the Union but delays on the Union side allowed the Confederates to strengthen with an abatis – an obstacle constructed with tree branches and sharpened tops – a rather rugged, old school war tactic, if we think about it!

As the attack continued through August 5 and August 6, the abatis slowed down the Union a great deal and eventually the Union was repulsed with heavy loss in their attempt to get through the main line to the railroad. On August 7, the Union shifted position to their right and entrenched. There they remained for August – almost the full of the month. Attacks continued off and on near to the location of the Atlanta Christian College but, ultimately Sherman decided to change his operation and move toward communication and supply lines. The Battle of Utoy Creek that began the long siege of Atlanta after the battles of Atlanta and Ezra Church, left nearly 1,000 Union casualties and about 345 Confederate ones over the period of August 4 through 7, 1864 with more casualties, though lesser number in the weeks that followed. And it was during those weeks that the mind of the soldiers tried to make sense of what was happening and found themselves suffering unimaginable nightmares that sometimes turned out to be real.

Arguably, one of the most moving ghost stories out of the Atlanta region during the war came from a Union man named John Downey of the 11th Michigan Volunteers. The story printed in *Fate Magazine* and uncovered by Mr. Miles, explained the tale of a young man who had enlisted early in the war as soon as he turned 18 and was thenceforth ordered to attack the Confederate Line at Utoy Creek on August 7. Unsuccessful, in the night, the 11th Michigan and others reversed their exterior ditch they occupied so they could withdraw behind lines on August 10. Downey had several companions with him in war, including his friends, George Lockwood, George Quay and his best friend Daniel Baldwin – all of whom had gone missing in the fray. It was on August 10 as they settled for breakfast when Lockwood, suffering multiple wounds staggered into the encampment. Downey described the vision of him that even

> "his eyes were sunken far back in his head, his cheeks were hollow, the ghastly pallor of death was upon his face and he was so weak that he reeled and staggered

> as he walked. A dead man from the grave could not have startled us more."

Later, the same night, another of the missing, Daniel Baldwin came into camp and looked upon Downey while demonstrating a gentle gesture of a finger upon his lips cautioning him to be quiet and not to alert everyone to his presence. Downey recalled, the moon nearly full, showed Baldwin was also badly injured but nevertheless Baldwin summoned Downey to follow him, perhaps to find the other missing. Both men, silently walked into the woods until Downey began to demand explanation and received no response. At long last, in what felt like eons to Downey, Baldwin opened his shirt and revealed a

> "great blotch of blood,"

a mortal injury over his heart and pointed to weeds among the stream before he suddenly and shockingly, vanished. Downey did not go into the weeds he was pointed to by Baldwin straightway, deciding instead to go back to camp to grab another friend named Tim to accompany him. Together, they went to the area his best friend had pointed to. There they found two bloated corpses belonging to Baldwin and Quay and in fear of what the entire situation meant, Downey swore his friend, Tim to secrecy as they recovered the remains.

Downey survived the war and had a long professional life as a scientist and professor across the globe, never sharing his experience until 30 years later where he confessed that despite all his efforts, he could never find a scientific explanation for what happened to him that night. And that, is because there wasn't one.

As, we discussed these matters are of the heart and soul, and a soldier's worst fear was to be left behind, unrecovered on a battle landscape. To us, it seems, it was just a friend begging his friend to bring him home – no more, no less, but a trust even in the afterlife demonstrates a companionship strong enough to defy earthly bounds.

Dalton

Immediately after Utoy Creek, the Confederate Cavalry and a Union troop at a garrison found themselves up in north Georgia, in Dalton again – the same location where they had skirmished in February of the same year. On August 14, the Confederate cavalry under General Wheeler raided north Georgia to destroy Sherman's supply lines just as he was attempting to destroy theirs and demanded the surrender of a Union garrison at Dalton. Fighting occurred overnight on August 14 through to the 15th when Union reinforcement arrived. Wheeler had ended his attack by that point, but skirmishing continued for four hours, and the railroad was briefly out of commission but working within two days. The Confederate strength of 5,000 lost to the smaller Union strength of 800 and Confederate casualties numbered 150 to the Union's 95. The battle site no longer remains and has been developed over by the city of Dalton. The first battle at Dalton in February had been a Confederate victory and likened to intense skirmishing but the second was a decidedly Union victory.

Lovejoy's Station

Less than a week after Dalton and over 100 miles away in Lovejoy, Georgia, the Union continued to circle Atlanta and the Confederacy continued to try and salvage as much of the Deep South as they could – moving further and further away from the Chattanooga gateway. The Confederacy was growing desperate, leadership change had come too late, movements were slow and the Union was getting ahead of them and outflanking them. For every victory, they suffered more losses.

On August 20, it was deep summer and unbearable heat south of Atlanta in Clayton County at Lovejoy's Station when conflict would erupt again. General Joseph Wheeler of the Confederate cavalry found himself a bit further north at that time raiding the Union supply lines in North Georgia and in the Chattanooga region trying to salvage any protection of the gateway possible after the battles around the Atlanta area. And in Wheeler's absence, Union General Sherman saw the perfect opportunity to raid the less protected Confederate supply lines. As such he sent cavalry under General Kilpatrick to do just that.

Kilpatrick and his men left on August 18 and hit the Atlanta & WestPoint Railroad in the evening before disabling a small area of track. They then made their way to Macon & Western Railroad which had long been their goal. On August 19, they arrived at the Jonesborough supply depot and burned several Confederate supplies before arriving to Lovejoy's station on August 20 with destruction in their sights. Confederate infantry from Arkansas under Cleburne's division made it Lovejoy's Station swiftly and fought off the invading Union Calvary. Cleburne's infantry fought the cavalry throughout the night eventually forcing Kilpatrick's Cavalry to withdraw.

The Confederates were able to resume railroad operations within two days. Casualty counts were estimated to be about 240 men on each side though official numbers are not known. It's debated whether it's considered an actual battle, or battle site. Though historian opinions differ, the area itself is pretty built up around with modern development and is only marked by signs and plaques.

For a time, the people in the farming community and in Henry County, neighboring to Clayton County tried to protect the site and opened Nash Farm Battlefield Park over 200 acres wide but it was closed permanently in 2017. The battlefield had just been placed on the Civil War Trust's Most Endangered Battlefields list in 2008 and the park was to help that. At that time, the controversy remained over the little land that's left and the significance of this event in the Atlanta campaign. No prominent hauntings have been reported but perhaps it's worth a visit to see if the spirits are longing for their story to be told in absence of having a park in which to share their story. The lack of stories could just be from pure lack of visitors!

Jonesborough

As August made way to early September, the armies were still engaged around Atlanta, the South trying to defend their home and the North trying to put an end to the rising of the rebels. Quiet had not come, victory was not yet defined for anyone, and the South still had supply lines that remained open and supported Hood's army. Union raids like at Lovejoy's Station were superficial damage that had been easily repaired. Sherman still had his eyes on the railroads and knew that if they could be destroyed, the Rebel army would be forced to evacuate. About five days after the attack on Lovejoy's Station, Sherman's Union Army began to make their way to the railroad in Jonesborough and once more, Hood sent his General Hardee with two Corps to halve their movement.

The two armies confronted each other on August 31, 1864, just west of Jonesborough. The Confederates, with Hood now in command attacked first this time. The artillery attacked at 3:00 PM alongside Cleburne's skirmishers. The young General Lee mistook the skirmish fire for attack signal and his attack centered on Union soldiers in Hazen's division. The first line troops made it over the

Union line when they were immediately and viciously repulsed. In fact, the intensity of the attack and repulse was so violent, Confederate General Deas's brigade fled the battlefield. Much like seen in other battles – the next line had to go forward anyway for the Confederates and suffer the same ill fate. It was described as a one-sided slaughter. At that point, the Confederates refused further orders to attack.

There were, of course, exceptions. Confederate General Anderson bravely continued fighting until he was shot and wounded. Even the Union admired his determination. Hardee ordered another attack as he did not want to give up. But young General Lee told him, the troops were in no condition to attack. They dug their heels in and declined to charge as the Union fired upon them with

> "terrible accuracy."

The Confederate's ill luck continued when the Union cavalry in the northwest, armed with the deadly Spencer repeating rifles attacked Confederate General Lowrey's Division forcing them out of the main line but this did give them some advantage. The Confederates were able to capture two guns and force men in Kilpatrick's cavalry to retreat. Shortly thereafter, Union General Smith and his men recaptured the guns. The Confederates attacking the Union left flank met the same deadly roar of gunfire and took cover in a ravine and also dug their heels in refusing to go any further. The Confederate generals began to realize that the Union position was too strong and so they canceled Cleburne's assault and organized withdrawal.

The Union had lost in casualties only 179 out of over 14,000 engaged but the Confederate casualty count was already at 1,725 despite their increased number of nearly 24,000 engaged. The Union only issued half force to repulse the rebels and were feeling

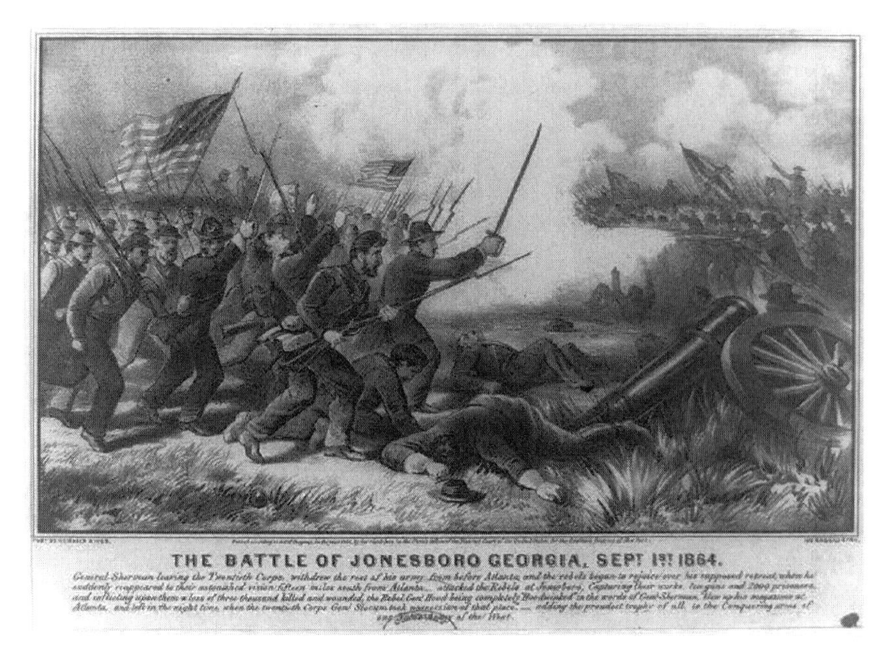

The Battle of Jonesboro, Sept. 1, 1864 (Library of Congress)

optimistic and began to move south toward Jonesborough with Sherman destroying the railroad as they went. The rebels feared that the Union would come right into Atlanta to attack directly and the tensions for the last months showed that the civilians and army wanted anything but that. As such, Hood withdrew one of the corps from Hardee – Lee's Corps. Lee's Corps was sent that night to protect Atlanta and he assigned Hardee's Corps to protect Macon and communications in the rear. By midnight when Hood heard from Hardee that his attacks failed, he knew Atlanta had to be abandoned.

On September 1, the battle resulted in the Union breaking through Hardee's troops and forcing them to flee south. Thomas's men marched for Jonesborough in the afternoon of September 1. They watched each other's movements and skirmished throughout the day trying to figure out who was where. Hardee reinforced his right with troops from the left and Sherman got hot-headed when he figured out that not all of Hardee's men were in Atlanta. But some say, he was aware of this and was simply frustrated that Hardee's Corps hadn't been completely destroyed. In all the fighting on September 1, the Union Commanding General was angry that they had 1,272 casualties in the XIV Corps even though the Confederate supply lines and railroads had been cut/destroyed on August 31.

The Confederates lost another, 1,400 including 900 prisoners on September 1. Hundreds in Cleburne's division were missing. Casualty estimates are unclear to this day what the total is for one or two days of battle. In total, the Battle of Jonesborough had an estimated 3,149 casualties with 2,000 belonging to the Confederacy. On the evening of September 1st, Hood evacuated Atlanta utilizing the Georgia State Militia to assist in evacuation with his troops and the next day, September 2, he surrendered the city of Atlanta.

Several Georgia men continued their fight at home including the 46th & 65th Georgia, 8th Georgia Battalion, 2nd Georgia Sharpshooter Battalion, 54th, 67th and 63rd Georgia, 37th Georgia, 4th Georgia Sharpshooter Battalion, 25th, 29th, 30th and 66th Georgia, Havis' Georgia Battery, and Howell's Georgia Battery in Cleburne's Division under Hardee as well as the 34th, 36th, 39th, 56th Georgia, 2nd Georgia State, 40th, 41st, 42nd, 43rd, 52nd and 1st Georgia State, Cherokee Georgia Artillery and Stephens Georgia Light Artillery in Lee's Division in Lee's Corps. Every list of men subjected to death in a war that came into their backyard who were left on battlefields just miles from some of their homes is a continual, harrowing, and haunting reminder of the true cost of the Civil War.

After the Battle of Jonesborough, the Atlanta Campaign had ended and Sherman and the Union had won the Deep South city. But the Army of the Tennessee and the Confederacy were not done yet and the war was definitely not over in Georgia.

To visit the battlefield of Jonesborough is like visiting most battlefields in the Atlanta region and involves a walk among a more suburban or urban landscape to find the plaques throughout town. However, when you visit Jonesboro there are places that you can check out that are of note on your quest for history and mystery.

The Patrick Cleburne Confederate Memorial Cemetery is home to the remains of approximately a thousand Confederate soldiers who perished in the Battle of Jonesborough. All of them are unidentified and the origin of the cemetery has unknown factors, but the cemetery memorial arch was constructed in 1872, eight years after the battle with a grant by the State legislature so that the soldiers would not be scattered about town in their resting places. The unmarked stones form the shape of the Confederate flag, and the cemetery is maintained by the Daughters of the Confederacy.

Patrick Cleburne Memorial Cemetery, 2022

The cemetery is located near to the train depot that was constructed in 1867 after the burning of the depot during the Atlanta campaign in 1864. When you find yourself going through Jonesboro and communing with the dead, it's worth a drive by of the Stephen Carnes house on North McDonough Street. Constructed before the war, the home survived the nearby battle and had an operating wagon and carriage shop behind it. Stephen Carnes, the owner, also ran a wood shop where he made trim for his home but also used his woodworking skills to support his Southern brethren and constructed caskets for the Confederate army. He was the very man hired by the state of Georgia to re-inter the Confederate soldiers that were buried around the city and place them in the Patrick Cleburne Confederate Cemetery.

Jonesboro seems to indeed be a place that centers around the Confederate dead even as they don't relate to battle. Just down the same street from the Carnes house is the site of the Pope Dickson & Son Funeral Home that houses the hearse which carried the Confederate Vice President and Georgia Governor, Alexander Stephens from his mansion to his resting place in Crawfordsville. On North Main Street in Jonesboro, the 1859 Johnson-Blalock House sits as the home of a signer of the Georgia Secession Ordinance but also the site of a field hospital used during the war. The Warren House on West Mimosa Drive built in 1860 by a railroad agent also served as a hospital and headquarters for Confederate troops until their loss at Jonesboro led the 52nd Illinois to take possession of the house. The home itself even still has signatures from the Illinois soldiers on the walls in their downstairs parlor.

Jonesboro is a big inspiration for a timeless novel with a town by the name of Tara. Margaret Mitchell's *Gone with the Wind,* of course was set to take place just five miles from Jonesboro. And many of the characters were confirmed to have been influenced by people she knew from the community. Mitchell did much of her research in the town as well. Her research took place at the 1898 Courthouse on S. McDonough Street and legend states the RK Holliday Office building was where the cousin of Margaret Mitchell's namesake was and he was the father of the woman who inspired the character of Melanie Hamilton. The town is home to the Road to Tara Museum and the town hosts Tara Boulevard on the Clayton/Henry County line in honor of the novel.

Hollywood and the Civil War combine in a fascinating trip through Jonesboro for any visitor. But, is it haunted? When walking through the memorial cemetery, despite the developed area around it, it was eerily quiet and my husband and I heard continual footsteps behind us in the closed off area coming through the stones. I felt called to a few as if the spirits were trying to tell us their names, or perhaps plead that they were close to home, but no one recognized them. A peaceful cemetery with an underlying call for help definitely seems a contradiction.

The Warren House and hospital, unlike the other homes mentioned is one that can be visited and has claims of a haunting. Locals believe that the ghost of one of the soldiers can be seen at night standing near the windows. It remains unknown in the shadows just which side of the war the spectral soldier fought on.

Interestingly, when looking through old accounts of soldier's time in Jonesboro, I reflected on *Gone with the Wind* and the havoc upon the southern civilians and their homesteads shown by "raiding Yankees," and one story tugged at my heart strings and compelled me to go on reading it despite its lack of "spooky," theme. There was something quite spiritual and romantic about it.

The story came from a man named Sarge Plunkett, an Ohio native and was entitled "The Story of a Spy," when it was printed in the December 28, 1889, issue of *The Valdosta Times* originally printed in a publication entitled *The Confederate Veteran*. The young, teenage Union soldier confessed his rather feminine and fine features made the local men in his hometown suggest that he could be an excellent army spy. Plunkett consulted an army officer about the matter, and they agreed and sent him to General Sherman in the Atlanta region in 1864. He, on assignment, just a couple days away from the Battle of Jonesborough dressed as a Southern belle and was sent into the woods alone to gather information. However, as the night wore on, feeling vulnerable in lady's clothes and riding alone in the woods, the young man, in his women's clothing went to a house and posed as an unassuming lady looking for hospitality. He encountered the lady of the house who provided food and shelter for the lady that showed on her doorstep unawares.

The soldier-spy had made up a tale of an injured brother and trying to make way to Atlanta to tend to him. And given the hostilities and battles, this seemed plausible. The siege was still in place. The young mother had all her daughters with her, tending to the visitor, making coffee, putting wood on the fire and lamenting the horrors of war. Plunkett began to feel guilty as the young girls waited on him hand and foot believing he was one of them. He knew if he revealed the truth death would be upon him. He noticed only two beds in the home. Mom kept some children in her bed and said that two of the girls could share the other bed with him…believing, of course, it was a her. The girls embraced their visitor and snuggled in. He, afraid of being exposed for who he really was did not show much affection back but felt their warmth surround him and watched their innocence, guilt still overwhelming him.

Plunkett wrote,

> "I looked at Lucy, with her long hair streaming down her back, which she had just begun to braid, preparing to get into bed, and then I cast my eye over in the corner at Mary who was just untying her garter, and as I looked she skinned the stocking down and

> off at the toes, displaying a pretty, naked, plump foot. My heart smote me for what it was now death to undo…It was a trying time, and it was only the angelic innocence of those girls that kept me from being detected and suffering the penalty for being a spy."

He described their sleep with such warmth,

> "Mary had pulled the cover up and tucked in around us, they both gave me a generous, loving hug. I did not, could not return their embraces but in a few moments, each of them with an arm laying affectionately across my body, were sleeping the sleep of the innocent, while I was suffering the tortures of hell for an imposition that it would have been death to reveal."

He repeated to himself,

> "To be truthful, would be death."

He continued his journey the next day and said when the war was over, he returned to Georgia and to the family he met and the young lady, Lucy, who was once the innocent young girl, he had shared a bed with dressed in spy clothes was all grown up. The pair fell in love, and he made her his wife and together they raised children he described as "half-rebel, half-Yankee." Does one story of love, trust, and hospitality, or innocence change what happened around Atlanta in 1864 and the shadow of violence? Of course not, and it was not the rule but rather the exception. Still, the heartwarming tale reminds us all that we are on this journey of human experience together and we always have been. And sometimes our common humanity and our love is more important than any war.

Suffice to say, with all that in mind, on your Civil War tours, the suburban town of Jonesboro is absolutely worth a visit, and perhaps, some day we can identify the spirits who roam its streets and still feel the heart of those who lost their lives in 1864 and the homes and streets around Atlanta.

Though the Atlanta campaign was at an end, the fighting in Georgia wasn't and it was only about a month later when the Franklin-Nashville Campaign made its way to Bartow County in the northwest corner of Georgia, and back in the Atlanta metropolitan region, just a little more on the distant and wooded side near Acworth.

Allatoona Pass

How does a battle with only 5,000 engaged become one of the most haunted sites in the Peach State? Georgia legends tell us, that regardless of number engaged, the Battle of Allatoona Pass left behind a haunting that is unrivaled by most.

To be sure, there is something lurking in the dark woods on the lake at Allatoona Pass. Is it a ghost? A wild boar? Both? My answer for you is both. And I can tell you that those who visit never forget going to the site. The Battle of Allatoona (Pass) occurred about a month after the end of the Atlanta Campaign and was the kickoff for the Franklin-Nashville campaign that took place mostly in Tennessee and would ultimately end in the death of the beloved "Stonewall of the West," Major General Patrick Cleburne himself – just 36 years old at the time of his passing.

Of course, his death in Franklin, Tennessee was heart-stopping for the Confederacy in many ways but for the beginning of this campaign Cleburne was still present and oddly always up against the Rock of Chickamauga, Union Major General George H. Thomas – always in the same battles but oftentimes at opposite flanks – perhaps their strength was known by each side, and they could not risk them being pitted against each other. Thomas and Cleburne were already in the Tennessee region or headed that way after Sherman captured Atlanta and it's important to note that they were not at the eerie and bloody site in the northwest region of Atlanta known as Allatoona Pass. Perhaps, what made it particularly haunting is that the Siege of Atlanta had ended in Union favor after several Confederate losses and few victories that came with high casualty counts for them in their home terrain. And what they could not yet know is that Sherman's destructive March to the Sea would begin in November 1864.

The Franklin-Nashville Campaign was waged in Tennessee, Alabama and close to northwest Georgia throughout Sherman's March making the last few months of 1864 nothing short of panic and disaster for civilians in the south. Nevertheless, in many ways, Allatoona set the tone as the beginning of last effort for the Confederacy to protect their home, one last gasp for the Deep South and for them, one gasp was a glimmer of hope. And if Cleburne was still on their side, there was no reason to give up hope at all.

Atlanta had been the center of transportation and supply lines. The Union capture of Atlanta was difficult for Georgiana and Confederates to wrap their mind around, but they had to watch for Sherman's next move. Sherman had noticed the location of Allatoona Pass in the skirmishes and battles bringing his army to Atlanta because of its proximity to the railroad. In fact, the railroad tracks go right through Allatoona Pass and that is where the parking area is even located today – on the railroad tracks. These railroads connected Atlanta and Chattanooga through the Allatoona Mountain and thus its importance did not escape Sherman. As such, he had sent his engineering chief Captain Orlando Poe to design the fortifications along the pass and keeping the supply depot as its entrance and supervise the construction. Poe did that and included a series of trenches for the Union army and filled the earthworks for artillery. The website ExploreSouthernHistory.com describes Sherman's move here as prophetic, that he knew in advance this would come of importance to plan that far in advance and with such confidence. This was more than just instinct.

After the fall of Atlanta, Confederate President Jefferson Davis met with his General, John Bell Hood and they determined that the Confederacy had to take a strong position astride the Western & Atlantic line between Chattanooga and Atlanta and break off the Union supply line that had helped Sherman and the Union in Atlanta. The plan, in theory, for the Confederacy wasn't bad because the March to the Sea was not set in stone and Sherman was almost waiting to see what Hood's next move was. Ultimately, Hood pulled back a bit on his orders to Stewart and his decision to go to the rail line in Allatoona Pass was going to be charged to one division – one division totaling 3,276 men under General Samuel G. French. This was Hood's selection and order to Stewart for French. French's orders were to take the pass, fill it in, destroy the bridge at the Etowah River and reunite the army at the site of their previous victory at New Hope Church. Between October 2 and October 4, the Confederates under Stewart in other divisions were attacking minor garrisons and damaging tracks but the orders for French and his men included over 96 miles of marching in two days in addition to his list of orders. Typical marches during that time were about 15 miles a day. They endeavored to do their best.

As French's men deployed, the Union observed their movements quickly and notified their headquarters to send Union forces to Allatoona Pass. Lieutenant Colonel John E. Tourtellote was in command of nearly 1,000 Union soldiers at Allatoona Pass and he was alerted to the Confederate attack through signal flags that also promised him that help was coming. The Christian song,

"*Hold the Fort,*" was inspired by this.

Battle of Allatoona Pass, GA, 1864 by Alfred Waud

By 1:00 AM on October 5, Union General Corse, his men and over 1,000 reinforcements now numbered 2,000 in anticipation of the attack and assembled around their earthworks. By 3:00 AM, just two hours later, the Confederates had arrived but given the darkness, French awaited any attack until there was light. In the light, he could better ascertain the landscape as he faced the "mountain fortress." Trying not to be intimidated by what Mother Earth had provided the Union troops geographically, he came up with a plan to have some of his division go to the left and to have his men attack Union positions east of the deep valley like-area while the pother portion attacked west.

Several men from the 39th Mississippi attacking in the west were unable to successfully storm the Union trenches at the area of earth known as the "Deep Cut." Minnesota and Illinois Union men were too strong and well-fortified. As such the Confederates focused on an open group and up a steep ridge where their enemy lay in wait, in a position of advantage with their rifles and cannon facing them.

The 39th Mississippi again found themselves in the bloody carnage and their movement uphill was considered disastrous due to the casualties of men pinned down in a gully and taken prisoner including their commander, Colonel Durr. The other Confederates continued to try and attack the walls to no success. Men from the 36th Mississippi met a similar fate to their companions in the 39th being fired upon from other side of the railroad by men from Illinois as they tried to make their way to the ridge.

Eventually, following French's plan and orders, the rebels attempted to converge from three directions into the "Star Fort," and encountered Rowett's redoubt by the main fort held by Iowa and Illinois and a 12-pounder. Brigades from Missouri, Texas and North Carolina stormed the redoubt and engaged in hand-to-hand combat reaching the earthworks. The fight turned brutal as they began to hit each other with rocks, physically beating each other with anything they could find available including weapons or their own hands. The Confederates took the redoubt and the Union and their cannon fell back. Heavy fire continued from the main Union fort upon the Confederacy and the Confederate line moved forward as the morning hours began to sink away. It was around 11:00 AM when the Confederate plan to attack from all three sides took place. They made four attempts to attack and capture the star fort but it was too fortified by cannon and men. They poured all they had into it and hit the U.S. flag nearly 200 times.

The Confederates were in a weak position, hammered upon far too often and Union reinforcements continued to head toward Allatoona Pass. They put up a mighty fight and there were approximately 706 Union casualties. Confederate casualties outnumbered Union due to the ridge assault and numbered nearly 900 including many Mississippi men and those in the gully. That was over 30 percent of French's division that was gone in the severe battle. One of the battle roads was reported by soldiers to have "ran with blood," after the terrible fighting that day and Union soldiers took three weeks to locate and bury those they lost among the carnage.

Battle of Allatoona Pass Louis Prang & Company, 1897 (Wikimedia Commons)

No Georgia men fought or died in the Battle of Allatoona Pass but plenty of their Confederate brethren from Mississippi, Tennessee and other neighboring states came to call Georgia their final resting place because of the Battle of Allatoona Pass and many were left buried on-site and can be felt there today. Some may have been removed to home or Confederate cemeteries but records of that remain murky.

There are two 19th Century antebellum homes that were witness homes to the event. One is the Clayton/Mooney Homestead, a private family residence (owned by descendants of the family) and is located at the entrance to the battlefield. The home had stood for over twenty years prior to the battle, however, in 1864 the Union troops commandeered the house as their command post for the garrison. The home would go on to serve as a field hospital after the battle as well. With an estimated 1,500 casualties total out of just 5,400 troops, medical help would have been greatly needed.

The Clayton/Mooney house still stands and maintains bullet holes in the boards of the house – primarily upstairs in the gable. Behind the home, there are the graves of 21 soldiers, Confederate, who died at the hospital and were buried on the grounds, and it is considered a small cemetery of sorts. The family patriarch and property owner, John Clayton, died just one month after the battle having been sent into shock by everything that occurred on his doorstep and subsequently his home and is buried at the nearby New Zion Baptist Cemetery. Residents of the house have continued to find artifacts that relate to the battle and those who died there making it a local fascination in Acworth.

The other historic home is popular inn and wedding site overlooking the lake and is the Lake Allatoona Inn. The home had been lived in by the town's postmaster Thomas Moore before it was reconstructed in 1893 a few years after his passing and thus it looks a bit different than it once did in the late 19th Century, though visitors say there is still evidence in the home of soldier's being near it and that perhaps also bullet holes lay beneath the renovation or shadows stand in the window showing their presence. Locals we interviewed insisted that there are reminders of the battle all over the Inn and the reason that the homes could have been preserved and not destroyed by the Union would have included having a freemason's flag upon the home if the families were involved – something that both sides respected.

Truth be told, the Lake Allatoona Inn is well aware that Allatoona Pass is considered one of the top ten haunted sites in Georgia and in fact, boasts this title proudly on their website. Lake

Allatoona Inn and the battlefield itself have been places where folks sight the most well-known ghost of the Civil War in Georgia, having been reported starting within days after the battle. The phantom's identity remains unknown. In trying to sort out, who it could be, we look at the houses. Part of the rail lines going through the pass were removed after the war and the energy surrounding those and clinging on to the rail that remains by the lake have been the center of such sightings. One wonders if the neighboring house with the small Confederate cemetery in their backyard or the bodies buried on site are perhaps from where the spectral figure surfaces. One grave has remained the center of topic though it's hard to say if it's the rail spirit as the accounts different on this. This gravesite is known as the man buried in the tomb for a "Southern hero." In 1949, a man from Texas visiting family at the time recalled that he was just six years old when the Confederate was buried. He stated that the Confederate actually arrived in Allatoona on a train a few days after the battle in a coffin listing only its destination. The man named Abernathy went on to explain that his female cousins opened the coffin to look at the man inside, wearing a gray uniform and holding a black hat. The girls dug a grave and carried the body through the pass toward the deep cut only about one foot from end of the cross ties. In 1880, surveyors who found the body gave it a headstone. However, this account is challenged by a man named Robert White, the stationmaster at Cartersville and historian Joe Head. They believe there are two graves – one that Abernathy, just a boy at the time described and the second belonging to a soldier who fell at the battle and who was buried where he fell by those tracks at the deep cut. This, they claim, is the Confederate hero who the railroad employees cared for. In 1950, nearly a century after the war, the grave was relocated near the tracks at the south end of the cut and an iron fence was built around it and he was officially commemorated as the "Unknown Hero." Newspaper accounts from the *Atlanta*

An Unknown Hero Grave at Allatoona Pass, 2023

(David W. Googe photo)

Constitution in 1938 refer to the body and the iron fence as having already existed. Are there more than one? Is the same one getting confused? Some local historians believe the deceased's name is Private Andrew Jackson Houston of the 35th Mississippi. Age and ailments had kept him off the battlefield in the first couple years of the war and even in June of 1864 he was registered in a military hospital in Macon, Georgia. Returning to his company in late August, he disappears from record and does not come up on the list of confirmed dead after the battle which is not uncommon. You can visit the unknown grave passing the battlefield toward Old Allatoona Road and crossing the railroad tracks by taking a right on Oak Hollow Road where the Unknown Hero is interred.

One sign on the battlefield reads a Poem about the Unknown soldier and sits close to where the initial burial was discovered and reads:

"The Soldiers Grave" by Joseph Brown: In Allatoona Pass, by the Western and Atlantic railroad, is the grave of an unknown soldier who fell in the battle there October 5, 1864," and is followed by the poem,

> "In the railroad cut there's a lonely grave/which the trackmen hold sacred to care/ they have piled round it stones and for it they save/every flower, when their task calls them there./Away from the home of his love/away from his sweetheart or wife/away from his mother, whose prayers went above/he gave for his country his life/ We know not if, wearing the blue, he came/ "Neath the "bright, starry banner," arrayed/and, dying, that it o'er the mountains of fame/might forever in triumph wave prayed./Or we know not if, "neat the bonnie blue flag,"/he rushed forth his country's defender/valiant, smote those who her cause down would drag./and only to death did surrender./That God only knows/and so in his hand/let the secret unfathomed e'er rest;/but this we know, that he died for his land/and the banner he thought was the best./Heav'n pity the dear ones who prayed his return/Heav'n bless them and shield them

from woes/Heav'n grant over his grave to melt anger stern/and make brothers of those who were foes."

The poem expressed by a Georgia Governor Joseph M. Brown was somewhat of an attempt at reconciliation. Some expressed disdain at the bringing up of the blue. Some understood why that was necessary.

The poem shows a unity among the people who were grieving the lives lost in the war among brothers and among states. There was a sense of honor for the soldier's cause and patriotism regardless of sign – "and the banner he thought was the best," which encourages all of us today to look upon the men who fought with peace in our hearts and to see each one as an individual with a home that they didn't get to home and see one last time and a beloved that they didn't get to grow old with. Though it is presumed that grave marks a Confederate, the poem made sure to insist upon the respect and dignity of any soldier buried – be they rebel or Yankee. Allatoona Pass seems to commemorate this sentiment of unity and peace in death more than most places in Georgia, at least in spirituality. Perhaps it is the spirit of the battlefield and those that linger desperately trying to get home that that makes it so in that regard.

With bodies on the field, down the road, in unmarked cemeteries and unknown names – it's no strange thing that hauntings would take over – remember our recurring theme, that people feared being forgotten, them not brought home and worse yet their name unknown, all of which happened at Allatoona Pass, especially to the Confederate soldiers. And it explains why our famed ghost of Allatoona Pass remains unidentified.

The first major ghost sighting at Allatoona is detailed in a December 1872 edition of the *Atlanta Journal* and was described as a repeating occurrence having happened over several months. The trains coming between Tilton would cross near Dalton and

Allatoona Pass when suddenly the employees of the railroad noticed a figure riding atop the car.

> "For some months, railroaders – conductors, engineers and brakemen have been noticing between Tilton and Allatoona, that when their respective freight trains would enter on to that portion of the track named, that their number would be reinforced by an extra train hand, who of course the officers of the W and A Railroad cannot persuade to sign the "death warrant." This individual appears suddenly on top of the freight cars, takes a seat, and remains for many miles, then the unknown brakeman disappears. Conductors seeing him, have often gone out to collect his fare, but on nearing him, he would vanish like mist."

A conductor even recounted approaching the figure vividly, seeing him and taking caution not knowing what the mysterious passenger's motive may be,

> "The engineer approached cautiously, with both eyes fixed on the form of the man, but as he neared his ghostship, he gradually faded from view, leaving the engineer completely bewildered, but who still tried to unravel the suddenness of his disappearance by passing over the entire train and looking in every place, which was capable of concealing a man, but nowhere was the man to be visible."

After a full search, convinced the man may be hiding, the engineer went back to the place where he spotted him and there he was,

> "In the identical spot where he first discovered him. It was all incomprehensibly strange and unaccountable to the engineer but his intrepid courage never failed him....and as he approached again the apparition dissolved into nothing."

Rail workers claimed the ghost continued to appear for many years and stories were continually told of him – the ghostly passenger atop the train who vanished when approached. His physical description varied but most assumed due to his arrival in Allatoona that he was a man killed there, trying to get home on those rails that were so hotly contested. The area the train ran through is part of the public battlefield that you can visit today, a state park, and you can see if you sense the man still trying to get home on the pathways or if he found the nearby rail lines and migrated that way – that remains to be seen. Perhaps he remembers the Great Locomotive Chase that went through Allatoona in 1862 ... but more on that to come. The old railroad bed became a lake levy and its proximity to Lake Allatoona perhaps is what allows the spirits to make themselves so vividly known. Water is a conduit for spirit activity and I daresay, that is the case at Allatoona Pass.

Though we don't know who the train passenger is, many have also seen a phantom looking man in Confederate clothing near to the initial burial places of the "Unknown hero." They also report cries of wounded Confederates and phantom soldiers in the mist – all remaining unidentified as sadness and darkness surrounds them.

When speaking with rangers who work at other state sites, they all claimed to have had their most vivid experiences at the Allatoona Pass Battlefield more than any other place of battle. Something about the setting of this battle, toward the end the war, this being one more big move from the Confederacy seemed to trap so many souls there waiting to turn the story around. Not to mention the elevation that the Union soldiers had at the rocks firing down upon the Confederates so violently. One ranger, recalled walking through the battlefield pass, getting near to the Deep Cut region when he felt a shove upon his shoulder so strong that it almost pushed him, a sturdy, grown man on a hike completely off the path. He looked around and confirmed that he was indeed alone, as far as he could see but he could feel and hear someone behind him. And as he turned around swiftly to make his way out of the pass nervously, it was as if he could hear that someone following him.

I've read a few reports about being pushed at Allatoona Pass and luckily, I did not have such an experience on my visits. I confess; however, I did visit in the cloak of darkness toward the Star Fort area that the current Union memorials mark and not as close to the Deep Cut. On my first visit to Allatoona, I brought some of my "ghost hunting" equipment and the moment we set up the EMF detectors and REM pods that detect or react to electromagnetic energy, they both began to indicate that they were picking something up. I decided to try and communicate with the spirits and see if any would give a response. Upon my inquiry as to whether anyone could near me or needed help, myself and my family members who were assembled with me, began to hear an awful cry and yell echoing across the lake. We all froze in fear and stayed put for a moment as the cries and moans got louder and humanlike yet also not quite. One of my cousins suggested that it was wild boars and my husband in his infinite wisdom decided to go down by the water and assess the situation accordingly. Warning, do not try this at home – don't go into the dark after a sound that sounds like a wild boar or a screaming ghost. Luckily, my husband saw nothing and all the houses that surrounded the pass on that March evening were quiet, their lights flickering off the lake in the distance. We contemplated leaving the scene when we noticed a shadow figure approaching our group which

Battle of Allatoona Pass Marker by Lake Allatoona, 2022

confirmed that leaving was the right decision. I wanted to try and find the spectral train passenger but perhaps that was not our night.

I returned in December on another quiet, winter evening and began to investigate again accompanied by my family. As we approached the circle beyond the tracks against the lake surrounded by monuments, the equipment turned on again indicating a reaction to something and this time we used a communication device called an Echovox to try and capture vocal responses from the spirits. Luckily, did not hear wild boars in the distance this time, or whatever was crying before but my sister noted that the shadow figure by the ridge emerged almost giving this likeness to a banshee or reaper who collected the dead from that area as the energy did not seem to emit anything human-related. The figure loomed and the Echovox began to bring forward the voice of a man, saying he owned property in Tennessee and that he was so happy to see his wife here. I asked him if "our home" was nice and he responded,

"Well, I certainly think so,"

and sounded confused as to why I asked. So, I didn't press any further. The spirit directed the entire conversation to me, speaking directly to me, and saying that I was his wife and how glad he was that I had come to get him, and that we would get home. There were some additional voices from the soldier spirits remarking at all the females that had come to the site (myself, my sister, and my female cousins were there) and though my husband and male cousins with there – they received no audible feedback from the ghosts or spirits. In fact, one electronic voice phenomenon seemed to say,

"There's girls here."

Perhaps, the soldiers thought that we were an aiding expedition to bring home survivors, or a group of families come to collect their family. But that broke my heart. Are they there, waiting for someone to come get them? Do they not know that they have passed? Was the trauma and violence of Allatoona Pass holding them there so much so that even their souls did not want to recognize the truth about the devastation that had occurred? I left after about an hour of back-and-forth conversation with the spirits there and felt comforted, that maybe there was a sense of familiarity running through history that connected us that night. And though they were intelligent spirits, they didn't seem troubled or to know what had happened in any horrible way. But I also felt sadness and grief that perhaps I could not help them to move forward from their station at Allatoona. I did not feel it was appropriate for me to tell them that the war was over for some time and I wasn't one of their wives. It seemed as if it would confuse them, as if their mission was still giving them purpose and the hope of people coming to assist was still very real for them. The identities of the men we spoke to, like the train passenger, the unmarked graves and more remains unknown, but their presence shows that whether we know their name or not, their existence cannot be denied.

The paradox of Allatoona Pass, one of the most haunted places in all of Georgia is that it's haunted but also beautiful, seated in the mountains, upon a lake, surrounded by wilderness and history. It's a paradox and a flood of mixed emotions can overcome you upon your trails there. Be sure to take note that when you walk there, you are anything but alone and perhaps your companion is just trying to make the train home or get to see their family one last time.

March to the Sea

Sherman's March to the sea is considered a military campaign, technically, however the controversy regarding this campaign cannot be overstated. This was the first large example in America of the modern warfare tactic of total war and scorched earth involving civilians and soldiers alike. The campaign enthusiastically embraced destruction and havoc throughout Georgia and many descendants and people of the South today look upon General William Sherman as their devil figure, their Voldemort. And it is with good reason. There were fair battles of soldiers gallantly marching toward each other and keeping their violence to the tactical fields throughout the war to this point. The March to the Sea changed this.

Again, this was an all-embracing march from Atlanta to Savannah. The troops following the "Scorched Earth," policy were allowed to destroy industry, infrastructure (transportation) and civilian property, whatever was necessary to squash the Confederacy logistically and financially. There is continued debate whether the March to the Sea was Sherman's brainchild or if future

Drawing of Gen. Sherman and his troops on parade in Savannah, GA, Jan. 1865 (Library of Congress)

President and then Union Commander, General Ulysses S. Grant had control of this decision or planned this. However, locals, (and I, a Grant aficionado) believe Grant was not the type to believe in total warfare. It had never been in his wheelhouse despite his companion, Sherman being more of an all or nothing mentality (especially after the loss of his young son, Willie Sherman). You may recall, Sherman was, more or less, assigned to Georgia and when the Atlanta campaign had concluded and the Franklin-Nashville campaign was continuing in the west, Grant ordered Sherman to do what was necessary and to destroy, essentially, anything in his way (more rail lines, etic). Grant felt this symbolic and logistical destruction of the Confederacy, would frighten them into backing down. To Sherman, frightening them that much was a call for total war. The Confederacy had not backed down in nearly four years, despites several losses in their home terrain, high casualty counts and more. They continued to find a way to persevere, and this march was intended to stop that.

Some may argue that parts of Georgia have never recovered from this military action and people refer to the March to the Sea as if it was yesterday. Though there weren't many events that were considered battles in the March so much as there was the destruction, battles and large events did take place throughout as the Confederacy tried to protect their home as best as they could from these perceived monsters. Sherman was not messing around when he set forth. His march was supported with 60,000 Union troops. Devastation was left in their wake and the movement started close to Macon, Georgia, south of Atlanta in a landscape encountered by Stoneman just months before. And then, that path brought them to a more rural area that was then known as Griswoldville. Today, Griswoldville is part of Jones County and close to Gray, Georgia and Dunlap Hill is part of the Ocmulgee Mounds State Park in Macon, Georgia.

Second Battle of Dunlap Hill/Walnut Creek

Not as brutal as the first encounters in Macon, Georgia, Dunlap Hill once again found itself in the center of conflict. Union General Kilpatrick and his cavalry were able to "pin down" several Confederate troops in the city. The local Georgia militia and some other Confederates did not want to leave Macon undefended. So, they remained in defense of Macon rather than aggressively preventing Sherman's march in an offensive move. They arguably missed some vulnerable opportunities for Sherman that they could have taken advantage of, had they not remained there. Nevertheless, the Second Battle of Dunlap Hill also known as the Battle of Walnut Creek developed when Kilpatrick swept in close to Macon to screen movements of Sherman's right column and straighten it out. Kilpatrick set a nearby jail to "explode" and tore up rail track as he made his way to the Macon defense line. Repeating Stoneman's moves, it was a very similar event as a whole. The Confederates watched from their post at the old Fort Hawkins and used enslaved people to surround Macon with trenches and earthworks. Crossing Walnut Creek, the Union captured two confederate cannon and temporarily overran the area. The Union began to assault Fort Hawkins. Confederate General

Cobb was prepared with artillery and was able to return fire commensurately with nine cannons included. Once more, Confederate forces assaulted the Union in their well-fortified structure. Confederate reinforcements began to fill in on November 20, 1864, as the battle ensued. When Kilpatrick was losing at Dunlap Farm, he tried to attack the rail trestle at Walnut Creek but was quickly stopped by the Confederate defenders. Ultimately, Kilpatrick and his men fell back, and Kilpatrick felt his mission for the column was accomplished and he was followed by General Joseph Wheeler's cavalry in his withdrawal. The Union fall back brought them to Griswoldville alongside Wheeler's cavalry and the battle on November 22, 1864, was ultimately, "scheduled," as was the destruction of the budding industrial complex and town.

This march start at Dunlap Hill was not considered a battle for the March to the Sea (though the timing was commensurate), however, the next engagement between both armies would constitute as a deadly battle and the first of the march.

For hauntings of Dunlap Hill, please Chapter 3K in Part 1, under Atlanta Campaign in Battlefields.

Griswoldville

> "It was a terrible sight, we moved a few bodies and there was a boy with a broken arm and leg – just a boy, 14 years old and beside him, cold in death, lay his father, two brothers and an uncle. It was a harvest of death."

The above paints the haunting picture of The Battle of Griswoldville. Griswoldville was an industrial village located on the Central of Georgia Railway hence its position on the path of Sherman's soldiers just days after the March began. This was the last station before Macon on the railroad from Savannah. Griswoldville primarily manufactured cotton gins and Confederate rifles during it's time and a map of what the town looked like can be seen in the preserved field now. Griswoldville was named after a Connecticut native, Samuel Griswold, who was member of a very prominent New England family. He and his parents moved to Clinton, Georgia when Griswold was about 28-years-old in 1818. It was Samuel who created the cotton gin factory. And by 1830, it had become one of the largest producers of cotton gins in America. In a way, he started a movement, as a friend of his named Daniel Pratt also left New England for Georgia's neighbor, Alabama and became an industrial figure at the time as well. Pratt influenced Samuel in naming the town for himself. Griswoldville developed around the factory and became a company town fully equipped with a cotton gin plant, soap and tallow factory, candle factory, saw and grist mill post office and non-denominational church by about 1850. There was also a blacksmith and foundry, and Griswold's gin factory was uniquely steam-powered. Samuel did have enslaved people living in his custody and in the town and the enslaved people had dwellings along a stream at south of the village's southern end.

In all, people thought Griswoldville was scenic, beautiful town and reporters spoke of it as handsome and

> "lying in ambush among tall, graceful pines."

It was when the Civil War began that Samuel Griswold paused gin manufacturing and began weapons manufacturing answering the Georgia Governor's call for manufacturers to produce pikes. Pikes are the medieval torture device weapons with steep tips on wooden shafts and pikes would primarily be used against the cavalry. By 1862, however, Griswold teamed with A.N. Gunnison to manufacture firearms styled after the Colt revolver. Well-supplied in production and workforce, as well as enslaved mechanics given wages, Griswoldville produced nearly 3,700 "Griswold and Gunnison" revolvers. They were one of the largest Confederate weapons manufacturers.

You may recall Stoneman had gotten close to the region in 1864, and at that time the pistol works were threatened but did manage to escape with minimal to little damage. However, that July, Capron's men, prior to their incident at King's Tanyard, had orders from Stoneman to attack Griswoldville on their way to Atlanta. They caused railroad destruction and unable to enter Griswoldville took a captured train and built it to full steam before sending it backwards into town slamming into a passenger train and splitting a wooden car in half. Griswoldville would not be destroyed by that attack, however. Instead, they would continue manufacturing until the late fall when they met with the Union Army again.

So, let's flash forward to the late fall, shall we? The Harvest of Death was upon Georgia and Sherman would not be stopped at Griswoldville. Just days into the March to the Sea, on November 20, 1864, the same day as the Second Battle of Dunlap Hill, Captain Frederick Ladd of the 9th Michigan Cavalry and "100 handpicked men," burned down the factory complex and much of Griswoldville.

A Confederate force of primarily Georgia militia men, "on loan," made up the army that was trying to protect their region. Most of the men were either older – and far from prime fighting age or incredibly young boys and teenagers with no experience – even younger than the soldiers out in the field for the last few years. They marched to attack Shermans right wing at Duncan's Farm east of Griswoldville and they were marching along the line of the Central railroad to meet a train to carry them to Augusta where they believed Sherman was heading. The Union troops had dug in along a ridge astride one of the train approaches which is indicated now by historical markers. They were slowed by heavy roads and were headed toward Gordon. The Union was waiting for a Confederate cavalry attack that didn't come. Instead, they faced young boys and old men in the Georgia militia charging them on an open field who thought their Union opposition was only to be a small cavalry.

Prior to the march on the field, the 9th Pennsylvania had captured eighteen of the Confederates; killing one and wounding two and had charged them back a mile across a creek where they found the rest of Confederates in force, in order of battle there. The Confederates tried to drive off the Union skirmishers, but the Union had a saber charge that ended that. After this, Union General Walcutt's infantry and artillery joined the cavalry and threw out a strong skirmish line that had driven the Confederates back through Griswoldville. Union General Woods fell back to Duncan Farm and kept position on the edge of the woods and threw up a barricade of rails, logs, and battery of artillery. By mid-afternoon at 2:00 PM, was when the three brigades of the Georgia Militia made their appearance on the battlefield under the orders of Confederate General Philips. They were very unassuming and as stated, truly thought that they were headed to Augusta for Sherman. This was an accidental meeting.

Again, thinking it was just a small cavalry and not a force of 3,000 trained soldiers they were up against, the ill-equipped militia formed three compact lines and marched the open field where they were met with the Union army equipped with Spencer rifles that they promptly unloaded upon them with showers of canister causing imminent death and dismemberment. A state of shock fell upon the boys and men. The Union recalled their firearms allowing them to keep continuous fire. They made it to a ravine in face of all this field just 75 yards from General Walcutt who ended up being wounded and having to be taken off the field and his command given over to Colonel Catterson.

When the militia reached the ravine, they re-formed the lines that had been scattered and made three charges with all they had on the Union but were quickly repulsed time and again. They faced the Union flank well protected by cavalry and as such went back to the ravine where they hid until dark before leaving the field. The battle had lasted for a few hours from mid-afternoon until dusk with 650 casualties out of 2,300 Confederates and Union troops of somewhere 1,500 to 3,000 total suffering only 62 casualties,

Battlefield at Griswoldville, 2022

mostly wounded, not fatalities. The Union felt guilt-ridden about this battle as the Confederacy had at Pickett's Mill and one officer remarked,

> "I hope we will never have to shoot at such men again."

The men of the Union walked the field after their victory and were heartbroken by what they witnessed. One wrote,

> "Old grey-haired and weakly looking men and little boys not over fifteen years old, lay dead or writhing in pain."

Another followed up and said,

> "It was a terrible sight, we moved a few bodies and there was a boy with a broken arm and leg – just a boy, 14 years old and beside him, cold in death, lay his father, two brothers and an uncle. It was a harvest of death."

Griswoldville never rebuilt or repopulated as a town. The battlefield is maintained as a state historic site that can be visited. Historical markers commemorate the lives lost as best as they can, especially their innocence, and one at the battle site even reads:

> "The Confederates, mostly old men and boys, attacked with great courage and vigor, but failed to change any part of the Sherman's plan in the only pitched infantry battle on the March to the Sea."

The plaque confirms the other battles in the March were just not the same and not often spoke of as the March was mostly destruction.

The battlefield sits just off the road and is well marked and visible for the tree lines are far beyond the fields and there's a residence that abuts one of the sides of the field where many informational markers are.

Upon my arrival there, the resident's dog watched us as if he protected the soldiers of those who died there, ensuring we were there to pay respects. Animals always have a sense of knowing when it comes to spirit. I felt a deep sadness as I looked at the wood line where men would emerge from and across the way at what was then so unclear to them and their untrained eye. I looked at the obelisk commemorating the Confederate forces of the First Division Georgia Militia including the Georgia State Line, 2nd, 3rd and 4th Brigade, and a battery and militia surrounded on the ground by bricks of those descended from those lost, and I felt even more

Monument at Griswoldville, 2022

unbearable heartache. These men were considered defenders and honestly at home, in Connecticut where I reside, the home state of Mr. Griswold, I saw that name Griswold and the word defenders and thought of a site local to my home named Fort Griswold where local militia men defended an attack from Benedict Arnold in the American Revolution (the Voldemort of the North), and many young boys and many old men, fathers and sons also lay on that field dying among each other. The parallels were abundant and clear.

In my mind's eye or perhaps reenacting in front of me I could see them marching and hear them screaming and felt a pit in my stomach while at the same time looking at the sunshine, the dog, the quiet field and feeling quiet and solitude. I talked with Tim Mosely of Middle Georgia Haunted History who had suggested my visit to the battlefield at Griswoldville, and he spoke of his time there with his team as being one of the eeriest investigations he had ever had in relation to the Civil War. Tim mentioned they heard cannon fire throughout their hours there, screams for help, and a continual replay of the battle as if an epic residual haunting was pressed on repeat.

I think back to the accounts and the guilt from the Union troops, the scenes of families with children and elderly laying upon a field just a couple miles perhaps from home, and I think that's the ultimate sadness and horror one thinks of when visiting the field and there is no phantom sound or eerie apparition that can replace the haunting nature of the brutality of war.

On your Civil War journeys, be sure to travel just ten miles from Macon and give the boys of the Georgia militia a moment of your time and perhaps, say a prayer, intention or whatever your spirituality leads you to do that they are reunited with their loved ones beyond that veil on the other side and brought a sense of peace that their tragic passing most certainly did not provide.

Buckhead Creek

Less than a week after Griswoldville, Confederate Cavalry General Wheeler was playing catch up and tried to make his way to two Union regiments who were lagging ahead of him. North of Savannah by Buckhead Creek, near to the Big Buckhead Church in Jenkins County, Wheeler did meet up with Kilpatrick's men. The church at Buckhead Creek near this convergence still stands and the transpiring events would become the second "battle" in the March to the Sea/Savannah campaign.

Kilpatrick ended up in the area after Sherman sent out a cavalry force under his command, who had been known as the "Kill Cavalry." Their job was to try and free prisoners of war from Camp Lawton in Millen. They were to burn the railroad bridge over Briar Creek and head toward Millen in that order. Kilpatrick had set out from the left of Sherman's men on November 24 with the goal in mind and to get there he was going to try to fake out the Confederacy and make them think Sherman was heading toward Augusta (the former state capital), not Savannah. (Throughout the war, Milledgeville was the capital of Georgia and seat of government for the state). Nevertheless, Kilpatrick tried to deter the Confederacy and Sherman made his destructive run for the coast. Kilpatrick did deter several Confederates to Augusta, but General Wheeler known for the Confederacy as "Fighting Joe," realized that move very quickly and began his attempt to catch up to the Union and what they were doing immediately. He moved south toward their route to Savannah where Kilpatrick found out all too late that the prisoners were removed from Camp Lawton and his mission at that time was pointless. So he began to head back to Sherman.

It was on November 27, 1864, that the Union camped near Buckhead Creek and it was the next morning that Wheeler's CSA Cavalry found them and attacked. Wheeler almost captured Kilpatrick himself as they made their way to Buck Head Creek. Quickly and swiftly Kilpatrick and his men crossed the creek with the 5th Ohio Cavalry utilizing their artillery and severely wounding the Confederate troops with canister fire and burning the bridge behind them as they went. Wheeler made it eventually with his army; however, it was too late as the Union had hidden behind barricades at the Reynold's plantation near the Buck Head Creek Church and were able to halt the Confederate movement and force them to retreat. Kilpatrick ended up making it to Sherman with his forces having only suffered 46 casualties out of 5,000 men. The Confederates estimated a loss of 600 out of their 2,000 men. The Battle of Buckhead Creek was far more devastating for the Confederacy than the Union and evidence of their grasping at straws to try and prevent Sherman and his associates from continuing their path of horror lays in the bloodbath that ensued for them.

Kilpatrick's troops were rumored to have taken pews from the nearby Buckhead church where some of them were set up, to aid their horses in crossing high rivers before returning them after their successful mission and legend states that if you look closely at the front pew in the church today and the back two pews you can make out horseshoe prints left by the Union horses. Legend further states that it's the horses who seem to haunt the church and that you can hear their hooves clanking on the wood and the horses snorting as you hear the efforts in some sort of residual haunt of them trying to cross the creek with their Union soldier companions.

Charlie Taylor Films on YouTube posted a video in 2018 featuring an interview with his uncle about a time when he and some friends and family went to the church to check out the strange and supernatural rumors. They were preparing to try to get into the church through locked doors when they heard an engine coming toward them. They looked around – having only noticed a small Confederate cemetery with a handful of graves behind the church and nothing else of note. They were surprised to hear something coming so rapidly. Quickly, they got into the vehicle and turned around only to have a deer walk in front of them that they barely evaded and to never lay eyes on the supposed vehicle that they heard and thought for certain was there. Who was trying to stop them from entering? And was this deer like the deer I encountered, a spirit animal correlating with a soldier? One can visit the Buckhead Creek Church that still stands today (perhaps during open hours is my suggestion) to investigate the pews for horse hoof prints or anything else strange. A historical marker stands not far from the road marking the site on the Civil War trails though no official battlefield remains.

Honey Hill

The third and arguably one of the largest battle-type engagements of Sherman's March to the Sea took place just over the Georgia Border in Jasper County, South Carolina and once again, Sherman went unhindered on his march and this battle like the others was a breakoff group that was sent to cut off the Charleston and Savannah Railroad so that Savannah would be prepared for Sherman's arrival. Sherman sent General Hatch on these orders. Hatch having been in Hilton Head prior, left on November 28 with 5,000 men including two brigades, one naval and three batteries of light artillery. They traveled via steamboat on the river to cut the railroad, however due to heavy fog the troops did not arrive until late the following afternoon and had to start immediately.

They grew frustrated when their maps pointed them in the wrong direction, and they didn't end up on track until the morning of November 30. It was then that they arrived at Honey Hill and encountered Confederate forces under Colonel Colcock who had a battery of seven guns on the road. The now famed, 54th and 55th

Massachusetts Colored Troops led a determined attack but could only use one artillery at a time and with well entrenched Confederates, it was impossible to dislodge them. They continued their fight until dark until Hatch realizing the futility of it, withdrew to Boyd's Neck having lost 89 men killed and nearly 700 wounded or missing. It was almost a reverse of what happened at Buckhead in casualty count as the Confederate force of only 1,400 reported just eight killed and only 39 wounded in comparison. It was a small Confederate victory by the rail lines on the Georgia border. Several Georgia men were present at Honey Hill, including the 1st Brigade of Georgia Militia with the 1st, 2nd, and 3rd Militia as well as the Georgia State Line Brigade with the 1st and 2nd State Line. Also present were the 32nd Georgia infantry who were under the division of General Gustavus Smith once again.

The battle anniversary of November 30th seems to dictate the ghostly activity at Honey Hill. Apparently, between November and January is when most haunting activity occurs, and it's been reported that it's mostly audible paranormal activity such as sounds of gunfire or the screams of injured and dying soldiers. The site is marked right of Highway 336 by a marker and several earthworks remain as well as the 1864 road network that was in existence at the time. Should you find yourself on the highway, don't' be too surprised if someone staggers out looking for a ride.

Waynesboro

Just a few days later as the March to the Sea was nearing an end and Sherman closed in on Savannah, Kilpatrick's and Wheeler's cavalries collided again. In fact, Kilpatrick felt that Wheeler had become a nuisance despite his lack of numbers and continuing losses as he persistently traveled with his cavalry to stop the Union from burning bridges as much possible. He was not going to give up. Wheeler drove off the Union cavalry on November 26 after they reached a railroad bridge near Waynesboro. And as such on December 4, Kilpatrick set his eyes on attacking Waynesboro and destroying Wheeler's command.

Kilpatrick had reinforcements of two infantry brigades from Thomas' station and they were ready to burn bridges and attack Confederates. The Confederates were on the road when Kilpatrick attacked the skirmishers at the front and suddenly the Union encountered a strong line of Confederate barricades. Though a substantial obstacle for the Union they did overrun the barricades and eventually outnumbered and surrounded the Confederates until they pushed back into the city of Waynesboro and put up barricades in the street.

Wheeler tried quickly for his troops of Texans and Tennesseans to have enough time to cross Brier Creek and block Augusta where he considered Sherman's objective and a fight occurred between the two armies to prevent that. Eventually, the Union broke through again and Wheeler had to withdraw. Kilpatrick made it to Brier Creek instead and burned the rail lines and wagon bridges before bringing his men to rejoin Union troops. Continual fighting as they made their way back toward Sherman and Savannah ensued over a few days just south of Augusta in Burke County that early December. The townspeople were able to save much of Waynesboro from being destroyed from the battle despite it going into the center of the community. No hauntings of Waynesboro as they relate to this skirmish have been widely reported however residents of the town have often stated that they see shadow figures on the streets or in their homes and feel an eerie presence at the local cemeteries. Many have come to surmise that it is linked to the battle of Waynesboro.

Tulifinny

The Battle of Tulifinny also takes place not far from the Georgia border in Jasper County, South Carolina and was a unique battle in that it's the only Civil War battle that involved the U.S. Marine Corps fighting for the Union and one of only eight involving the South Carolina Military Academy Corps of Cadets fighting for the Confederacy. Several Georgia men fought in the battle as well including the 5th, 32nd and 47th Georgia infantries as well as the 1st and 3rd Georgia Reserves.

The Confederates were able to somehow muster a victory here despite being outnumbered five to one. And this engagement was not just cavalry as so many others in the March were. By early December of 1864, Sherman and his 62,000 men were close to Savannah and thus the South Carolina border. His scorched earth tactics were destroying farms, homes livestock and ultimately causing havoc and destitution in their unapologetic wake. Slowly he was destroying the South's morale while logistically stunting their ability to fight. Ultimately, the Union was headed for the rail lines once more and wanted to destroy the Charleston-Savannah rail line.

The South Carolina cadets met up with Major Jenkins of the Confederacy on December 6, 1864, and were sent toward the Union troops advancing toward the railroad. Sadly, the cadets found that the Union was already entrenched on the peninsula and within striking distance of railroad trestles. General Jones of the Confederacy assigned the cadets to protect the bridge at Tulifinny. There the cadets assisted in building entrenchments and fortifications and gathered their weaponry in preparation of attack. By dawn on December 7th, the skirmish line of cadets and three companies of Georgia's 5th advanced. Then the arsenal cadets and the 47th Georgia advanced on the right and the skirmish line advanced into the wooded area. As they approached thc Union, a brisk exchange of gunfire began. Eventually the Confederates shifted to engage the entire Union line. Utilizing the woods, the cadets and Confederate troops were able to pour heavy fire into the enemy and because they used the element of surprise the attack drove the Union troops back to their original entrenchments.

One Georgia man remarked on the ability of the cadets and said,

> "Dang, them fellers fight like Hood's Texicans,"

a high compliment from his time with General Hood. One cadet was killed, sadly but ultimately, the Confederacy only suffered injuries in addition to that. By December 9, the cadets had repulsed the Union counterattack. And were pushed back through thick swamp. Ultimately, sometime later Sherman's troops burned down the Arsenal academy and seized the Citadel Academy (the South Carolina Military Academy,) but on that early December morning, in the battle of Tulifinny, the Confederates numbering 900, half of which were cadets were able to defeat a Union force of 5,000. And thus, they proved the morale of the South was not yet gone and there was fight left within them to protect their home.

In 2019, the Sons of Confederate Veterans established the Tulifinny Crossroad Memorial on Frontage Road in north Jasper County, just off I-95. They wanted to mark the service of the Citadel cadets and a beautiful marker can be visited today. Though, the site, like Honey Hill doesn't have a terribly sordid history of death as so many other battle sites do, it was historically significant and I can't help but think that the spirit of the one cadet who didn't make it back to the academy with his mates, might still be fighting the war on the other side and trying to prevent Sherman and his troops from making it to Savannah.

Fort McAllister

By December 13, the March to the Sea was in its final stages. In fact, Sherman's armies were on Savannah's doorstep by December 10th and needed supplies. Off the coast in the water was Union Naval Admiral John Dahlgren's fleet with the supplies and six weeks of mail for Sherman's men. However, the Confederacy had fortified Savannah and prevented that delivery. Sherman began to deploy forces to begin the invasion of Savannah and on their reconnaissance mission to find out weak points, Sherman's troops alerted him that Fort McAllister was lightly defended and could be taken by infantry attack. Sherman liked this idea – if they captured Fort McAllister, then the Union Army would gain control of Ogeechee River and have access to the coast. Sherman ordered Union General Howard to "reduce the fort," and Howard ordered Union General Hazen to lead these efforts with a 4,000 man-division that would storm the fort. Howard watched on the top of an abandoned rice mill at what would happen next. Hazen's Division was ready in the afternoon of December 13 and in line for the attack. The fort was run by Savannah native and Confederate

Major George W. Anderson and a 230-man garrison (mostly local men). They were grossly outnumbered by the Union, however they thought strategically and began to plant explosives throughout the site.

Fort McAllister Earthworks, 2022

When the Union army was ordered to advance, Hazen's men came from the woods and surrounded the fort spaced apart so that the Confederate artillery would not be as effective. The Union rushed forward evading abatis and torpedoes buried in the sand and captured Anderson's men and 15 guns in just 15 minutes. Sherman had gained the supply line; it was open for him, and the siege of Savannah was imminently his at that moment. It looked like he was going to meet his goal to be in Savannah by Christmas. Later that night as Sherman was overjoyed, he and Hazen had supper with Major Anderson and during this meeting Sherman complained about the land mines around the land route and told

Anderson it was not gentlemanly and then ordered the Major to clear the mines out with other captured Confederates. Now, Anderson could have been petty then, heck, I know may have been, but he wasn't. He was only a gentleman. In fact, later when he observed Union soldiers marching on the fort toward unexploded ordnance, Anderson took their hand and led them out of harm's way leaving behind fond memories with Union soldiers. Meanwhile, in the day after the battle Sherman rowed out to greet the Admiral on the supply ship and spoke highly of his men who he commanded at Shiloh, Vicksburg and now at Savannah.

Major Gallie & The Ironclads of 1863 at Fort McAllister

December of 1864 was not the only time that Fort McAllister had seen action during the Civil War though it was the last. The fort was attacked seven times by ships within two years of its inspection by Lee in 1861 before Sherman reached there in 1864. In fact, in 1862, there were four naval attacks by Union ironclads.

The following year attacks began on January 27, 1863, when the Union utilized the ironclad monitors, Montauk Passaic, Nahant and Patapsco. The Montauk had an 11-inch and 15-inch cannon (record-breaking size for that time) and bombarded upon the fortification for five hours. The fort however had seven cannon emplacements, a bombproof area with a hospital, supply barracks officer's quarters and gun powder and more weaponry and well as 10-inch mortar on the exterior of the fort – so despite this large intimidation the strengthened earth walls that the garrison had tended to for two years were able to absorb the artillery shells and damage was minimal and fixable. The fort even struck the ironclad Montauk fifteen times but with its strength – the blows didn't damage the ship. The Montauk retuned twice more on February 1 and March 3, the February 1 appearance killing respected Scotland native and Georgia local, Major John B. Gallie. Legend says he was beheaded as he went from post to aid the men in manning the cannon and tried to help them to maintain a sense of calm. Papers at the time stated rather that though he was struck in the head, his face was "slightly damaged." Gallie was known to be capable and courageous – and one student concluded that

> "Hardly a week passed without his name being in the news at least twice,"

in a good way and this even before he maintained the rank of Major. In fact, his funeral was a lavish affair, full of military honors and incredibly well attended on February 3, 1863.

Site of Major Gallie's Mortal Wound, 2022

Tom Cat

A March 3 engagement in a seven-hour bombardment had the same results as the first. There was a tragedy for the men of the garrison, however, on March 3 and it was the sole casualty that

Tom Cat Plaque at Fort McAllister, 2022

day. Their beloved mascot, Tom Cat was a large, black cat adored by the men. He would always run and back forth when they were attacked dodging the musket fire and cannonballs playfully helping uplift the men's attitude as they watched their pet having a grand time. And Tom Cat had done this successfully on January 27 and February 1, however on March 3, a stray bullet took out the beloved cat. As stated, he was the only Confederate casualty of the day, and he was buried with full military honors. In fact, a full report of the action of his death was even reported to Confederate General Beauregard as it was considered such a tragic loss. Some say the men carried on their defense of the fort in his honor which is why the Fort McAllister stood so strongly until Sherman and his men came.

Ghosts of Fort McAllister

Ultimately, Fort McAllister is thought to be one of the most haunted locations in Georgia despite its minimal casualties and the two most frequently seen ghostly specters walking its grounds? Major Gallie and Tom Cat, of course. Fort McAllister is now a state park that you can walk in its entirety to see the woods in which the Union emerged in 1864, to walk the cannon pits where Gallie aided his men in 1863, to walk through the earth works where Tom Cat played and to see reconstruction of how the men in the garrison lived. You can also go underground into the well protected earth to see where they stored ammunitions, kept hospital rooms open and kept their food and important items. Albeit the hospital room is a bit eerie – almost like a modern-day haunted house, you can appreciate the strength the Fort gave and most certainly feel as if you are accompanied as you go through.

I felt oddly at home at the Fort, the soothing sounds of the water, the quiet nature, and the sense that people had called this home and filled it with their loved pet made me feel welcome there and had a sense of "homeyness" rather than the cold starkness that abounds in so many old military forts. But I did, of course, feel it was truly haunted. Who is the most famous of ghost of the fort you may ask?

Well, several visitors and staff report to see a black cat running around the lines of the earthen ramparts and works and even through the bomb proof shelters underground as if making his rounds to see all his people and playing about, or even out on a feline hunt. Re-enactors have even witnessed the spectral cat peering out at the river peacefully, watching. Some have seen the cat so vividly that they have inquired with the staff regarding his presence there or if the park still allowed a cat to live on-site perhaps in and out of the visitor's center. The staff of the park has always and continues to deny presence of any living cats on the park grounds.

Interior View of Fort McAllister, Ogechee River, 1861-1865
(Wikimedia Commons)

I inquired, of course with the staff about their hauntings when I visited, and they brought out a little brochure they keep behind the desk about the ghost of Tom Cat. The brochure confirmed what the visitors and staff have seen but also felt, the touch of a cat rubbing against their leg with a

> "furry arched back,"

as cats affectionally do still happens over 150 years later. They embrace the ghost of Tom Cat, one of the major casualties of Fort McAllister and are open to the idea of their other resident spirit –

John B. Gallie Gun, Fort McAllister, 1864 (Library of Congress)

Major Gallie himself. Major Gallie's ghost could be the very reason folks believe he was totally beheaded for it is the phantom of a headless man that has been seen walking the park grounds at night, pacing the ramparts in the exact positions where Gallie was walking to and fro when he was mortally wounded. The legend regarding the ghost of Major Gallie is thought to have originated in the 1930s when Henry Ford had acquired the grounds with an interest in historical preservation of the amazing fort that remained in remarkable condition. Ford invested in his own money in the reconstruction of the fort thus earning it a title as the best-preserved Civil War era earthen fortification in the south. However, Ford's workers during this vital time were none too pleased to hear strange noises in the darkness of night, noises they felt were emanating from the grounds but were never identified. They heard shouts of military commands coming from places they saw no living person at all hours and then suddenly they'd hear cannon in response or someone sounding as if injured. The panic that surrounded the workers about all of this as well as their sighting of Major Gallie in his headless form which they deemed to be ghastly, caused high turnaround in Ford's workforce and a lack of willingness to work at all when it was not daylight hours as well as a blatant refusal to say on the premises.

Altamaha Bridge

Just a couple days before the conclusion of Sherman's March to the Sea, on December 19, 1864, another battle broke out in Wayne County, Georgia near the Doctortown Railroad Trestle and Altamaha Bridge – a battle whose name goes by both trestle and bridge names, but is better known as the Battle of Altamaha Bridge. Despite Sherman's success in making it to Savannah's doorstep at this point, the Confederates had another victory presenting the destruction of a railroad bridge that was vital to them during the Savannah siege by the Union if they wanted to keep supply lines open.

Weeks prior to the battle, the 4th Brigade Georgia Militia under General McCay arrived to prepare defenses of the Atlanta and Gulf Railroad at the Altamaha River. They built earthworks bisecting the rail north of the river and set up two 23-pounder rifled guns on the south side in Doctortown, as well as a light gun at the lake. On December 16, some of Shermans troops were stalled outside Savannah and sent troops from Ogeechee River to destroy the bridge. Kilpatrick's Cavalry was back at it when his brigade under

Col. Atkins and his "Kill Cavalry," when they attacked the bridge destroying part of the trestlework. However, due to Confederate defenses and the battery at Doctortown, the Union had to withdraw to Ogeechee River. The Union strength was an estimated 1,000 and the Confederate Georgia militia brigade just 200, however the casualty count remains unknown but is thought to have been minimal due to the effective weaponry.

Several supernatural stories surround the region and the bridge including even a sea monster in the Altamaha River. Tragedies have occurred there as well with an actress being killed by the rail bridge as recently as 2014 filming a movie about the Allman Brothers. None of the ghost stories seem to liken back to the battle which ultimately was perhaps just the spiritual boost the Confederacy needed just before the Siege of Savannah.

Fort James Jackson

Just three miles east of Savannah on the Savannah River sat what was thought to be the indomitable Fort James Jackson, constructed in 1808 under President Thomas Jefferson's coastal defense initiative. The brick fortification was established on an earthen battery that had once been known as the Mud Fort and utilized during the War of 1812 before it further expanded in the 1840s to 1850s, not too long before the Civil War began. The fort is considered to be the oldest standing brick fortification in Georgia and the height of its activity was during the Civil War. The Jackson fort includes a moat, drawbridge, barracks, privies, a back wall and a powder magazine. Overall, it was well established and well supplied which in turn, kept it protected.

When the Civil War broke out after the attack at Fort Sumter in 1861, the local Confederate militia units with mostly Georgia men occupied the fort and by 1862 it became headquarters for Savannah's river defenses when it's sister fort, the once powerful Fort Pulaski, fell into the hands of the Union army.

Fort Jackson, Savannah, 1992 (Wikimedia Commons)

The Confederates maintained control of Fort Jackson until Sherman's March to the Sea had arrived to Savannah and commensurately, the sea. On December 17, Sherman demanded the surrender of Savannah and the surviving forts. Ultimately, his capture of Savannah would be just in time for the holidays on December 21, 1864. Confederate General Hardee who commanded the forces in Savannah did not respond immediately to Sherman's demands and utilized the delay in response to give the Confederacy time to build temporary bridges and escape to South Carolina in the cover of darkness. The Confederates abandoned their trusty post that had served them so well over the years and also had to think about what to do with their Naval ships including the casemate ironclad CSS Savannah and ironclad warship CSS Georgia. The Georgia had only seen action, possibly, once in its protective position having been rumored to fire a volley at a smaller Union vessel. The Savannah and Georgia never saw battle until Sherman's siege and even then, the Confederates were not

THE DESTRUCTION OF THE REBEL RAM "SAVANNAH" BY THE ENEMY ON THE EVE OF THE FEDERAL OCCUPATION OF SAVANNAH.—[Sketched by Captain [illegible].]

Destruction of the Rebel Ram Savannah on Union Occupation (Ft. Jackson)

going to allow that to happen.

Though the Confederates abandoned their post at James Jackson leaving it open for Union takeover, the last thing they had wanted was to supply them with strong ironclad war ships to strengthen their offensive position in the city upon which they had invaded. The USS Savannah that had been transferred to service with the naval forces in the Savannah River under command of Flag Officer William Hunter and Commander Robert Pinkney and she was considered the most efficient of the squadron. When Sherman came to town, the Confederates, on December 21, 1864 as they were making their escape and surrender burned the CSS Savannah. On the same day, they looked at their other ironclad that was anchored as a floating battery to protect both the city and Fort Jackson. She was in service for nearly two years when Sherman made his capture of Savannah. The Confederacy scuttled the ship which is the intentional sinking of the ship so that she could not be utilized.

A year after the conclusion of the war the ships iron armor was partially salvaged but the wooden hull was destroyed in the process and the wreck was left alone for nearly a century until she was rediscovered in the dredging of the Savannah River. Several cannon, casemates, ordnance, boilers extra were deemed to be surviving by 1992 and in 2012 the US Army Corps of Engineers budgeted to raise the remains and artifacts discovered. In 2015, in excavations and efforts to get the CSS Georgia – they were even able to recover a 9,000-pound Dahlgren rifled cannon. Even in the 21st Century, the ironclads are providing remarkable artifacts.

CSS Georgia, Ironclad (Wikimedia Commons)

The Union took over the Fort and sent the 55th Massachusetts, the noted "colored regiment" to live in the quarters. Today, the Fort is run by the Coastal Heritage Society. The 55th were the last soldiers to be stationed there and the War Department abandoned the fort in 1906. The building remained vacant until the state of Georgia operated it as a maritime museum from 1965 to 1975 and in 1976 the Coastal Heritage Society opened the and operated the site as Old Fort Jackson. Fort Jackson is a wonderful walk back in time as they have staff and re-enactors on a daily basis giving demonstrations on 19th Century weapons and life with daily rifle firings, cannon firings (a light cannon), reviews of types of ammunition and lessons on 19th Century medicine. In full character, the soldiers will take you back to what life was like living in a fort, the diseases they were exposed to and worries they had. And as they light the firepits and fire the cannons with the Savannah River in the distance – despite the ever-changing water lines, you can sense that their efforts keep the spirit of Fort Jackson alive. The fort may not have seen battle, but it was a heart of fortifications for local Georgia men in the March to the Sea. And, if you ask the staff at Old Fort Jackson if the place is haunted – it's an unequivocal yes.

Reenactor on Parade at Fort James Jackson, 2022

Even at the visitor's center, they boast a bit about the spirit of a man named Private Garrity just as the reenacting staff do. The reenactors claim that they have heard footsteps marching lock in step behind them as they go to demonstrations and see shadows pacing back and forth by the entrance door. They've even had guests report a cranky man in uniform, in the room where security guards used to stand – looking like he's part of the staff but not treating visitors like he is. Rather, when he is encountered, he is treating them with a disgruntled nature and when the visitors tell the other staff about him, they learn there's no one in the security room or on staff matching that description. The folks at Old Fort Jackson are fairly convinced and with good reason that the ghostly specter is that of Confederate soldier, Private Patrick Garrity.

During the war, one evening as Private Garrity was standing guard near the drawbridge, some say on the floor above it which means the parapets on top of fort, he saw a figure approaching the fort. In a panic, not recognizing his own Lieutenant Dickerson, who had been meeting with other officers, he began to fire upon him; and when he missed, he ran out in a fit of panic or rage to attack the figure. He bludgeoned him with his musket and heard a crack of the skull. Garrity had crushed Lieutenant George Dickerson's skull in four places and broke his own musket in the process. It's unclear whether he was taken over in the heat of the moment and didn't recognize his superior until it was too late and he had come out of the hysteria he was in or if there was some intention behind it, or encounter they had that prompted the attack.

Nevertheless, at this time in the armies, officers were elected by popular vote and Dickerson had been quite popular among the men at Fort Jackson. As such, there are different theories on what happened next. We know, the men tended to Lieutenant Dickerson, and he survived. He had fought prior to his station at Fort Jackson and even lost two fingers on his left hand. He was resilient and strong despite this ungodly injury that at first it didn't look like he would survive. We also know he never fully recovered and was unable to recall the incident. Private Garrity was found days later washed up from the Savannah River close to the fort, beginning to decompose. The men stated he must have jumped into the moat and killed himself, guilt-ridden for what he had done. However, some of the staff believes, that the men handled Private Garrity and tried to dispose of him, wanting to defend their beloved Lieutenant and seek vengeance for the attempt to murder him. As such, it's quite possible the men of Fort Jackson, "took care" of Private Garrity.

Fort James Jackson, Site of Private Garrity Incident 2022

In the century-and-a-half since the death of Garrity and attack on Dickerson, the staff has seen a silhouette of a man on the casement walls on top of the fort several times looking out. And reenactors who visit for special awards often have their awards get broken or end up missing when they go to the area where the attack on the Lieutenant occurred. The ghost story has been talked about on national television.

Though Fort Jackson has a dark history, there is also a sense of peace in portions as well and during one of the re-enactments, we witnessed a rare eagle pass overhead, perhaps the eagle of a soldier keeping post from his fort. As you know, I always believe in spirit animals representing someone coming from the afterlife.

Ultimately, the question remains, are there other spirits at For Jackson other than Private Garrity? Possibly, though the fort did not see war conflict directly, some men succumbed to disease living in such close quarters with only rudimentary medical treatments available. Reports of disembodied voices, soldiers staring at visitors that walk through before vanishing and many uniformed phantoms abound at the fort making the Old Fort Jackson a step back in time in more ways than one.

Sherman's Time in Savannah, Special Field Orders No. 15 & Ebenezer Creek

Confederate General Hardee refused to surrender on December 20 while Sherman was gaining control of the forts and waterways, Hardee and his men planned their escape on a makeshift pontoon bridge. Savannah politicians such as the mayor and several alderman and ladies rode out to talk to Union and make a proposition. Enroute, the Confederate cavalry had taken their horses. Nevertheless, they arrived and let the Union General Geary know their plan to surrender the City of Savannah to the Union in an effort to protect the city's citizens and property. General Geary of the Union Army having made that deal convinced Sherman to accept the offer, which he subsequently did and then the Savannah Mayor offered Sherman the keys to the city. Sherman's men, led by Geary's division occupied the city of Savannah on December 21, 1864.

After his arrival, Sherman sent a telegraph to President Lincoln offering Savannah as his Christmas present,

> "I beg to present you as a Christmas gift the City of Savannah, with one hundred and fifty heavy guns

and plenty of ammunition and about twenty-five thousand bales of cotton."

Entrance Hall of Green House as occupied by Sherman, 1865 (Wikimedia Commons)

Sherman set up his headquarters at the Meldrim-Green House – then just the Green House at the home of Charles Green. Charles had offered this home in the initial meeting with the Union troops; however, Sherman was inclined to refuse a private home due to his fear of getting blamed for any potential destruction of personal property. He hesitantly accepted and was glad he did. Sherman incredibly impressed with the spacious, Gothic architecture. He didn't show much suspicion of his host despite his host having been an Englishman and Confederate sympathizer. His son Benjamin Burroughs Green was a member of the Confederate Cavalry and was incredibly sick with tuberculosis at that time and close to death. Green too had lost other children which seemed to gain some empathy from Sherman who suffered the loss of Willie.

Charles Green had made a name for himself as a cotton merchant which how he made his fortune. He, in fact was so committed to providing provisions to the South earlier in the war, he had even been imprisoned spying for the Confederacy and was put at Fort Warren in Boston Harbor for three months before the British consul intervened on his behalf. Green had gained respect from Sherman perhaps for his business etiquette and his elegant home, and he had gained the empathy of Sherman for their mutual familial losses to the war. Plus, Green, offered the house in the initial handing over of Savannah to protect it from destruction so there was no reason, he would suddenly be doing anything that would compromise that.

Sherman, had made it to Savannah, he had his headquarters, he had impressed Lincoln who himself confessed in his response a little nervousness and stated that he didn't want to question Sherman's methods of getting to the point where he had Savannah and the sea. In fact, Lincoln wrote in his December 26th correspondence,

> "When you were about leaving Atlanta for the Atlantic coast, I was anxious, if not fearful; but feeling that you were the better judge, and remembering that 'nothing risked, nothing gained,' I did not interfere."

Once Sherman was set up in Savannah, the people of Savannah were inherently anxious. They knew they had saved their city from ruin but at what cost? They had always been supporters of the Confederacy in Savannah and made no bones about getting rid of Yankees in their midst. At the Savannah City Hotel in 1860 – now the location of the Moon River Brewing Company, a Northern man named James Sinclair stayed at the hotel. When it was revealed that he was a Yankee that people of Savannah pressured him to leave town to which he refused, and mobs started to form in the street and into the hotel where Sinclair was dragged out. He was then stripped and beaten near to death. Now the Moon River Brewing Company which was also a hospital during the Civil War boasts several ghosts including they say the ghost of Sinclair. This is, of course, but one example of the Confederate passion for their cause and desire to protect their home from the perceived threat of Northerners at any cost. So, Sherman's presence caused disdain.

In fact, on a guided tour that I attended through the city of Savannah, a story was told about a little girl who was charged with delivering a message to Sherman and when she returned, she told her parents she was surprised to see that he didn't have a tail considering everyone had told her that he was the devil.

Sherman did have his allies in Georgia – mostly in the form of women both Union and Confederate who he always seemed to make peace with or deals with and perhaps it's some of those Southern belles who also helped to protect Savannah from the demon Union general.

One must remember in the scorched earth policy; he burned and captured all food stores Georgia residents had for the winter and left the citizens in a terribly vulnerable state. Ultimately, the army wrecked 300 miles of railroad, bridges and telegraph lines and seized 5,000 horses, 4,000 mules, 12,000 heads of cattle and confiscated 9.5 million pounds of corn, 10.5 million pounds of fodder and destroyed numerous mills and well. Some considered it psychological warfare and he carried the same mentality into South Carolina while he set Stoneman to do so in Tennessee and more in his raids -a campaign against civilians.

Sherman stayed in Savannah until about the end of January using it as his place of rest and remember for all those in the south who saw him as a villain, there were those in the north who praised him as a hero. It's more than worth mentioning that in Sherman's time in Savannah and at the Meldrim-Green House he met with several former enslaved people and created Special Field Orders No. 15 on January 16, 1865. But history is a … gray area.

Green-Meldrim House Front, 2020

It was estimated that about 10,000 former slaves followed Sherman's Army in his March to the Sea suffering from starvation and disease, and were disheartened at some of the war tactics they saw having suffered rape and other abuses themselves. It was said when they arrived having no care from those they were following,

> "Weary, famished, sick and almost naked."

So how can Sherman be considered a hero? On December 19, he dispatched several of these former slaves to Hilton on an Island serving as a refugee camp but by December 22, every cabin was full, and population had swelled to 15,000. Slaves who had freed themselves and enslaved people who had escaped and would be free as the Union won, were going to be homeless and uncared for if measures weren't taken. Secretary of War, Edwin Station and General Sherman as well as General Saxton consulted with about twenty leaders from the black community at the Green House on January 12, 1865. Spokesperson for the black community, 67-year-old Garrison Frazier, a pastor had bought freedom for himself about five to six years prior. When he was asked the question by Sherman,

> "What do you want for your own people?"

Frazier suggested the former enslaved people needed to have land that they took care of with their labor for their own households and that the young men of those communities would support the union in war while women and children care for the land. Almost everyone present, including Sherman agreed and the special orders utilized land not inhabited by the Sea Islands totaling 400,000 acres and divided into 40-acre plots each with a mule. This became known as the "40-acres and a mule" provision and became a landmark moment for African-Americans and their freedom, something that reflects a hero-type energy onto Sherman.

However, in speaking with historians, they say Sherman had to act benevolently and with such a big order like this because he had to atone for what he had done, not just to the civilians of Georgia and those he and his army would devastate in South Carolina but for what had happened at Ebenezer Creek on December 8, barely over a month before. Confederate General Jefferson Davis, not to be confused with the Confederate President was establishing a pontoon bridge to cross the creek with his men and Wheeler's cavalry engaged in some shelling with the Union lines. By midnight, they had completed the bridge and Davis and men began to cross. Over 600 freed slaves were anxious to go with them but

Davis, under Sherman's scorched earth policy, made a swift and cruel decision, and ordered his provost marshal to prevent them and tell them they could cross later. The Union abruptly ripped away the bridge before any of the former enslaved people could cross. A panic set in and the 600 freed enslaved people stampeded into the city water – old, young, men, women, children, and those who could not swim. Many drowned quickly. Some tried to create rafts to help others in acts of pure desperation. The Union men who were helping those in the water were ordered to leave the scene as Confederate cavalry arrived. Some had made it across, some had died, and the others left behind were captured and enslaved again. This event was brought up in the aforementioned meeting, but Sherman supported Davis's actions as a matter of military necessity. There is a sign now at the site marking the tragedy. By all accounts, it was a dark and rainy day at Ebenezer Creek on December 8th and if you visit on a dark and rainy day, you will still hear the cries of those drowning in the river trying to make it to freedom – or so, the local legend goes

Sherman's March for better or worse, was written about in the war song, "Marching through Georgia," where the 40 acres and a mule is referred to and the Union time in Georgia as heroic,

> "Hurrah! Hurrah! We bring the jubilee! Hurrah!
> Hurrah! The flag that makes you free!
> So we sang the chorus from Atlanta to the sea!
> While we were marching through Georgia!"

Even at the time, everyone's truth was different.

The South's encounter with Sherman is relevant to all who still live there. They still find "Sherman's neckties," which were trail rails bent around trees so they couldn't be repaired, they carry the ancestral tales of raping, pillaging, and looting among their families in the name of patriotism and in a way and mourn the loss of so many homes and structures they will never have again. In Georgia, Sherman will always be a symbolic villain of the freedom they felt they had lost in Georgia and in the south.

As for Sherman, he would carry on with his scorched earth policy even after he left Savannah and knew quite well what the people had thought of him. Sherman was not big on equality, and in fact, it can be argued that he didn't believe in any equality and many of the Union men didn't. But they were men of war. Sherman and some of his men were often cruel to the black community who they were supposed to be fighting for. Ebenezer Creek is a reminder of that strange gray area of history and the characters within it.

Sherman's ghost is thought to haunt all sorts of places important to him and places he destroyed, but suffice to say, the real Ghost of Sherman sits in the heart of all Savannah ever since 1864 and it is the looming memory of his destruction.

*Fort Pulaski, a noted Civil War site from Savannah dating to action before Sherman's March as well as more details on the Green-Meldrim House and Moon River Brewing can be found in Section IV, Homes, Museums and Places.

Columbus

Fort Tyler & West Point

The last battle of the Civil War, on April 16, 1865, too place in Western Georgia on the Alabama line, southwest of Atlanta and months after the March to the Sea had concluded. The Battle of Columbus sometimes went by the name Battle of Girard because the town of Girard, Alabama bordering Columbus, Georgia is where much of the battle took place. This last large-scale land battle of the war began because Columbus was the last surviving industrial city in the South and had avoided battles, the March to the Sea, and most conflict up until this point. Columbus was the location where a new ironclad ship was being constructed called the CSS Jackson. As such, the city was protected by earthworks and forts in anticipation of Union attack. The ridge of protection went into Alabama and followed the Chattahoochee River.

The only issue for the Confederacy at that time is that there weren't enough men for the entire line they had established. A week prior to the battle, Robert E. Lee and his army of Northern Virginia had surrendered in Appomattox, Virginia and Confederate General Cobb had learned at the time of Lee's surrender that Union Army General Wilson and his men had taken over Montgomery, Alabama and were heading toward Columbus,

Georgia. Cobb had about 3,500 men, some seasoned veterans, and others not as much. as well as local laborers that had been working on the ironclad. He ordered them all into the fortifications to prepare for the attack. It was Easter Sunday, April 16 at 2:00 PM when Union General Alexander passed through some of the Confederate defenses to capture the Dillingham Street Bridge leading into town. Quickly, the rebel defenses pushed them back.

The Union waited for reinforcements while a second unit from the Union attacked and captured Fort Tyler, a square redoubt atop a high hill in West Point which served as a protector of the vital bridge over the Chattahoochee. The redoubt had a 32-pounder, two field guns and three cannon. Upstream from Columbus it was in a protective position. When Union General Wilson came in from Atlanta and defeated Confederate General Forrest (who you may recall was quite a well-respected strategist) prior to moving in on April 14 as Wilson headed for Columbus, there was a lack of information provided to the rebels as well as a shortage of manpower. By their arrival on Easter Sunday, the Union force of nearly 4,000 men reached West Point and Southern General Tyler, having lost a leg at Missionary Ridge in the Chattanooga Campaign, was assembled with 120 men and fought anyway. Nearly 150 local men and boys helped the soldiers despite being from local hospitals and sick or wounded themselves. Many were from local militias.

Legend states that a flag flew above the fort that was gifted to General Tyler and that the General himself promised the ladies of the town that he would die before dishonoring their flag. The Union took West Point Bridge and the 32-pounder responded by killing Union Officer LaGrange's horse and stunning the Colonel himself. They were trying to prevent opening a path to the Confederate hold of Macon. But after that firing, the Union opened fire on the field and the Confederates responded in kind. The Union cut the rope holding the flag to its staff with their shell and witnessed 17-year-old Charlie McNeil amidst the bullets climb the flagpole and nail it back in place. The Confederates knew they were only buying time, and General Tyler knew that he was a man of his word and would have to become the ultimate sacrifice to end the battle. He knew where the Union snipers were, and he walked into the gate of the fort where they could see him and took his last breath as he was shot down and killed. His men still did not want to give up and fought until the evening when they surrendered and took down their flag. The Union lost about seven men and have a couple dozen injured men whereas the Confederates lost 19, had a couple dozen wounded well and reported 218 missing. The deceased Confederates and General Tyler lay buried in the nearby Fort Tyler Cemetery.

Meanwhile in Columbus, as the bridge at West Point was taken and a second column moved for Lagrange encountering the all-female Confederate unit known as the Nancy Harts, the main body prepared for their assault by Columbus that night. At 8:00 PM via the Summerville Road, General Cobb ordered his troops into the fortifications and at 9:00 PM they began to attack in the darkness. Men from Iowa and Missouri Cavalry stormed the Confederate works and thought they had captured the main line but found that they were isolated from their own men and now behind the Confederate lines. The Confederate line opened fire on the Union with artillery and musketry as explosions and flashes of fire could be seen in the night sky. The rebels also ensured they had their cannon positioned on the east bank to fire at the bridge though ultimately in the confusion of the night, it was never used. The Union troops who had not been isolated came across to assault the lines and it was only 10:00 PM when Columbus fell into their hands.

The National Civil War Naval Museum preserves the CSS Jackson and the story of the battle and can be visited in Columbus today as well as markers that represent the earthworks and battle

Photograph of General R.C. Tyler, CSA by Francis Miller (Wikimedia Commons)

sites on the Summerville Road. The National Civil War Museum is thought to be incredibly haunted, perhaps one of the most haunted museums in Georgia though they believe their ghosts come from the CSS Tennessee whose flag is in their inventory and that saw combat and death in the battle of Mobile Bay. The museum has had visitors and staff report sightings of men in uniform walking through the halls of the museum and hearing their footsteps on the old ships at the museum. They've also reported voices being heard in the distance. The activity has gotten so frequent that even some local Alabama ghost hunters have started conducting tours there on the matter. US Army Fort Benning also sits right outside Columbus and is thought to be home to ghostly soldiers not necessarily dating to the battle but possibly so. The Battle of Columbus/Girard estimated 151 Confederate losses and sixty Union, not the highest casualty count, however a significant event by being the concluding land battle of the war and the attack on Fort Tyler was one in which the last General was killed in action for the Civil War.

In fact, General Tyler seems to be the center of enigma in the Confederacy, if you will. With relatively vague unknown origins placing in him Walker's filibusterer army in Nicaragua in 1857, living in Baltimore, then Memphis where he had never been before in 1861, Tyler had been termed the

> "Mystery General…the South's Shadowiest Figure."

There were 425 Confederate Generals and he seemed to have

> "Stepped out of obscurity and then dropped back to oblivion,"

according to historian and author, Ezra Warner. Outside Tyler's career, we don't know very much about him. His soldiers claimed he was one of the bravest men they ever saw, and General Bragg had appointed him as provost marshal of the Army of Tennessee. Tyler had been at Chickamauga leading the 15th as well as at Shiloh and Perrysville doing the same. He was buried with his longtime friend, Captain Celestino Gonzalez of the 1st Florida – perhaps one of the only people that knew him and took any knowledge about Taylor's life to his grave.

Grave of Gen. Robert C. Tyler, CSA (Historical Marker Database)

Seeing as General was hospitalized near the location of his last fight and buried near to the site where he died, if anyone was to haunt West Point or Columbus area, my guess is it would be, General Tyler, himself. And I can't help but wonder if maybe a seasoned paranormal investigator might get more answers out of the General posthumously. I haven't yet had the opportunity to try as of the writing of this chapter, but it is most certainly on my list as something to endeavor to do. Ghost or no ghost, General Tyler, the mystery General and the last land battle of the Civil War remains legendary.

Fort Tyler can be visited off Highway 85 and is open year-round with a marked trail leading visitors to a small earthen fort and is part of the Civil War Discovery Trail.

PART II

GEORGIA REGIMENTS

Georgia Regiments, Units, and Legendary Soldiers in Significant Battles

Let's start the regiment chapter with a little rundown of the order -- regiments form Brigades which form Divisions and then there are wings and eventually armies. Georgia had several regiments, dozens more than smaller Union States but many of them more scarcely populated. It's important to remember that there were approximately 750,000 Confederate soldiers to the Union's two-million and the South had a much lower population. Overall, the casualty rates of Confederates were more devastating. There were approximately sixty-six infantry regiments in Georgia, nine infantry battalions, and four sharpshooter battalions as well as twenty or so cavalry, forty-eight Artilleries, approximately thirty-four state guards, seven regiments or battalions of State troops and seven legions. Not to mention there were over 129 reserve units.

Georgia's population at the time of the war was just over one million totaling, 1,082, 757 and of that one million, just over half were free – 620,527. Of that 620,527, there were 120,000 Confederate soldiers and 2,500 Union – accounting for an enormous portion of their population. It's estimated at least 25,000 Confederates from Georgia died with thousands more injured, sick, or missing. Georgia also had several high-ranking officers and

Generals. In fact, of the 425 Confederate Generals, Georgia men accounted for over 13% coming in at a whopping fifty-six Generals with home bases in Georgia most before the war and a couple immediately after the list of Generals includes (not in ranking order):

- Edward Porter Alexander – Washington, GA
- George T. Anderson – Covington, GA
- Robert Houston Anderson – Savannah, GA
- Cullen A. Battle – Powelton, GA
- Henry Lewis Benning "Old Rock," – Columbus, GA
- William Boggs – Augusta, GA
- John S. Bowen – Bowen's Creek, GA
- William M. Browne – Ireland & Athens, GA
- Goode Bryan – Augusta, GA
- John Carter – Waynesboro, GA
- James Holt Clanton – Columbia County, GA
- Henry DeLamar Clayton – Pulaski County, GA
- Howell Cobb – Cherry Hill, GA
- Thomas Reade Rootes Cobb – Jefferson County, GA
- Alfred Colquitt – Monroe, GA
- Philip Cook – Twiggs County, GA
- Alfred Cumming – Augusta, GA
- George Doles – Milledgeville, GA
- Dudley M. Dubose – moved to Washington, GA
- Mathew Ector – Putnam County, GA
- Clement Evans – Stewart County, GA
- William M. Gardner – Augusta, GA
- Lucius Jeremiah Gartrell – Washington, GA
- John Brown Gordon – Upson County, GA (Governor)
- William Joseph Hardee "Old Reliable," – Camden County, GA
- Joseph L. Hogg – Morgan County, GA
- James Thadeus Holtzclaw – McDonough, GA

- Alfred Iverson – Clinton, GA
- Henry R. Jackson – Athens, GA
- John K. Jackson – Augusta, GA
- James Longstreet – Gainesville, GA "Old Pete"
- Lafayette McLaws – Augusta/Savannah, GA
- Allison Nelson – Fulton County, GA
- William F. Perry – Jackson County, GA
- Isaac M. St. John – Augusta, GA
- Thomas M. Scott – Athens, GA
- Paul Jones Semmes – Wilkes County, GA
- James P. Simms – Covington, GA
- Martin Luther Smith – Savannah, GA (moved after war)
- William Duncan Smith – Augusta, GA
- Moxley Sorrel – Savannah, GA
- Marcellus Augustus Stovall – Sparta/Augusta, GA
- Bryan M. Thomas – Milledgeville, GA
- Edward Lloyd Thomas – Clarke County, GA
- Robert Toombs – Washington, GA
- Edward D. Tracy – Macon, GA
- David E. Twiggs – Richmond County, GA
- John C. Vaughn – moved to GA after war ()Washington, GA)
- William H. T. Walker – Augusta, GA (died Atlanta)
- William Stephen "Live Oak" Walker – Atlanta, GA
- Henry C. Wayne – Savannah, GA
- Joseph "Fighting Joe" Wheeler – Atlanta, GA
- Claudius C. Wilson – Effingham County, GA
- William T. Wofford – Toccoa/Cass Station, GA
- Ambrose Ransom Wright – Louisville/Augusta, GA
- Pierce Manning Butler Young – Bartow County, GA

Now that you have a rough estimate of how many Georgia men, units, and leaders there were going into it, it's important we take some time to feature some of the known regiments, known battles and fascinating facts as they relate to Georgia's men in the Civil War.

Troup Artillery & Charlie the Canine Cannoneer

Artillery units were specialized branches that would support the infantry and existed on both sides of the Civil War. Their specialty, of course, was cannons and artillery weaponry. Typically, an artillery was organized into battalions, batteries, sections and cannons and some men often had horses. Depending on the artillery, they would have smoothbore cannons or rifled cannons which were more accurate and started off acquired in higher number by the Union rather than the Confederacy. Artillery could fire multiple types of ammunition. Unlike the Union's six guns per battery, the Confederate batteries typically existed with four and in the Confederacy, the batteries were attached to infantry brigades until they reorganized in the second half of the war and batteries were put into battalions assigned with direct support of infantry. Light artillery would use guns and howitzers of smaller caliber than their artillery comrades.

The Troup Light Artillery (Carlton's Company, Georgia Artillery) also known as Troup County Artillery was organized early on in the war in 1861 in Athens, GA with men from Troup County as it's so named (the name hailing from former Governor George M. Troup). Part of Cobb's Georgia Legion when first organized, the light artillery was ordered to Virginia and then became an independent unit before serving in H.C. Cabell's Battalion of Artillery in Robert E. Lee's Army of Northern Virginia.

Since artilleries/batteries were specialized units, had much smaller forces rather than the 800 to a thousand or more that would be in an infantry regiment, Troup Artillery had a total of 288 men serve during the war. There would be 49 deaths out of the 288 in the artillery, most due to disease, the more common form of death during the war and the rest due to injury in battle.

The thing that most captured my attention about the Troup Artillery was their dog, Charlie that was with them throughout the entirety of the war. What struck me next was that the Troup Artillery from Athens, Georgia was in almost every major combat of the Eastern Theater including: Sharpsburg/Antietam, Chancellorsville, Gettysburg, Cold Harbor, the siege of Petersburg and even surrender at Appomattox with a section reporting to the dangerous Battle at Crampton's Gap as well.

Troup Artillery/Battery was briefly called the National Artillery in Athens, Georgia with Franklin Hill as Captain but when the name was changed, Captain Hill was also on his way to become an officer in the first Georgia Regular Regiment and as such, the battery elected Marcellus Stanley as Captain and Dr. Henry Hull Carton as First Lieutenant in January of 1861. The battery left Athens for Savannah, Georgia in late April of 1861 for a two-months drill and brought with them a twelve-pound howitzer, two six-pounder smoothbore howitzers and a James Rifle. Two days after they left Athens for Savannah on April 26, 1861, they were mustered into Confederate service. After their drills on July 5, 1861, they arrived in Richmond and then were sent to western Virginia. It was here on August 1st that the battery met Charlie, the small dog or rather Charlie met them.

The members of the artillery considered August 1, 1861 the day the little dog "enlisted," into the unit on the march in Staunton, Virginia. Decades later, Private George Baber Atkisson wrote a tribute to Charlie in the *Athens Banner* printed on April 29, 1911. Atkisson was merely 18 years old when he enlisted, a graduate of the University of Georgia who was forever changed by the war. Young George wrote of Charlie's arrival,

> "At Staunton in the afternoon of August 1st, a little friend came into our camp, a visitor who seemed inclined to make himself sociable with the boys. He was small and uncouth in appearance but showed a genial, friendly disposition and such winning ways that he soon won the friendship of the company. He was invited to spend the night and a bountiful supper was given him, also a comfortable bed...the next day when we took up the line of march, he signified his desire to become an independent member of the company and was cordially accepted as such. From that day until the closing days, at Appomattox, he remained a faithful member of the company, loved and petted by every member of the same."

Are you tearing up yet? Me too. But that little dog truly was just beginning his journey with the men and so was the Troup Battery with him and the war. They went through war together, the triumphs, the losses, the aches, pains, the laughter, and the tears – the 288 men and their little dog, Charlie. They remembered Charlie's endurance on the long, hot marches,

> "He endured fatigue and privation without a murmur, participated in every battle in which the company engaged, was always in the front rank where the shells

and bullets fell the thickest. He seemed to enjoy the whistling of the bullets, shrieking of shells and to go wild with delight as the combat raged. He was too small to take an active part in the work, but would dart back and forth from gun to gun, cheering the men with his clear, ringing voice, which could be heard distinctly above the din of battle."

Charlie the Canine Cannoneer of Troup Artillery, Artist Rendering
JackMasters.Net & Civil War Talk

Ah, a bark louder than bullets, you say? Reminds me of my own Beagle-Jack Russell mix named Buddy – whose bark is the same. In fact, the description of him reminds me much of my dog, as I'm sure you too may think of dogs you have loved when thinking of Charlie. Atkisson continued,

> "In this little four-legged comrade beat a heart warm with affection and bravery as in any of his "comrades," even if he was only a little dog. We named him, "Charlie," and today he is well remembered and his memory cherished by every surviving member of the company."

Atkisson could not speak enough of Charlie. He described him as,

> "a small dog, not very pretty and could boast of no illustrious pedigree. He had a soft, pathetic expression, yet, with no tail worth mentioning, but we loved him and wept for him when he died."

Before you worry too soon about his death – please remember, he does see most of the war with his men and they remember all of it and do their best to protect him. In December of 1861, after some months travelling with the artillery, and being at Camp Marion near Yorktown, Virginia, the men decided to have a raffle for Charlie to decide who would be his owner. He was won by Sergeant Motes who became Lieutenant Motes, but

> "Charlie was of an independent nature and refused to be the special property of anyone. In camp he would select the particular "mess," he wished to spend the night with. Gently scratching on the door, he was always sure of a welcome and a comfortable bed."

Even as I write this – the dog is scratching at the door to my office for his warm bed next to me. Perhaps, he's bringing Charlie with him. They recollected in the early war when they were at "dam number one," on April 16, 1862, that one of their guns, "Olivia," and Lieutenant People had to engage in an all-day attack from firing from the Union batteries. When the firing was happening at 8:00 AM,

> "Captain Stanley and Charlie were back at the camps. As soon as the captain heard the firings, he rushed to the front. They say one might have played marbles on his coattails, as he flew to the gun. At his heels was Charlie, just as eager as Captain Stanley to take part in the fray and at every shot would dance and bark with delight."

As time drug on and the army crossed the Potomac, they wanted to protect Charlie and placed him on the foremost caisson for safety since he couldn't swim in such a wide, fast-moving river. I confess, the veteran's recollections of life with Charlie gives us a unique first-hand glance at life with a traveling unit of the Confederacy so far from home and their love and companionship and their human nature to protect their animal companion.

Charlie was the first to step foot in Maryland and when he did, he

> "danced and barked with delight, till the last gun had crossed, and then bravely took up the line of march with the company."

It wasn't long before the Troup Battery found themselves at the battlefield of South Mountain and then Antietam. In South Mountain, which was also known as Crampton's Gap a two-gun section of the battery was in action and one gun was captured as well as one member killed and one wounded. A marker stands for them at South Mountain. Two days later was the Battle at Sharpsburg, (Antietam), known as the deadliest and bloodiest day in American History – September 17, 1862. Confederates often called battles by what town they were in as opposed to any another name for natural landmarks, etc. which is why you see differing names from the Union for some battles (i.e. Bull Run/Manassas; Antietam/Sharpsburg). Antietam is a name that lives in United States infamy. It was presumed that the full Troup battery wasn't able to be present at Antietam and were shorthanded with as little as one officer and twenty-six men present since they likely left guns in Leesburg and had one stolen at Crampton's Gap.

There were nine casualties for the Troup Battery – one death and eight injuries (one injury including Atkisson who had his thigh bone fractured by gunshot) at Antietam which was devastating for such a small force of men. The death was that of Benjamin Carlton, the brother of Captain Carlton and George Augustus Carlton of the same artillery. Benjamin was a 23-year-old brick mason, shot through the heart on the fields of battle and buried near a large walnut tree in Smith's field to later be disinterred by friends. The Troup Artillery location at Antietam was at the High-Water Mark noted as Greene's High in the West Woods from 9 AM to Noon, though some likely remained through the evening hours. You can visit the battle site and see a tablet for McLaw's Division in Longstreet's Command which was their chain of command commemorating their presence. Atkisson spoke of Charlie at Antietam and said,

> "At Sharpsburg, Charlie was in his glory. He ran up and down the line from fun to gun. He would wiggle his little body with joy, whilst his bark rang above the roar of battle. He seemed to know no such thing as fear, and as the battle grew fiercer so did his joy."

Charlie seemed to take pride in protecting his men and intimidating his enemy.

Months later, the Troup Artillery served in the Battle of Fredericksburg on December 13, 1862. Southern artillery were placed near the tops of Willis Hill and Marye's Hill and it is presumed that is where Troup Battery was. In the spring of the next year, they were at the Battle of Chancellorsville leaving Fredericksburg and the deceased private, Thomas Aaron who had a fatal wound to his left thigh. They said, of their friend,

> "The only thing he could do without stuttering was to shoot,"

but they missed him and grieved for his wife and child. Much of the artillery here was at Hazel's Grove and the Troup Artillery suffered eleven casualties. It was at Chancellorsville, that the Confederates lost their beloved General Stonewall Jackson as well.

By July of 1863, the Georgia battery including Charlie were at the Battle of Gettysburg. The War Department markers on the battlefield show their placements. The markers indicate their placement on Southwest Confederate Avenue on the right or west side traveling west, and north of the position is the Confederate Avenue Watch Tower.

On July 2, their section with two ten-pounder parrots took position around 3:30 PM, the second day of battle and engaged until dark. On July 3rd on position in the main artillery line in front of Spangler's woods, they took part in great cannonade and after repulse of Longstreet's assault, advanced 300 yards and aided in checking pursuit, then retired from front after dark. They remained the next day, inactive and short of ammunition before removing themselves at night. Losses included one death, six wounded and 17 horses killed or disabled. The death was a man registered as a substitute (paid to be there by someone else), John H. Adams and was buried on-site. One wounded man, Private William Biggers received a fatal wound he tried to recover from for two months and is buried on a Gettysburg farm having tried to recover there. Records are unsure if his body was moved to Laurel Grove Cemetery in Savannah or left on a farm in Gettysburg. Another of the wounded was Captain Henry Carlton from who First Lieutenant Motes took command. Captain Carlton returned to the battery almost a year later recovered from his wound on April 3, 1864.

On May 31, 1864, the artillery was at Cold Harbor in Virginia – one of the most haunting battles of the entire war where Captain Carlton was injured again. As war raged on in 1864 through Spotsylvania and the Wilderness (bringing them back through Chancellorsville) and then to the Siege at Petersburg, the men showed their resiliency and Charlie accompanied them without fail. Atkisson wrote,

> "At Fredericksburg, Gettysburg, Spotsylvania and in every engagement, he was always present and always exhibiting the same wild joy and courage."

Even General Lee knew of Charlie.

> "When General Lee held grand review of the "The Army of Northern Virginia," at Brandy Station, Virginia, prior to the Pennsylvania Campaign (Gettysburg), Charlie was given the place of honor upon of the "the Caissons," and as he passed was honored with a grave [?] salute from the general commanding. Charlie acknowledged the honor by a wiggle of his body, and a loud bark. He would have wagged his little tail off, if he had one."

Well, if that's not the cutest thing – I don't know what it is.

Though the Troup was part of Longstreet's Corps, some of the infantry men who rivaled with them would kidnap or steal Charlie, according to the artillery, but they needn't worry of their loyal companion.

"He was true to his "first love," and in a few days would find his way back to our camp to be hailed with shouts of joy."

In fact, their canine companion was known to go and try to get food for the men, especially when food was scarce.

> "Charlie was a good forager and many a rabbit fell victim to his hunting prowess, to say nothing of a few stray chickens. He brought his game into camp, giving it to the one he thought needed the most. He was impartial in bestowing his favors."

They said the little dog knew how to take orders as well,

> "During the Maryland campaign he strictly obeyed General Lee's orders, refusing to leave the ranks. Some of the boys would say, "Charlie, go bring us a chicken," but he would pay no attention to the request and jog along the guns. He looked upon the people in Maryland as friends; refused to steal from them."

A dog of empathy and caring – a smart dog, indeed. The men of Troup Artillery think Charlie knew he had reached enemy territory in Gettysburg, however as he behaved differently.

> "He was on the enemy soil and he plundered accordingly. Many a Dutch wife bewailed the loss of her chickens."

Some even went to the Captain and said,

> "Leetle dog vot belongs to your company steal mine chickens and bring dem to you mens. I vants my chickens, or you pay for them."

The Captain would suggest to the farmer, that the man point out the dog and men who did it and he would pay if they could do so, but it was impossible to know who ate the chickens and Charlie would hide during those times, leaving the Dutch to curse the rebels. As the war waged on, Troup Artillery men were running scarce on rations and Charlie's contribution could not be overstated.

> "Charlie spent most of his time at the guns, but was always going to camp for his meals." The men would always call Charlie for dinner and he would dart off to camp immediately upon his summons barking and wiggling."

Atkisson said of Charlie's dinner,

> 'If all was ready, the cooks would say, "all right Charlie, here we go," and away they went, Charlie showing his joy by barking and dancing around the bearer's heels."

Even when food was scarce, Charlie was provided for as he provided for them. If dinner was running late, Charlie would sulk in a corner until ready and only when he was sure would he summon the men to dinner as his orders said. And, upon eating, he would be happy once more.

Ultimately when the men ended up at Petersburg with Charlie, many chapters were coming to an end for the artillery, for the war and for Charlie. The siege of Petersburg lasted from June 9, 1864, to March 25, 1865. Two days before surrender and the end of the siege, there was a slight engagement and Atkisson heartbreakingly wrote,

> "A shell strikes a tree by which he was standing and exploded. When the smoke cleared away, little Charlie was dead. For nearly four years, the faithful little fellow had been our constant companion, enduring every hardship, sharing every danger, loved and petted by all. But now he was gone and the Confederacy is gone too. Perhaps it was not unmet that his little life should end with the closing scenes of our "Lost Cause." His grave was dug at the foot of a tree and the body of our faithful little "comrade" was consigned to his last resting place. I can safely write, that there was not a dry eye among that group of war-worn veterans as the clods fell upon his little body. Rest in peace, little comrade, for nearly four years you were our faithful companion and loving pet. You shared our dangers and our pleasures. Your mouldering body lies beneath Virginia's sod, but your memory is yet fresh and green in the hearts of every surviving member of the Troup Artillery, Carlton's Battery. I fondly fancy that the trees cast a loving shade, that the winter winds wail less mournful and the wild flowers blossom more lovingly over your little grave."

In 1911, Atkisson and any surviving veterans, growing in age, finally got to eulogize their friend and member of their unit. When he had passed, Charlie's entire battery fell in line for his funeral and vowed to hold him in their hearts forever more. I confess, as I write this, I can't help but cry myself. Charlie had come to them precisely when they mustered out and no one knew from where but he was there when the war started for the men of the Troup Artillery and it was clear that it was by some act of fate and higher purpose. Then as the bloody conflict concluded, the young dog rested peacefully under a tree and fate again stepped in but this time the war was over and his purpose with the men, the dog's soul purpose – yes, *soul* purpose – had ended. He had served with loyalty and love and forever changed those who knew him.

The Civil War was a time of fear and loss, and for the men of the Troup Artillery, they were blessed with smiles and laughter from their protector, Charlie – an angel sent to them for precisely how long they needed it. Of course, now Atkisson and the others have passed on, but I know as do you, dear reader, that Charlie was on the rainbow bridge, I imagine the bridge for him going over the Potomac River and there he waited for every member of his artillery to cross the river with him, the comrades who passed in war waiting on the bridge with him, and Charlie the first to arrive once more and step foot into heaven as he had into Maryland, waiting for his comrades to join him one final time. Now, they are all indeed crossed over together and are gazing out at the wildflowers that grow on the fields of all those souls lost in the Civil War grounds upon which they once trod.

As for the war, at the end of Petersburg, with the heart of their unit and their cause gone, on April 8, most of the battery was captured with Walker's artillery park at Appomattox Station and the next day on April 9 at Appomattox Court House many of the men disbanded near Lynchburg under Captain Carlton's orders just before Lee's surrender. Ultimately, only seven men were surrendered at Appomattox from the unit. Many of the men, university graduates, laborers, husbands, sons, fathers and friends went on to resume work, get involved with their communities, work on their farms and try to live with the injuries both physical and emotional that the war had given to them, until they were called to meet one another and little Charlie once again.

The true spirit of the Troup battery/artillery would remain on always through their hearts and despite their loss but most of all the soul of Troup Artillery was kept alive in the spirit of a little dog named Charlie, the Canine Cannoneer.

Troup Artillery Veterans Reunion Oconee County – Jennings Family Collection Courtesy, Georgia Archives, Virtual Georgia Collection, VRG110

Nancy Harts Militia

As you may recall from the battle segments, Georgia has no shortage of militia men, taking up arms to defend their home especially when the Union Army invaded the Deep South, but it wasn't only men that formed the local militias. In La Grange, Georgia during the very first weeks of the Civil War, a female military unit organized by wives of enlisted Confederate soldiers, at that time all volunteers, formed a unit to protect the home front. On April 26, 1861, the men of the LaGrange Light Guards of the 4th Georgia Infantry in Troup County (same county as the aforementioned artillery) left home and fought for the Confederacy. Nearly 1,300 men left the small town of LaGrange and left it quite vulnerable to Union attack because of its location between the train and supply hub of Atlanta and the first capital of the Confederacy in Montgomery, Alabama.

After their husbands left, two women, Nancy Hill Morgan and Mary Alford Heard formed the company and met at the schoolhouse located on the grounds of U.S. Senator Benjamin Hill's home. Nearly forty women attended wanting to learn more about how to protect their home and support the men who were away.

The fighting women formed their ensemble almost a century before Rosie the Riveter came into public eye. They felt as I do that women were not content to be quiet, meek and hide. This was especially true for rebel women who often served as spies in addition to forming militias such as this. They held opinions as strongly as their husbands did as well as a fierce patriotism and loyalty for their home. Women, were often inexperienced with firearms as they didn't do most of the hunting and military training hadn't been shared with them, so they educated themselves. They networked and turned to Dr. A.C. Ware, a man who stayed in town due to his disability and asked for his help in training them. Initially, they appointed him a Captain but quickly decided that the founding women should be their own officers with Nancy Morgan serving as Captain and Mary Heard as First Lieutenant. The ladies decided to call themselves the "Nancy Harts," or the "Nancies," in honor of the female Patriot spy who outsmarted a group of Loyalists and killed them in her northeast Georgia cabin during the American Revolutionary War, the century prior – a local, fearless woman of war was the perfect namesake for the group of bold women. The *Southern Confederacy* paper wrote of their formation in June of 1861,

"We have no doubt they will provide as true as did Nancy Hart if the emergency ever presents itself, and therefore, we do not think a more appropriate name could be suggested. The Nancy Harts of LaGrange! That's it, ladies."

The women started off their training using William J. Hardee's *Rifle and Light Infantry Tactics* published in 1861. They would leave their homesteads twice a week, meet up and have drilling and target practice. As with anything, there were prizes to the best

Officers of the Nancy Hart Militia (Ladies Home Journal 1904)

markswomen. Legend says that familiarity with their weapons came quick after one accidentally shot a hornet's nest and the other a cow. I laugh a little because typically women are known to be better shots than men! They were absolutely working their way there. Nancy Morgan reflected on their practice,

"I am sure this company presented a curious, odd, and singular spectacle as it met in Harris Grove, a beautiful and picturesque spot, with its magnificent trees to shelter them from the glare of light or sultry heat of the midsummer days, where they went often went for target practice or drill…They met twice a week at the grove in the day, and at night on the courthouse square, with the moon and stars looking down with their majestic and glorious illumination to light the earth with their radiancy; while the captain could be heard in clear voice giving commands: "Shoulder arms, right face, forward, march!"

She described their practices and drills as ongoing throughout the entirety of the war, even when they served as nurses. Unlike other militia, they did not wear uniforms for practice or service. Nancy Morgan described their clothes and increasingly good marksmanship and stated,

"The Nancy Harts did not have uniforms, as all the gray cloth and brass buttons available were bestowed upon their fathers and brothers; but in feminine dress of ruffled skirts and flowered or feathered heats, their hearts beat in unison to the captain's command as they boldly marched, "Hep, hep, hep," to the time of the battered

Nancy C. Hill (Mrs. J. Brown Morgan) Captain of the Nancy Hart Militia (Troup County Archives)

drum, guns on their shoulders, banners flying, ready and anxious for combat or to be called to field duty. In a modest way they made many conquests, for they were watched with adoring eyes of women and children, and black as well as white were proudly envious of the military genius they displayed and the achievement they wrought. They patrolled the town for four long years, their reputation as expert marks-women becoming widespread…"

The war hadn't called upon the women to be directly involved in combat yet for most of the 19th Century, but they were getting ready just in case; all of this was defensive preparation, of course. So, to provide service in the ongoing battles that were not yet in Georgia or in La Grange, many of the women served as nurses, especially in the second half of the war when people in need of medical help and refugees came to La Grange due to its existing, intact rail line and the crossroads location to so many battlefields. In fact, the women were kept busy as it's reported the four hospitals in town were often full and the Nancy Harts as well as other residents were even taking patients into their personal homes.

In June of 1863, the *Georgia Journal and Messenger* reported that the ladies had quite a scare. There were rumors afloat that

> "a party of Yankee raiders were approaching the city from Lincoln county (an ominous name,) where they now are and the information declared to be pretty authentic….Now the story was just about as improbable as one would have been in Atlanta that a Yankee raid was approaching to burn down the Stone Mountain,"

they go on to discover it was indeed an innocent hoax from the beloved Nancy Harts and others. A few members of the Nancy Harts dressed in "male habiliments," and

> "pounced upon some negroes at a ferry,"

who told them,

> "Federals coming,"

and soon the Mayor of Augusta heard word. The "raid," was more or less fictionalized but persuaded people in the region to prepare for invasion.

The Nancy Harts were one of the only female militias that actually faced their enemy's army. When the last battle at Fort Tyler, the Battle of Columbus had come to the small town of La Grange, the Nancy Harts actually took up arms in the conflict of mid-April 1865. It's unclear if they are the women, General Tyler made their promise to, but I assume so. When some local Confederate cavalrymen had fled the scene in some fear, it was the Nancy Harts who stepped in to protect the town. On April 17, 1865, the Nancy Harts marched to the campus of LaGrange Female College on the edge of town and met with enemy force and peacefully surrendered to the ironically named, Union Colonel LaGrange. Their negotiations allowed the private homes and property to be spared though factories, rail lines or stores with Confederate supplies would not be as lucky. Nancy Morgan proclaimed,

> "Thus it was that the girl soldiers rendered the Southern cause valuable service. They were never called to field duty, it is true, but they stood ever in readiness and rendered a service equally effective as guards over the defenseless and their homes."

The women had used their knack for diplomacy to save as much of home as they possible could.

Many of the Nancy Hart's husbands did not return from the war and the women continued their mission to protect their home and formed the LaGrange Chapter of the United Daughters of the Confederacy. Decades later, Leila Pullen Morris, just 18-years-old in 1865 gave a first-hand account of what the Nancy Harts had done in a La Grange years prior to a UDC meeting in Atlanta. The Nancy Harts have been honored in La Grange with a marker in front of the La Grange Courthouse and there have even been reenactments of their activity. The Nancy Harts also have a tree commemorating them in the town's Stonewall Confederate Cemetery planted by a local Garden Club.

Legend wonders if it wasn't the Revolutionary woman, Nancy Hart herself who had some influence over the ladies and their unique role in the military. They channeled the energy of strength and war – proving that a woman can be just as their ancestors said, a woman of love *and* war – prepared for battle and nurturing all in one. The Ghost of Nancy Hart and her influenced descendants is still felt in LaGrange today and when you visit the small town and walk the wood-line, look out for a female figure dressed in men's clothing or a tattered dress. If anyone is fighting after death to protect their homeland from invaders, it would be the Nancy Harts.

5th Georgia
The Poundcake Regiment

I often tell people that I don't choose which people/spirits to write about – regiments, soldiers, battlefield spirits – they choose me and sometimes they must hit me over the head spiritually to make sure I pay attention. As I was working on my research, I had music on in the background by American bluegrass band called The Steeldrivers (see chapter on Kennesaw Mountain), and it was on shuffle lightly in the background. At the end of a song I had paid no mind to, I suddenly heard a fiddle playing, "Dixie," an instrumental version immediately segueing into a banjo rendition of "Yankee Doodle." The songs oddly melded into each other beautifully. Curiously, I looked at the song and played it from the beginning. The song was entitled "River Runs Red," and as I listened to the verses, the story of a Civil War Battle fought in Murfreesboro, Tennessee at Stones River unfolded. Beautifully written, it brought stories to the men of the battle in a way that truly touched the soul. But the battle having been in Tennessee, I took this as a hint to just move along with my work and go back to Georgia.

COPYRIGHT, 1911, REVIEW OF REVIEWS CO.

CONFEDERATES OF '61

THE CLINCH RIFLES ON MAY 10TH

NEXT DAY THEY JOINED A REGIMENT DESTINED TO FAME

On the day before they were mustered in as Company A, Fifth Regiment of Georgia Volunteer Infantry, the Clinch Rifles of Augusta were photographed at their home town. A. K. Clark, the boy in the center with the drum, fortunately preserved a copy of the picture. Just half a century later, he wrote: "I weighed only ninety-five pounds, and was so small that they would only take me as a drummer. Of the seventeen men in this picture, I am the only one living." Hardly two are dressed alike; they did not become "uniform" for many months. With the hard campaigning in the West and East, the weights of the men also became more uniform. The drummer-boy filled out and became a real soldier, and the stout man lying down in front lost much of his superfluous avoirdupois in the furious engagements where it earned its title as a "fighting regiment." The Confederate armies were not clad in the uniform gray till the second year of the war. So variegated were the costumes on both sides at the first battle of Bull Run that both Confederates and Federals frequently fired upon their own men. There are instances recorded where the colonel of a regiment notified his supports to which side he belonged before daring to advance in front of them.

Clinch Rifles, May 1861 (Wikimedia Commons)

Then, as I was reviewing regiments to write about, I was looking at the Poundcake Regiment who seemed to have so much attention due to the included unit affectionally called the Clinch Rifles and I began to read old newspaper accounts about them. I immediately pulled up an article from January 13, 1863, in the *Macon Telegraph* from Georgia entitled "The Fifth Georgia at

Murfreesborough." I read the distressing accounts of the men who fought valiantly, impressing their officers and suffering so much death on December 31, 1862, in the Battle at Stones River.

The lightbulb went off – that song had been no coincidence, me stumbling upon the 5th had been no accident – the men of the 5th needed to tell their story. And so, I shall endeavor to tell you of their bravery and the haunted land they left behind, though I'm not sure anyone can do them justice.

Clinch Rifles, Co. A in Camp (ResearchOnline.net)

The 5th Georgia Infantry was organized on May 11, 1861, with additional companies joining in 1862 as well. The companies included Company A, The Clinch Rifles from Richmond County, Company B, The Griffin Light Guards from Spalding County, Company C, The Irish Volunteers from Richmond County, Company D, the McDuffie Riflemen from Warren County, Company E, the Dawson Volunteers from Terrell County, Company F, the Cuthbert Rifles from Randolph County, Company

G from Schley County, Company H, the Hardee Rifles from Decatur County, Company I, the Georgia Grays from Muscogee County, Company K, the Upson Guards from Upson County, Company L and Company M from Bibb Count and Company N from Clarke and Richmond Counties. Companies without nicknames only were missing them because they joined later in the service.

The 5th Georgia was known as the Poundcake Regiment and the nickname was given to them by General Braxton Bragg. Early in the war, especially, most of the companies wore differing outfits, many with green which made them stand out distinctly and also many with light blue trousers and a dark blue frock coat with a CR badge and Georgia State belt-plate. As the war went on, the 5th Georgia was issued standard dress uniforms though some men still wore their colors. Where did the colors come from? Some of the company's history is well-documented and talks about their time in battle and the colors they would wear. But it was the mix of colors, so varied in appearance that led to Bragg deeming them the Poundcake Regiment.

Company A, the Clinch Rifles were perhaps one of the most well-known companies of the war and donned the green colors that the 5th was often seen in. The Clinch Rifles named after General Duncan Clinch of the Seminole Indian War was formed in 1852 and fought in almost every engagement their regiment was present in for the Civil War. Upon their formation in 1852, the unit comprised of men wearing a simple, elegant uniform of rifle dark green single-breasted frock coat and matching trousers. Green kepis were also worn as well as French cuff flaps that were outlined in regimental color for enlisted and gold for officers with black leather equipment. However, as stated eventually these colors would blend into the Confederate regular uniforms. The company flag was presented on March 10, 1861, with a surviving example that still exists in Savannah as the small silk First

Clinch Rifles Co. A 5th Georgia, Macon GA, May 1861 (Library of Congress)

National flag, with the word "Clinch" on it.

Company B, The Griffin Light Guards were the line company with blue cloth caps and white plumes with blue frock coats, brass buttons, silver lace trim and blue adornments including blue trousers with a white stripe. The company flag, dating to December 11, 1860, is similar to many modern flags in the USA and has Revolutionary War influence from Benjamin Franklin as well including one side with the coat of arms of Georgia and the other with a rattlesnake coiled around a tree with the words "Don't Tread on Me." The flag was issued before Georgia's secession and is believed to be the company colors for 5th Georgia.

Company C, the Irish Volunteers was so named because of their Irish heritage and their legacy was remembered for their sacrifices at Chickamauga serving in Jackson's Brigade of Cheatham's Division close to some of the bloodiest engagement in the first part of the Chickamauga battlefield. They had a sister company named the Montgomery Guards from Company K of the

20th Georgia. The Irishmen were known for showy uniforms and beautiful new banners. They had a flag too that was a handsome Confederate States Banner and like the men of Company A, they topped it with a wreath of flowers.

Company D, the McDuffie Rifles were known for their time fighting in Chickamauga and Atlanta and had been the first volunteer company from their county of Warren. Their nickname came from notable Warren County resident Honorable George McDuffie. They were one of the very first volunteer companies in all of Georgia for the Civil War.

Company G, from Schley County doesn't have a lot of documentation outside their home county however a photo of Albertus T. Giuce who was made first Corporal of Company G shows that they also had unique clothing when the war started. Records state he was photographed in an ornate coat with three rows of buttons and a dark color with sergeant stripes as well as a shako hat with two brass emblems and pompoms. Corporal, later Sergeant Major Giuce was killed in the Battle of Resaca in the Atlanta Campaign.

Company H known as the Hardee's Rifles from Macon, Georgia mustered out on May 11, 1861, and also became Company A of the 2nd Battalion Georgia Sharpshooters with Companies N and L before merging with Company M of the 5th Georgia after casualties. Their nickname coming from their time with the Harrison Brigade who had served under General Hardee. Battle-hardened like the Irish Volunteers they too had a unique flag that was presented in April 1861, a wool bunting with seven stars and the left side of the circle open as a horseshoe. Eventually the flag was given to Annie Campbell who bequeathed it her local United Daughters of the Confederacy in 1941.

Company I, the Georgia Grays did seem to wear the gray color early on to their muster which may have been a little later than the other companies and gray was more mainstreamed into the

Confederate army. One notable member of Company I was said to have been photographed wearing the GG upon his kepi standing for Georgia Grays. He was William Lewis Salisbury and raised the 5th infantry, Georgia State Guard. After the war he owned a newspaper called the *Enquirer Sun* but in a feud over a remark in the paper that someone took as libelous he was murdered in 1878. I often look at my ancestry and the people who survived the war only to leave the world a decade or so later in such a peculiar way – a reminder that even outside of war, there is no sense of knowing when our time will come to cross into the spirit realm. William is a perfect example of that.

Company K, the Upson Guard had distinguished blue colors with a large brass state of arms and a dark blue shako on the headgear with the letters UG and a yellow pompom. Their coat also was dark blue and had several lace adornments like Company B as well as blue trousers with a buff stripe and plain kepis.

All companies had friends, brothers, and neighbors among them from their home region in the 5th Georgia and they became fast friends of one another in battle. The Poundcake Regiment was colorful and eager to begin their involvement in supporting the Confederate cause.

Upon the 5th Georgia mustering out, they spent the very beginning of the war stationed in Florida in Pensacola under General Braxton Bragg and were the first to be posted under him. It is in Florida where they received their training and had their first combat assignment on Santa Rosa Island off the Florida coast. The assault resulted in victory for the regiment and by early 1862 the regiment was posted to Knoxville, Tennessee and Corinth, Mississippi before being ordered to Shiloh. Perhaps, luckily for them, they arrived too late for the Battle of Shiloh in April and resumed post in Corinth where they fought around the region until the end of May 1862. Unlike many Georgia regiments who reported to the Eastern Theater, the 5th was known for their presence in the Western Theater. After their time in Mississippi, they were ordered to participate in the Invasion of Kentucky which had resulted in a major loss for them. It was then that the 5th was assigned to battle in Murfreesboro, and this is where the real heartbreak for the men first began.

The Battle of Stone River or Murfreesboro 1864 by AE Mathews (Library of Congress)

The *Macon Telegraph* reports of their time at Murfreesboro are haunting. In an editorial that was dated from January 8, 1863, in Alabama just a week after the battle and printed in Georgia on the 13th, the reporter wrote,

> "The papers are full of glowing accounts of the gallant deeds of different brigades and regiments in the battle at Murfreesboro, in which ample justice is done to the troops of Tennessee, Mississippi and Alabama, but very little has met my eye in reference to those from Georgia. This is probably owing to the

> remissness of Georgia correspondents. Being with those fresh from the battlefield and fully cognizant of its events I desire to briefly record the noble conduct of the Fifth Georgia under command of Colonel Black on Wednesday, the 31st of December."

The writer further states that despite Georgia's lack of correspondents, it's not fair that their service go unacknowledged. He then describes the scene.

> "The Brigade (General John W. Jackson's,) to which the regiment is attached, acted with every Division in the field during this memorable battle, being, at times, on the extreme right, then on the extreme left, and again in the centre of the line of battle. On Wednesday, this Brigade was ordered to charge a strong position of the enemy's centre, consisting of three batteries well sustained by infantry. Col. Black, believing himself sustained by other regiments, after skirting for a short distance in the [?] woods on his left and to the right of the enemy's position, ordered his men to charge through an open space immediately in range and about five hundred yards from enemy's guns."

The fearful scene was set … what would the 5th do?

> "The men sprang eagerly forward under one of the most galling fires of the whole battle. The color bearer (Thos. Brantley of Company E) was mortally wounded, and the colors immediately seized by A.P. Burr of Co. B. (Griffin Light Guards.) *Human fortitude could not stand such an awful storm of shot and shell and this*

> *gallant little band of Georgians only 117 strong, recoiled to the woods. Again they were ordered to the charge and again they sprang forward into the deadly arena with alacrity*. Here Colonel Black fell, shot through the head and A.J. Burr, still carrying the colors rescued on the first charge was wounded in the abdomen – Gen. Jackson, seeing this gallant little regiment insufficiently supported, some distance in advance of all other troops and perfectly enveloped with a murderous fire from the enemy ordered it to fall back, which movement was executed in time to save it from utter annihilation, but not until the third color-bearer, Lt. Eason of Co. G was shot down dead. On this last charge the regiment reached within two hundred yards of the enemy who were protected by a cut in the railroad and a natural barricade of rocks. Noting the gallant daring of this regiment, I am told that *General Withers remarked, if he had then thousand such men, he could whip the whole of Rosecrans' army,* and other officers spoke in high terms of praise for the regiment. Of it's sufferings your readers can judge when I tell you that of one hundred and seventeen actually engaged in the fight, sixty-one were killed and wounded and not a man missing."

The author then went on to present the list of casualties. Ultimately the battle at Murfreesboro/Stones River was a Union Victory (tactically) with over 76,400 troops engaged, casualty counts were high for both armies but the little band of Georgians from the 5th and their perseverance at the front of the lines, their suffering and sacrifice on the field of battle and their fortitude will always be remembered from that day – or at the very least should be. Perhaps that's why they played that song for me – to ensure

Stone River Rebellion Pen & Ink 1863 by Adolph Metzner (Library of Congress)

that they would be. The adjutant of the 5th Georgia remarked on the list of the dead,

> "We had two color bearers killed and one wounded. After the third was shot down, Private Monroe Stevens, (the largest man in the regiment, and as brave as big,) took it up and carried it through safely."

The imagery of imagining this brave soldier coming forward for his men and raising the colors is haunting and inspirational at the same time.

The song echoed in my head,

> "The thirty-first day of December
> Three thousand dressed blue and gray
> All sons of the heavenly father
> Lay in a watery grave
> And the river runs red
> The river runs red

5th Georgia Bloody Banner – the Second National Flag (Augusta Museum of History)

One shot woke the Tennessee morning
Soon fire and smoke filled the sky
Then rain came down with no warning
As sorrow fell down from all sides
The river runs red
The river runs red
No winners or losers
When you count the dead
We watch it roll by
We all bow our heads
The guns have gone silent
But the river runs red and the haunting final verse …
Some say you could see red for miles
And it flowed that way so many years
Now the water looks clean and untainted
But Stones River will never run clear"

In 1884, a Confederate Roll of Honor was released in official records and listed for their honor from Georgia's 5th in the Battle at Murfreesboro was Private Newton Rice, Company A, Corporal Michael McNamara, Company C, and Private Thomas J. Brantley of Company E – all of whom died in battle.

Stones River Battlefield reports no shortage of hauntings and in fact, many residents believe that much of Murfreesboro, Tennessee's paranormal activity can be correlated with the battle itself. The battlefield park that you can visit only accounts for 15% of the actual battlefield of 1863. The town and hospitals, shops and more have built over the top of where the fight occurred. You can visit on the park where the fiercest fighting occurred near limestone rock formations and was known as the slaughter pen for its resemblance of a slaughterhouse. Ghost soldiers have been seen by many park visitors and some believe them to be reenactors as we see is often the case, only to have them vanish without a trace in front of people's very eyes. They also report the residual haunting sounds of guns and cannon fire as well as footsteps marching in – I can't help but wonder how much of that is Georgia's 5th who left so much on the line there.

The field is also home to another ghost that overlaps peculiarly with Chickamauga's headless ghost, except this is where he should reside as it's where he died. It is Union officer, Lt. Colonel Julius Garesche who was killed by a cannonball that decapitated him whilst he was riding his horse and, of course, now he is believed to be the headless horseman on many civil war battlefields according to legend. Suffice to say, this is the one where he goes.

Perhaps my favorite paranormal legend from Stones River/Murfreesboro is from a reenactor himself – one I presume to be Union who was walking to get some water when suddenly he saw someone hiding in the bushes. It being nighttime and not wanting to be taken by surprise by a trespasser, he demanded the person come out and then a man in full uniform (presumed Confederate) raised his hands in surrender. Thinking that another reenactor was playing around, the first man who demanded the man appear pointed his rifle at him and then watched as the poor frightened, soul fell to the ground in panic and vanished in thin air – perhaps reliving his death and still seeking that final act of mercy. I wonder who the poor soul is and if it's one of the beloved color bearers or others from Georgia just trying to survive the battle and reliving it on repeat.

Ultimately, the battle in Murfreesboro caused 32% casualties of the 173 engaged from Georgia's 5th including their Colonel and the regimental battle flag. After Murfreesboro, the 5th pulled back to Shelbyville, Tennessee where they remained until their participation in the Tullahoma Campaign, a military operation lasting about a week and a half where Bragg's army faced off against Rosecrans again in June to July of 1863, the same time as Vicksburg and Gettysburg raged on. This was ultimately a Union victory as well.

By September of 1863, Bragg's army including the Poundcake Regiment found themselves in their home state, in the mountains of Northwest Georgia at Chickamauga, Georgia. Once again, they remained in Jackson's Brigade of Cheatham's Division in the Army of the Tennessee. General Jackson's Battle Report regarding his Brigade ended with the chilling line,

> "The greatest loss was in the fifth Georgia regiment, amounting to nearly 55 percent."

This division had been involved heavily in the in the fight since the outbreak of battle on September 19, 1863. Jackson described their arrival at Chickamauga as he came near Alexander's Bridge and a half-mile out joined Major General Walker's troops in line with his. He reported his men in good spirits when they were ordered to advance from line and when the Union fired upon them, they returned fire.

> "A charge being ordered, the troops responded with great intrepidity, driving the enemy before them from a half to three-quarters of a mile, capturing three pieces of artillery which were immediately sent to the rear; also, a large number of knapsacks from which the enemy had been driven."

He then reported the enemy stubbornly holding the ground at their breastworks. Jackson notes that his peer General Preston Smith's brigade of more men was pushed back leaving his left flank entirely exposed. His ranks were confused, fell back and then rallied back in line after learning the enemy was turning right. The fight, he said, had continued for two hours at an unusually severe rate. By nightfall, General Cleburne formed a line to Jackson's right and Cheatham was ordered to move up Jackson's brigade once more. It was then, the reports of severe small arms fire was described. They got confused in the dark at what angle Cleburne's line had formed and Jackson's brigade thought they had backup where they didn't and didn't realize how sudden and severe the firing had become. At night, after more moving in the lines and the ceasefire of this event, the men who survived fell back until morning.

In the morning, the flanks were moved as were the lines by orders of Cheatham and Hill. Sharpshooters of the enemy were reported and wanting men from Jackson's division, he was unable to fill the space to dislodge the enemy and ultimately, they couldn't do so. Jackson reported that he would expose his left flank by moving again and then he was ordered to move up in line anyhow. And so, he did, and

> "the enemy opened a galling fire from the front and left flank, enfilading the entire line with canister and small arms. The engagement now became terrific and

the position of my brigade extremely critical. The troops, however, stood nobly to the work before them and, steadily advancing, surmounted the hill on which the enemy's breastworks were, the battery moving with the line and rendering effective service,"

Georgia 5th Infantry monument at Chickamauga, 2022

described General Jackson.

Ultimately, the rebels had won that piece of ground. But the 5th Georgia was engaged in much of the highest combat of the Battle of Chickamauga. Today on the battlefield, erected in 1899 is a marker for the 5th Georgia marking their placement on September 20th at 5:30 PM at the intersection of Alexander Bridge Road and Battleline Road. I confess, every visit I go to the battlefield starting from the first visit I have, it's the location where I get out of my car and where I feel drawn to – hearing voices from the woods, feeling watched from behind the trees and I go and spend time on that line. Of course, when I looked at the stone and realized it read Georgia – it's a unique marker pointed at the top and looks like a large old gravestone – nothing too fancy.

Both times I arrived there, I thought immediately,

"Ah, so it was you who brought me here."

There I stood, pensive, feeling their sacrifice and thinking of the men so vividly that I was able to envision them. The men of Georgia's 5th have not been shy about sharing their story and wanting to be remembered for their sacrifices, for their lives, and most importantly who they were. Like I said, sometimes they must hit you over the head spiritually and here they did, insistently -- they had brought me to them at Chickamauga and played their song of Stones River over and over to ensure their lasting legacy was heard by me.

The haunting tales of Chickamauga are famous and though some can be debunked, it's well known to be one of the most haunted battle sites in the country, the 2nd highest casualty count of the Civil War, bodies left on the field for years, or forever and several tales of spectral phantoms appearing. As I said I always feel the ethereal the most where the men of Georgia's 5th were on my visits (the only exception being the Viniard Field) which rivals the spot just down the road. But the spirits of Chickamauga are throughout the battle landscape and for more details on Chickamauga ghosts please see Part I, Chapter 1, the Battle of Chickamauga in Battlefields.

Again, despite the Confederate victory at Chickamauga, it came at a high price of intense casualties, Georgia's 5th had suffered the worst out of any regiment in their home state, a tragedy that is often overlooked. Unlike the other Georgians, they had been engaged in some of the heaviest fighting. As Jackson stated, of the 317 engaged at Chickamauga they had a 55% casualty rate, even worse than Murfreesboro but with almost twice as many engaged. The Confederate Roll of Honor lists Private J. Kirby Brown of Company A, Private Thomas P. Wier of Company B, Corporal John Fox of Company C, Private James W. Hall of Company D, Corporal John B. Johnston of Company E, Private William Blackwell of Company F, Private T. H. Devane of Company G, 1st Sgt. John P. Chapman of Company I and Private James Torrence of Company K on their list of honorees for service at the Battle of Chickamauga. Of that list, Privates Brown, Hall, and Torrence passed away in battle as did Corporal Johnston.

Kirby Brown, from the honor roll, just 20 years old when he was killed was remembered deeply by his family and friends who, in fact, did more than their due diligence in returning him home became a legend of the 5th Georgia. Knowing that hasty graves had to be made for many on the 21st of September, Captain Joseph Cumming even told his wife,

> "Poor Kirby Brown was killed Saturday. I am afraid I cannot save his body."

However, Kirby, who had been employed as a draftsman for the Confederate Ordnance Department in Augusta, had his guardian, Judge Charles Jenkins of the Georgia Supreme Court and a neighbor of Augusta go to Chickamauga to search through the corpses for him. After closely walking through and examining the remains on September 30, they succeeded and wrote,

> "He had been more fortunate than many of the gallant dead whose remains will sleep on the field they so nobly defended."

His body was brought back to the Jenkins family plot in Summerville Cemetery and a death notice published on October 17. Heartbreakingly, Kirby Brown was even mentioned in a report from General Walker just four days earlier as doing well. Kirby's father had drowned when he was a young boy and his Aunt Emily married Charles Jenkins and when she moved in, she brought her nieces and nephews with her and thus the Jenkins became their guardians. The Browns had an illustrious background and even relatives in the Union who were dying in battle, with connections on the North and South – showing that this really was a battle of brothers, family, and fellow Americans. Here was the 5th Georgia again reminding us of the closeness. To think though, that his guardian would spare no expense or time to bring him home, shows the importance of love and family – no matter how that family may look. Family isn't always traditional. As for young Mr. Brown, Private Kirby Brown's legacy lives on at the Episcopal Church of the Good Shepherd in Augusta, Georgia where a stained-glass window in his honor let's in breathtaking sunlight daily.

After the Battle at Chickamauga, the regiment participated in the Siege of Chattanooga with the Battle of Missionary Ridge, driven from their position, and falling back with the rest of the Army of Tennessee. And then, they went right back into their home state of Georgia involved in battles through early 1864 and serving as prison guards before moving to the South Carolina coast in late 1864. It was there where they did their best to protect the Charleston and Savannah's railroad as Sherman's March to the Sea raged forth and ultimately were unable to as they lost the battle flag a second time. Then they retreated with the army to North Carolina and fought in the Battle of Bentonville in March of 1865 where again a devastating blow from the Union to their army caused them to fall back. The Army of Tennessee including Georgia's 5th surrendered on April 26, 1865, with a just a few members of the regiment present at the surrender at Bennett Homestead in Durham, North Carolina. In March 1865, Georgia's 5th just had 256 considered effectives out of over 2,000 in a total roster throughout the war, a harrowing statistic. The 5th Georgia, truly didn't make it home from the Civil War and gave almost all the souls they had to the fields of battle.

8th Georgia

The Goober Grabbers

I can't lie to you, it's hard to hand select regiments of note, when all have notable moments and incredible people but something about a regiment called the Goober Grabbers makes a person smile and shows you just how relatable people from history or the Civil War can be. Goobers are, of course, an abbreviated version of Goober Peas which is an iconic Southern term for peanuts. I recall, having grown up with a Southern dad, him shelling peanuts on the front porch and calling them goobers. I had no idea goobers were called by any other name until I was older. Of course, my husband and I were talking one day and I referenced goobers, to which he gave me a peculiar gaze of confusion. Then I threw the term, "goobers," at some other New Englanders and they too looked equally perplexed.

"It's what you call peanuts,"

I explained to them as they laughed. Then, of course, good ol' Google defended my position as did the Southern song "Goober Peas," which some believe was inspired by the 8th Georgia. The war song released in 1866 details a Southern soldier's take on the

GOOBER PEAS!

Words by A. Pinder. Music by P. Nut.

Sitting by the roadside on a summer day,
Chatting with my messmates, passing time away,
Lying in the shadows underneath the trees,
Goodness, how delicious, eating Goober Peas!

Chorus:
Peas, peas, peas, peas, eating Goober Peas!
Goodness, how delicious, eating Goober Peas!

Tell me not of glory, chatter not of fame,
Of men that live in story, winning them a name,
I'm content to sit down, wholly at my ease,
Free from care or sorrow, eating Goober Peas!

When a horseman passes soldiers' have a rule,
To cry out at their loudest, "Mister, here's your Mule!"
But another pleasure enchantinger than these,
Is wearing out your jaw teeth eating Goober Peas!

Just before the battle the General heard a row,
He said the Yankees were coming, I hear their rifles now;
He looked about in wonder, and what do you think he sees,
The Geor-gi-a militia cracking Goober Peas!

I loved a girl in Georgia, she was bright and fair,
And she was as beautiful as Georgia girls are;
We passed the time together, what happy days were these,
And in the nights we courted and eat up Goober Peas!

Now we are here in prison and likely long to stay;
They have got us closely guarded, we cannot get away;
The rations they are thin, it's cold enough to freeze!
I wish I was back in Georgia eating Goober Peas!

I think my song has lasted almost long enough;
The subject interesting the names are very ruff;
But when this war is o'er and we are free from grape and fleas,
We'll kiss our wives and sweethearts and gobble Goober Peas!

SOUTHERN ENTERPRISE.
Thomasville, Georgia, Wednesday, May 9, 1866.

Goober Peas Song & Lyrics, 1866 (Wikimedia Commons)

war while they're eating goober peas.

Today, Georgia is known as the Peach State, but it has also been known as the Goober State for all of its peanuts! During the war time, some Georgia recruits may have heard the term Goober Grabber but the 8th Georgia got to wear that badge of pride as they recorded proudly in their stories that were published later in a book by William Morrow. The legend states that in the summer of 1861 at the first Battle of Bull Run/Manassas in Virginia, the Eight Georgia, marching through the Shenandoah Valley with Joseph Johnston's army were passing a field of clover when they all remarked how much it looked like a field of goobers. As such, they went and started pulling the clover and finding just clovers…no goobers underneath the surface. The Virginia troops who witnessed this took to calling the Eight Georgia, "Goober Grabbers," and eventually the name was shared with all kinds of regiments from across the state.

The story of the 8th Georgia as evidenced by the tale of the clover in Shenandoah Valley enroute to Bull Run brings us back to the Eastern Theater where we left the Troup Artillery as well. And the Eastern Theater speaks more to the average Georgia soldier's experience as again, that's where most of them were placed. Unfortunately, their nickname may be where some of the fun ends for their tale – a roster of over 2,126 (in numbers of just at varying engagements 200-400 throughout the war) would have only about 100 men present, tattered and torn at the end of the war – even worse than the devastation of Georgia's 5th.

Our beloved Goober Grabbers were formed in Richmond, Virginia in May of 1851 out of several independent Georgia Companies including, Company A, the Rome Light Guard of Floyd County, Company B, Oglethorpe Light Infantry of Chatham County, Company C, the Macon Guards of Bibb County, Company D, the Echols Guards of Meriweather County, Company E, Miller Rifles of Floyd County, Company F, the Atlanta Greys of Fulton County, Company G, the Pulaski Volunteers of Pulaski County, Company H ,the Floyd Infantry of Floyd County, Company I, the Green or Stephens Light Guards of Greene County and Company K. the Oglethorpe Rifles of Oglethorpe County. Upon the organization of these companies into the 8th Georgia Infantry, they were under the command of Colonel Francis S. Bartow and West Point Graduate, Lieutenant Colonel William Gardner as well as Major Thomas L. Cooper.

On June 5th, the men left Richmond by railroad and arrived at the Manassas Gap railroad the next day where they marched to Winchester, VA and then caught a train again to Harper's Ferry, West Virginia (just Virginia at the time) for the Evacuation of Harper's Ferry where they then marched to Camp Johnstown between Charlestown and Winchester. At that point, they moved their sick by rail to Winchester before their March to Bunker Hill, then Camp Defiance and throughout Virginia in June and July. On July 18 they were ordered to the Battle of Manassas and arrived on July 20 where they marched to the rear of the army. Manassas would be their first brush with severe conflict as it had many of the men fighting in the Eastern Theater. This, of course, is also the time where they would grab their nickname at Bull Run/Manassas as well though the affection for that would come a bit later perhaps to liven everyone's spirits. Their Colonel Bartow took control of the whole Brigade while their Lt. Colonel commanded the regiment, and the 8th Georgia was stationed at the rear of McLean's and Blackburn's Fords before moving to House Hill where Colonel Bartow advanced to Matthew Hill. The 8th became engaged in intense combat and suffered heavy casualties of 201 – 42 killed and 150 wounded. Not only that, but Colonel Bartow was killed, being shot directly in the chest and Lt. Colonel Gardner wounded in the leg, leaving Major Cooper to take demand. Officers including John Cooper of Company H and Lieutenant Bartley Smith of Company F were also mortally wounded and two other lieutenants badly wounded. There is a trailside marker referencing the 8th Georgia on the Matthews Hill. Ultimately, Manassas was a Confederate victory despite the heavy casualties.

The 8th's slaughter did not go unrecognized, it was published in *The Weekly Telegraph* of March 14, 1884,

> "No regiment during the war displayed greater courage or rendered more enduring service than the Eighth Georgia. It was Beauregard who lifted his hat and said as the shattered regiment marched past after a terrific struggle on the field of battle: Eighth Georgia, I salute you."

Confederate fortifications at Manassas by Alexander Gardner, 1862 (Library of Congress)

In Richmond, says a war chronicler,

> "I heard hundreds of voices, old and young, exclaim 'There goes the Eighth Georgia – brave boys.'"

It's easy to get lost in the troop movements and officer movements but one thing that makes it all too real are the accounts of the men who were there. An online journal digitizing the sentiments of those who were there via their letters entitled *Bull Runnings*, truly captures what the men felt in trying to make peace with what happened and what they witnessed.

Lt. Melvin Dwinnell recalled the dedication of the Bartow Monument on September 5, 1861, just months after the battle and having to re-live the experience was nearly heart stopping,

> "Here one stood when he heard the first cannon ball pass in fearful nearness to himself; there he saw such a friend fall – his imploring look, and outstretched arms; yonder was the enemy's battery, and how their angry mouths belched forth the livid streams; what a shout there was when such a Regiment advanced to that point; how the heart sunk when our forces fell back there, how the enemies balls made the dirt fly around us as we passed along here; how good the muddy water in this little branch looked when we double-quicked across it; what horrid anxiety there was to know whether the Regiment yonder were friends or foes; here a cannon ball was dodged; there a bursting shell avoided; there was seen A leading off B, who dragged one leg; here came C, supported between D and E, and so awful bloody in face; yonder laid with his hand significantly on his breast, and at various points round about, were friends and strangers, lying fearfully still, some on their faces, some on their backs, some with folded arms and legs drawn up, and others with outstretched limbs… each one, naturally, seeks the place where his own Regiment had its severest struggle. Arrived there, he sees and hears once again, the indescribable scenes of bloody carnage, and fearful horror, which his memory now presents with most painful distinctness. He imagines that he again hears the whiz-z-z-z of the cannon ball – the zip–zip-zip-p-p-p of the musketry charge, and the quick whist, whist of the rifles. He sees where this and that friend *stood,* and where the other *fell.*"

That day they laid a marble slab that read, the name and last words of their beloved Colonel. Francis S. Bartow,

> *"They have killed me boys, but never give up the fight."*

After the ceremonies they returned to "Camp Bartow." The same Lieutenant recalled as processed the July battle how his mind was not allowing him the empathy and sympathy he would typically have in the middle of the catastrophe, as it was his brain's effort to survive. He remarked that he was fearful of his brain's ability to compartmentalize such trauma and wrote,

> "One of the most remarkable mental phenomena, was the sudden and strange drying up of sympathetic feeling for the suffering of the wounded and dying. I could never before look upon even small operations, or persons in extreme pain from any cause, especially when blood was freely flowing, without intense pain and generally more or less faintness. But on this occasion I beheld the most terrible mutilations, the most horrid and ghastly expression of men in the death struggle, men with one arm or a leg, shot off, others with the face horribly mutilated, heads shot through and brains lying about, bodies half torn into, and at the hospital, some 50 men with legs or arms jut amputated and a half cord of legs and arms, and men in all degrees of pain, from the slight flesh wound to those producing death in a few moments, and viewed all this with far less feeling that I would ordinarily have seen brutes thus mutilated. This obduracy I am truly glad, was only temporary. Only two days after the battle I caught myself avoiding the amputation of an arm."

Dwinnell's recollections give us but a mere glimpse into the humanity of witnessing such tragic events and losing our loved ones, witnessing such devastation close-up and what our mind does to save us!

After stationing at Camp Victory, the troop of Goober Grabbers movements continued around Virginia and by September, now Colonel Gardner was unable to return to service and new officers were elected as company captains. On September 25, 1861, the 8th was assigned to the 2nd Brigade of Major General Smith's Second Corps, Army of the Potomac. Skirmishes and small battles led to more deaths and Captain Couper of Company B was killed as well as L. Colonel Cooper who fell from his horse and died. Colonel Gardner was promoted to the ranks of General and the 8th was seeing a lot of quick change, death and more by the end of 1861. By April of 1862, there were only 251 men fit for duty in the 8th.

Manassas is no stranger to haunting activity and the battlefield built their visitor's center with National Parks Service upon one of the hills where much violence took place. Many report the residual haunting type activities of marching sounds, strange lights moving as if a gun was being fired off and report shadows walking in an area close to where General Stonewall Jackson hid his troops. One member of the Parks service staff recalls many strange sounds in the Visitor's Center built upon the scene of so much death including faucets turning themselves on and off as well as lights. He stated that he would just ask them to knock it off, and they would listen – so respectful spirits, at least!

Perhaps, one of the best stories of Bull Run comes from someone who was camping at the site in 1964 in a wooded area. They had some young boys that were about twelve with them and it was a couple families traveling together – so a couple sets of parents as well. When they started to sleep, they heard music coming up the hill to where they were. It sounded like a harmonica and someone blowing on a jug. Then they heard people talking and clapping along. Thinking it odd since they didn't see other campers, they looked about and saw one-hundred-feet or so away ten men seated around a fire kind of glowing in the flames holding rifles or something in their arms. As soon as they noticed the sight, the men began to fade away from vision. The families ran away, left their campsite to stay with family who lived nearby. They returned the next day to get all the things they had left and to check out the mysterious campfire site. No one was there and there was no sign of campfire – just underbrush that would have been too terrible to camp on. They knew what they saw were soldiers from the war and I'd like to think it's the brave boys of Georgia's 8th, having some joy on the other side and being among their friends but perhaps' that too romantic of a sentiment and I hold it because they hold a place in my heart. I confess though, losing Colonel Bartow and so much of their regiment – it's impossible not to feel the spirit of the 8th on the fields of Bull Run.

In the summer of 1862, the regiment was ordered to the Seven Days Battle in which Colonel Lamar was wounded and captured. Ailments, wounds and resignations seemed to dominate the early months and years of the war for the 8th as the men became accustomed to this new life as best as they could. How is one ever well accustomed the harshness of life in war? Before they knew it, by the end of summer 1862, the Second Battle of Manassas/Bull Run was upon them where two of their Company captains were killed and one wounded. Little did they know that this was just a preface for what was about to come in the war as they faced some of the deadliest battles ahead for the entirety of the conflict with Bull Run still on their hearts.

On September 17, 1862, they were at the Battle of Sharpsburg/Antietam – commanded by Lt. Colonel John R. Towers, whose son would later be the 2nd Lieutenant of Company H. They would witness true horror at Antietam but from a somewhat safer distance. Close to the worst, they would not be amongst the worse; the 2nd, 6th, 10th, 18th and 20th Georgia would see many more horrors at Antietam on the Cornfield, Sunken Road or at Burnside Bridge. However, for the 8th, it was a brush with the bloodiest day of history they'd never want to relive. Ensign Barnwell was killed as were some privates. Exact numbers don't seem to be recorded for the 8th at Antietam but we know Private Peter Frederic Kempson, just 19 to 20 years old, was killed in action and was buried on Smith's Orchard Farm and later likely removed to the cemetery at Hagerstown (all unmarked graves in a beautiful landscape with a monument) not far from Sharpsburg. Private S.C. Green was also mortally wounded in action, dying shortly thereafter; and buried near "Mrs. Lucker's barn," beforc presumably also being reinterred at Hagerstown over a decade later, the same for Private R.P Watters – a mortal wounding, dying shortly thereafter, though his burial was at Elmwood Cemetery in Shepherdstown, WV, also not too far away. Corporal William Smith of Company H was also killed in action. Sergeant William Henry Hartnett was wounded so terribly, eventually he was sent to guard duty in Andersonville, GA and deemed still unfit for duty even years later after furlough and being a guard. He was transferred to the First Georgia Reserves in early 1865. He lived but at what quality of life, one must wonder, especially after gunshot wounds and shattered bones.

The War Department marks the 8th Georgia's movements with Anderson's Brigade where they engaged with skirmishers until the morning of the 17th and moved left through Piper's cornfield toward the Sunken Road/Bloody Lane toward the rear side near Piper's Field and the Hagerstown Road. A marker near the Sunken Road tells of their placement beyond that point where it withstood several charges before retiring to Sharpsburg through the field and bloody lane so close to the slaughter. Their placement that day saved them from another regimental catastrophe like Manassas.

As fall laid into winter, the men were at the Battle of Fredericksburg commanded by Lt. Colonel John Towers once more and in May of the following year they were assigned to Anderson's Brigade of Hood's Division in the Longstreet's Corp just in time for the Suffolk Campaign. In summer of 1863, they made their way north. The infamous Battle of Gettysburg which would be one of their deadliest and most catastrophic engagements was their next engagement. They were again under the trusted command of Colonel John Towers. Most of their engagement was on July 2 – the second of the three-day battle and took place around the Wheatfield where they arrived, according to the War Department with Anderson's Brigade at 4:00 PM. They charged into the woods south of the Wheatfield and dislodged some Union forces from the stone fence before being outflanked and retiring to the crest of Rose Hill and advancing a second and third time before occupying the woodland around the Wheatfield. As I write about this and the horrors of it, I find myself smiling which sounds incredibly strange but the Wheatfield is where I tell people is one of the most haunted places in Gettysburg; the clashing of the men there, the surprises, and the open hand-to-hand combat was all brutal, it's true; but when I stand in the middle of the Wheatfield, as I so often do I find myself looking to the wood line, feeling watched, hearing voices from the trees – familiar voices, somehow. And knowing that's where the 8th Georgia was makes that sensical spiritually, being pulled to them, just as the 5th drew me to them at Chickamauga. Spirits will always find a way to reveal themselves to you when the time is right. And for the record, the Wheatfield is where I have most often captured sounds of cannon and rifle fire when no one else is there – no one living, anyway. At Gettysburg, the 8th Georgia brought 312 men to the field. 35 were killed, 108 wounded and 29 missing. Over half of the men they brought into Gettysburg were casualties.

After the campaign in Pennsylvania, the 8th returned to

Virginia and in September transferred to Hood's Division in the Army of East Tennessee. They did not participate in the Battle of Chickamauga that occurred thereafter and though engaged in small battles and skirmishes around Chattanooga and the Siege of Knoxville, TN as well as suffering the mortal wounding of Company A's Captain Hall at Fort Sanders, by the end of 1863 they withdrew from Knoxville to the Northeast. And in Spring of 1864, they fought in the Battles of Wilderness, Spotsylvania and Cold Harbor back-to-back. Brigadier General Benning was wounded in the Wilderness and as such a Colonel from the 15th Georgia commanded their brigade. They lost yet another Captain at the Battle of Wilderness. The Battles of Wilderness, Spotsylvania and Cold Harbor were some of the darkest that the war would ever see in Virginia and a turning point for the Union had occurred in Gettysburg leading to massive casualty counts for the Confederates and this string of battles had two battles that were inconclusive in victory. Just before the Battle of Wilderness the 8th had lost 96 to injury, disease, etcetera in that spring alone. The unit also participated in the Siege of Petersburg as the war roared to an end causing even more casualties for the 8th's officers and infantrymen alike, before most remaining of the approximately 100 were surrendered and paroled at Appomattox Court House in April of 1865.

One constant figure in the 8th regiment from 1861 until the war ended was J.R. Towers, commissioned as a Captain of Company E in May of 1861 from Rome, GA and appointed Lieutenant Colonel of the regiment on January 28, 1861. He was a merchant in Cass County and had a metal casting foundry. Towers lived with his wife Anna whom he had been married to for nearly 20 years and with whom he had ten children with by 1869. Towers was captured on June 28, 1862 near to Richmond, Virginia before he was held prisoner briefly in New York and then at Fort Warren, MA (the home of the Lady in Black whose husband was also imprisoned

Portrait 8th Georgia in Virginia (Freeenglishsite.com)

there at the same time – perhaps from Georgia's 8th) but by July 31, 1862, he was released for exchange and commanded the regiment in Antietam in September 1862. Then he received a promotion to Colonel in March of 1863 before he was wounded again, shot in the right hand at Gettysburg. He continued his time with the regiment and was surrendered and paroled at the court house. But that was not without heartbreak. His oldest son, Daniel Towers was killed near Petersburg, VA on September 30, 1864 and was just 20 years old and the 2nd Lieutenant of the 8th Georgia whom he had fought alongside for years. I can't imagine a father feeling as if he couldn't protect his son while they were right there together. His second son, also enlisted, did survive the war after serving as a cavalryman with General Forrest. Towers went home after the war and was incredibly involved in his community, serving as Sheriff for two years, owing a variety store, representing in the State Legislature for two years and running his metal casting business. He also served as the assistant keeper of the Georgia State Penitentiary for a time before becoming the keeper. After a year of that service, J.R. retired to Marietta, then promptly un-retired to sell cotton. He is buried in the Marietta City Cemetery.

In 1886, a couple of years after the war, Col. M. Lamar issued a call out to other members of the 8th Georgia in the *Savannah Morning News* in April 1886, but his call for reunion could be dated to as far back as October 1885 in the *Savannah Morning News* and the *Atlanta Constitution.* The call was a request to all who survived to attend a reunion to be held in May 1886 on the centennial anniversary of

> "That venerable and illustrious corps,"

He went on to say,

> "There are peculiar and potential reasons why it should convene in Savannah, our historic and beautiful city by the sea. The immortal Bartow, the founder of the organization lived there, and his fame as a soldier and statesman is interwoven indissolubly with its history. *The Eighth Georgia entered the war at Manassas, and continued to Appomattox. To it belongs the glorious distinction of receiving the first marked baptism of blood in the colossal struggle. No regiment did heavier duty or bore more of the dangers and hardships of the fight, and none passed through the four years of arduous and deadly ordeal with a better record for valor and patriotism.*"

Lamar then called for purpose in reuniting, a

> "peaceful fraternization and to take steps to redeem

> from forgetfulness the heroic career it achieved."

All surviving members were invited. On May 8, 1886, a report of the Survivor's Reunion was published in the *Savannah Morning News*. When Colonel Lamar spoke of the event, he said,

> *"The glory of our immortal corps is in it's heroic dead. The living brought from the conflict the supreme boon of life. The unfortunate dead, glorious in their sacred martyrdom, sealed their devotion to duty by their noble blood.* It is fitting then, that we as a specially imperative feature of these ceremonies and exercises should do full justice to be rave spirits of our organization that are in its most precious sacrifice and golden memory. They illuminate it's annals and canonized it's history....In reference to our dead, no mention would be just that did not hold up to living admiration the illustrious name of the immortal."

He went on to speak of Bartow,

> "around this chivalric spirit clusters the most shining radiance of the whole proud galaxy."

Colonel Anderson spoke as well, a profoundly haunting sentiment about being lost to history,

> "Died on the field of honor, our cemeteries will tell. Soon the wooden head boards will decay and the names cut by hand of affection will be effaced, as time spares not the beauty of the flower nor the majesty of the oak, and as in physical nature, vines and tendrils and flowers grow around ancient ruins,

> so around those sacred ruins of the heart amidst whose solemn shades we sometimes loved to wander, green memories…as we recall that glorified band of soldiers who Jackson, Bartow and others have crossed over the river and are resting in the shade of the trees."

The speeches bore on a heart of immortalization so strong that the souls of all those passed surely joined them and listened in, and surely, they were felt. For it was by August 1887, it looks like Colonel Lamar planned another reunion that was postponed until August 30 of that year and would include their friends the Macon Guards, according to *the Macon Telegraph*. They also announced holding a reunion in 1889 and 1890. The camaraderie among these men, the once innocent young "Goober Grabbers," lived for decades beyond the war's end – a band of brothers could have no truer example than the 8th Georgia Regiment brought together by loss and kept together by enduring loyalty.

In 1901, Private Pritchard thought back on the dead and tried to reconcile what he witnessed by thinking of his cause and the justness it had brought the 8th Georgia during and after the war even when he and the others arrived to surrender Appomattox. He thought of the purpose of war and death and wrote,

> "Probably 75 percent of those who received their baptism of blood at Manassas have solved the great mystery."

He remembered them as more than just soldiers – not just names in a history book,

> "It should not be forgotten that the Confederate was not such a soldier as comprised the regular army of a

> country. He was of a higher strain, and the purity of that strain finds no degeneracy in his issue. He claims lineage from: "the knightliest of the knightly race," Those who survive that regiment, and in weary steps pass to and fro amid the busy scenes of life, hold, as the French would express it, and embarrassment de richesse, resembling the sunlight and the shadow. "

And I, an author, can speak no better of the 8th Georgia and the enduring legacy of the souls of these young men than Pritchard, Lamar, Anderson or the others – once just fun, young men looking for goober peas in the clover who were baptized by blood and death in the youth of their early adulthood. Pritchard concludes,

> "Memories of picturesque scenes of jocund comradeship in the bivouac one day, and of death and burial the next; and it is 'for the touch a vanished hand, the sound of a voice now stilled.'"

18th Georgia

3rd Texas Infantry & Captain Lemon

The 18th Georgia was considered one of the wheel horses of the Confederate Army and affectionally referred to as the "3rd Texas," during their time in Hood's Texas Brigade with the Texas Regiments. They even learned to fight barefoot like their Texan comrades. And their General, John Bell Hood, was described poetically to look like a Viking who took with him the biggest men from Texas who were the strongest and most able-bodied for war and the 18th Georgia absolutely followed suit as they were thrust into the war as volunteers. An 1894 postbellum edition of the *Atlanta Constitution* recounts,

> "The Eighteenth Georgia had it's share of hard fighting. This regiment, the luckiest [?] of them all, went where the bullets came thick and fast over the field and did some work that marks its men who survived the war as heroes."

Who were they? How did they get to be such good fighters? Some say it was the influence of General Hood and his Texans and later fellow Georgian, General William T. Wofford. The regiment,

General John Bell Hood in Uniform, 1863 (Library of Congress)

one of the first to come together in Georgia was organized at Camp Brown in Cobb County, Georgia on April 22, 1861, and was at one point called the First Regiment, Fourth Brigade, State Troops under Colonel William Wofford, Lt. Colonel Solon Ruff from Georgia Military Institute, Major Jefferson Johnson and Adjutant John C. Griffin. They were all volunteers who trained at Camp Brown before transferring to Camp MacDonald in Kennesaw, a new facility where they drilled for two months. The Fourth Brigade was then broken up and sent north in August of 1861 and the 18th Volunteer Regiment was composed with ten companies and amounting to about 750 soldiers, a large regiment to start. Most were from Central Georgia and included Company A, Acworth Infantry from Cobb County, Company B, Newton Rifles from Newton County, Company C, Jackson County Volunteers from Jackson County, Company D, Davis Invincibles from Dougherty County, Company E – Stephens Infantry from Gordon County, Company F, Davis Guards from Bartow County, Company G, Lewis Volunteers from Bartow County, Company H, Rowland Highlanders from Bartow County, Company I, Dooly Light Infantry from Dooly County and Company K, Rowland Infantry from Bartow County.

On July 31, 1861, there was a Grand Review of the brigade in Big Shanty (Kennesaw) and the locals came to admire the troops as they prepared to leave for Richmond on August 9. They were mustered out as the 18th Georgia and were posted at Camp Scott, just outside the city of Richmond where their job was to guard Union prisoners from the first Battle of Bull Run/Manassas before they served garrison duty for two weeks in Goldsboro, North Carolina. By November of 1861, they were still making their way into the Eastern Theater and sent along the Potomac River near Dumfries, Virginia where they met their soon to be companions, from Texas and were attached to the 1st, 4th and 5th Texas infantry regiments to form a "full" Texas Brigade and they served with the Texas Brigade for almost an entire year. Thenceforth they became one of the most famous brigades of the Army of Northern Virginia and when Hood was promoted to General and put in charge of the Regiment (having been the Colonel of the 4th Texas), it was solidified in legend and infamy, they would be "Hood's Texas Brigade," and the 18th Georgia, the affectionally called, 3rd Texas Regiment. The Texas Brigade including the 18th Georgia would be used repeatedly as what were known as "shock troops' pushing the enemy (the Union) out of their earthworks and into open battle. As such, they were often assigned as a rear guard to protect the division's withdrawal. The brigade made their way to Fredericksburg to Camp Wigfall. After Marching through Virginia and erroneously arriving near Stafford House in Virginia to find no Union troops after being ordered to block a troop movement, the tired troops returned to camp, marched toward Yorktown on April 10, 1862 which was 85 miles away and arrived on April 19, 1862 (by foot and train) Here they continued training until a withdrawal was ordered and they served as rear guard again before heading toward Williamsburg with a stop near Eltham's Landing. General Hood wanted to block the Union cavalry here and sent some of his Texans to do that leaving 18th Georgia in reserve to protect them. After this brief engagement they headed toward the Richmond region and then Chickahominy Creek. In many ways, the 18th Georgia was likely getting anxious for their first brush with combat, and it was coming soon enough. Then the dominoes would fall, and the battles wouldn't stop after that.

Battle of Gaines Mill, Valley of the Chicahominy, VA, 1862 (WarHistoryOnline)

On June 27, their involvement with the Peninsula Campaign after the Battle of Seven Pines increased in the Battle of Gaines Mill, where the 3rd Texas broke the Federal lines, causing the wounding of Captain Armstrong and 106 others in addition to the death of 37 men. Baptism by fire had come by June of 1862 and then the battlefield engagements became relentless. By late Summer of 1862, on August 30, they were engaged in the Second Battle of Manassas and the regiment lost 37 men to death with 87 more wounded but were able to capture the colors of the 10th and 24th New York. Then just two weeks later they were engaged at the Battle of South Mountain in the Potomac Campaign on September 14, and just three days later they were at the Battle of Sharpsburg/Antietam, America's Bloodiest Day and one of the worst for the entire Texas Brigade. The evening before Sharpsburg/Antietam they had skirmished with advancing Union soldiers in Miller's Cornfield and by the next morning the Texas Brigade was under the command of Colonel Wofford and rested near the Dunker Church.

Hood's Texas Brigade at Sharpsburg Cornfield – "Lone Star" by Dan Troiani

(Penn State University)

They awoke on September 17, had breakfast and marched forward to the Cornfield, their goal to stop Union General Hooker's opening assault. The 18th formed the left of Hood's like right of the Hampton Legion and advanced into the Cornfield until the Union fire started across from the Hagerstown Pike. They faced off across the 4th US artillery and its infantry as well as the 80th' New York while the 18th Georgia shifted their regiments left and returned fire. Suddenly canister fire, infantry fire and close-range shots blew through their ranks and the Georgians could only try to survive and fire back as best as they were able. Colonel Wofford and General Hood looked desperately for reinforcements and brought them forward as the Union lines began to thin as well. Suddenly, more Union reinforcements arrived fleshing out their ranks. The Georgia men began to lose hope, nearly flanked on the right, under close-range fire and the 1st Texas who was being absolutely obliterated, slipped the bridle and began to march back leaving the 18th Georgia alone. When Georgia finally elected to retreat, 101 men of just 176 fighting from their regiment that day were left as casualties on the field – a nearly 58% casualty rate for the 18th Georgia. The 1st Texas who had slipped the bridle – had lost 180 of 226 men, with 82.3% casualties that day – the highest of any regiment on a single day, on either side for the entire war. When General Hood was asked about his division, he reported,

> "My division is dead on the field."

Texas Monument at Antietam Cornfield, 2022

And, ultimately Antietam did break up the division, at least with the Texas Brigade.

The 18th and their Texas comrades from the 4th and 5th, didn't even know how to process what had been lost and what they had tried to do – this was war, and it was hell on earth, and it carried on. I'm sure they longed for the days of rear guard and drilling once more, but they didn't have time to daydream. They would soon be parted from their Texas brethren, but like them they marched on and fought barefoot, stood tall, and remember all they learned from Hood on how to be aggressive. The 18th brought their fortitude with them when they were transferred to Cobb's Georgia Brigade in late November of 1862 and were part of McLaw's Division of the 1st Corps.

Cobb's and Kershaw's Troops Behind the Stone Wall at Fredericksburg by Allen Christian Redwood, 1894 (Library of Congress)

Just a couple weeks later, they were in the Battle of Fredericksburg where their new General Cobb, was mortally wounded and now their own Colonel Wofford took command of the brigade. At Fredericksburg they had forty-four casualties of 160 men. The following month, Colonel Wofford was promoted to the ranks of General and commanded the brigade, now so named as Wofford's Brigade. And the following Spring of 1863, they were in the wooded hellscape of northern Virginia known as

Chancellorsville, where they suffered 88 casualties of their regiment. Of course, they and all the Confederacy suffered the loss of beloved Southern General Stonewall Jackson at Chancellorsville, which hurt southern morale a great deal just a couple months before the Pennsylvania campaign at Gettysburg.

Wofford's Brigade assembled on the second day of Battle at Gettysburg on July 2 at 4:00 PM toward the right flank of Longstreet's Corps. At 6:00 PM they were ordered to the front and assailed troops on the loop and forced them back through the Wheatfield to Little Round Top where they were assaulted again by fresh troops and were forced to withdraw west of the Wheatfield. General Kershaw spoke of Wofford's Georgia men,

> "I feared the brave men around me would be surrounded by the large force of the enemy constantly increasing in numbers, and all the while gradually enveloping us. In order to avoid such a catastrophe, I ordered a retreat to the buildings at Rose's. On emerging from the wood as I followed the retreat, I saw Wofford riding in the head of his fine brigade, then coming in, his left being in the Peach Orchard, which was then clear of the enemy. His movement was such as to strike the stony hill on the left, and thus turn the flank of the troops that had driven us from that position. On his approach the enemy retreated across the wheat field, where, with the regiments of my left wing, Wofford attacked with great effect, driving the Federals upon and near to Little Round Top."

The next day the 18th was on outpost duty or in Peach Orchard Grove. Overall, 18th regiment casualties at Gettysburg were not nearly as monumental as some of their peers and was about 36 out of 300 but the Confederates suffered almost 29,000 casualties at Gettysburg alone.

After Gettysburg on July 23, the brave Georgia boys engaged at Snickers Gap and then by the fall were sent west with Longstreet to the Army of the Tennessee where they reported to the Battle of Chickamauga, but perhaps luckily enough for them, missed the battle arriving a day too late. They engaged in a small battle of October 1862 that took place mostly in Tennessee on the Georgia line near Dade County, where they then stayed in Tennessee for a skirmish at Little River in November and ultimately the Assault on Fort Sanders in Knoxville where their friend and comrade, Colonel Ruff was killed in the ditch in front of the fort as were several other Confederates.

The Confederate Medal of Honor was only handed out fifty times during the war, but the 18th Georgia had one of its own earn this esteemed medal after the Battle at Fort Sanders and that was Captain James Lile Lemon of Company A. Lemon led his men with "great determination," across an open field of fire, "crisscrossed by wire and blocked by abatis," in the early morning attack. It was written of the 18th under Lemon,

> "Charging into a hailstorm of musketry and canister, the Confederates pushed their attack to the very walls of the fort only to falter in the deep ditch surrounding the works."

At this point Lemon realized they needed to carry the parapet to stand a charge, and as such,

> "Captain Lemon took his sword and began digging steps in the frozen, slippery clay of the fortifications, among exploding shells and more, he reached the parapet. Although alone and perilously exposed in this dangerous position, he heroically assisted a number of others in getting out of the trench. Seeing his brigade commander killed, Captain Lemon courageously led the men with him to the top of the parapet and into the fort where he fell severely wounded, a 'prisoner of war.'"

Lemon became one of the Immortal 600 of Fort Pulaski, Fort Warren and Fort Delaware who refused to take the Union oath. Union medicine had saved his life but a prisoner exchange and release with parole would not come unless he did. After weeks of suffering, he took the oath and said,

> "I have done the unspeakable but I am now paroled and today set out for home. My duty to my country is done, mine to my family remains."

Captain Lemon's descendants report that in the war, he had traveled with a former enslaved man from his family named Bap, who was traveling as his friend. As Lemon traveled through North Carolina and obtained lunch inside, he found Bap, who had been waiting outside had vanished. It turns out Bap had been arrested and Lemon had to point his pistol at the Constable and Deputy and in response to them threatening to kill Bap in front of Lemon. Lemon disarmed the constable and deputy, grabbed his friend, and re-boarded the train. Bap was one of seven family "slaves," that Captain Lemon had freed when he turned 21 and kept employed instead as hired hands.

James L. Lemon saves freed slave, Bap in NC, August 1863 (Mark Lemon)

Bap and Lemon were also boyhood friends. Lemon it seems had a history of saving as many people as he could even before battle and is more deserving of the Medal of Honor than any I can think of.

During the war, Sherman used Lemon's house in Acworth briefly as his headquarters while in Georgia, where James' wife, Eliza was forced to wait upon Sherman and the Union in her own home, that her husband had built nearly a decade prior.

In June of 1864, the house served as a hospital after the Battle of Kennesaw Mountain. James and his brother were the first settlers of Acworth and James built the house in 1856 as a small farmhouse. The house with some 1890 porch additions is a

Mrs. James Lemon (Eliza), 1861-1865

beautiful home that still stands and was not burned by Sherman. In fact, it is still owned by descendants of Lemon who proudly documented his recollections and published his letters and memoir-esque writings in a book entitled, "Feed them the Steel" which has harrowing war-time accounts from the beloved Captain. Lemon returned home to Georgia when he was paroled where he lived and worked the rest of his days in his own business ventures as a farmer, merchant and banker and died June 12, 1907.

Back in our war-time chronology, Lemon is still imprisoned after his capture at Knoxville and the 18th is still in the war as 1863 slips into 1864. Ultimately, Longstreet's Corps wasn't able to capture the Union cavalry at the Battle of Beans Station that followed and after staying in Tennessee through the winter, McLaw's division began its return to the Eastern Theater under Kershaw's command while General McLaws awaited results of a court martial about actions at Knoxville. And though McLaws was vindicated, he and Longstreet were kept separate to avoid conflict for a time.

Back in the Eastern Theater on May 5 and 6, the 18th was thrust into the Battle of Wilderness, where Commander Longstreet suffered a terrible wound. Then there was the Battle of Spotsylvania Court House and not two weeks later the Battle of Cold Harbor. May to June of 1864 was encounter after encounter with the warfront for the 18th Georgia including several small

Lemon House/Sherman HQ, 1864 (Mark Lemon)

battles in early June 1864 in the Shenandoah Valley. By June 16, they were in the Assault on Petersburg. Their Brigade was commanded by Colonel Christopher Sanders that summer while Wofford was on leave for injuries and they were attached to the Army of the Valley with their new Colonel engaging in battles at Front Royal and Bunker Hill and then on October 19, 1864 in Early's Division, they participated in the Battle of Cedar Creek in the Shenandoah Valley as well. The next month, reassigned to the Army of Northern Virginia and back in Richmond and Petersburg facing off against Grant is where they stayed through most of the remainder of the war but suffered from disease running through the city. By 1865, only one officer and 52 men surrendered at Appomattox Courthouse from the 18th. The Rowland Highlanders of Company H had one man George Smith who surrendered in Kingston, Georgia where some of them had been in early 1865, and he had to prove later that he did not desert! Luckily, his comrades spoke up for him.

Our brave barefoot Georgians with a Texan Spirit had lost so many beloved friends and companions but had to do their best to resume their life in their home of the Peach State and try to pick up from the ashes that were left behind in the destructive wake. They, like the Goober Grabbers, and so many Georgia regiments, had several reunions over the years. *The Atlanta Constitution* of August 2,1882 reported on the second annual reunion of the 18th in great details as Generals Wofford and Longstreet were present and gave inspirational talks.

> "General Wofford's speech was a glowing tribute to the valor of his old comrades. Wofford declared that they hadn't ever retreated, but admitted to them that they had once made "a flank movement," but that flank movement gained the battle. He reviewed at length the second Manassas fight and described graphically the part the Eighteenth had taken in that terrible struggle. With pride he referred to the duel between the Eighteenth and the Zouaves in blue on that day and declared that that victory was gained by the Eighteenth. He told of the Battle of Gettysburg and how his soldiers in the midst of that fight sent up three cheers at the sight of General Longstreet on the battlefield."

Longstreet, who came to know the men at that point in the war, spoke and remembered his fallen comrades in war and post-war, and spoke,

> "If in it we could resurrect that grand old figure, R.E. Lee and restore to him his invincible Stonewall Jackson," to which there was great applause from the 18th veterans, "I would like to see a grand reunion of

> the north, the south, the east and the west in building up the grandest government of the universe."

And then he commended the bravery of the 18th. By this time, General Hood has passed and several others, so not much was written in speeches about their early fight at Antietam and their Texan brethren but for them, that was something that had come to define their very essence and soul – they didn't need reminding that their second name was the "3rd Texas."

Where can one most feel the spirit of the 18th? In Georgia where they lived and on the fields of battle where they fought from Maryland to Virginia and Tennessee. It was in these regions that they saw some of the most enormous conflicts the Civil War had and emanated a strength that was remembered for generations. The battlefields at which they fought boast to be some of the most haunted – Gettysburg, Antietam, Chancellorsville and more – for me, I believe they are most likely at Antietam, where they suffered such immense casualties and were taken by surprise at just how awful war could be truly for the first time.

Some say, the boys of the 18th who were captured at Cold Harbor and other Confederates who met death at the Elmira Prison Camp in New York, may be there, resting unpeacefully due to the conditions of "Hellmira," and not being able to return home to the safety of their family and loved ones. At least six men from the 18th Georgia perished in the prison and are buried near to the old camp. Elmira is considered one of New York's most haunted towns because of the terrible conditions of the camp, with over 3,000 Confederates dying in just one year. Showing a 25% mortality rate people hear whispers, cries for help and see flickering lights throughout the landscape.

Or, perhaps, you can visit James Lile Lemon's house in Acworth if they open it for visits. The current descendants and residents claim it to be haunted but only to visitors. Those who live there live peacefully among their family, but the spirits seem to stir things up when other folks come in. There's a small burial ground behind it with a CSA Marker though Lemon is recorded to be buried elsewhere? But perhaps the ghost of Lemon can tell us where he is buried, was it secretly at home? Suffice to say no matter where you find yourself in the Eastern Theater and in North Georgia, the spirit of the 18th infantry is alive and well. As for me, I'm going to ask them to join my protective entourage of spirits as they sound like some of the most remarkable men I can imagine to have in your corner.

Georgia at Antietam

Cornfield

Georgia's presence in Sharpsburg at the Battle of Antietam/Sharpsburg is defining for September 17, 1862. Georgia had 40 Regiments present, seven artillery batteries and one cavalry legion as well their native General James Longstreet. Some were in the worst of the combat, and some were able to avoid it. But the regiments who suffered the highest casualties and worst combat found themselves exposed to enemy fire at close range on the Cornfield, burrowed into the Sunken Road as they were trod upon making it a Bloody Lane or trying to hold off the Union from taking the Rohrbach (Burnside) Bridge.

The 6th Georgia, organized in Macon, in April of 1861 and mustered out May 27 of the same year. participated in at least 21 battles throughout the war and gained some fame for two reasons, their participation in Stonewall Jackson's Chancellorsville flank attack which became one of the most famous military moves of the Civil War, if not all time in Spring of 1863, and for the election of their first Colonel, Alfred H. Colquitt as Governor of Georgia after the war. They were 724 strong when they mustered out. Prior to Antietam, they were at nearby South Mountain as were several other Georgians and had also been in the Yorktown Siege, Williamsburg, Seven Pines, Seven Days, Gaines Mill and Malvern Hill – a very similar path to the 18th. In Yorktown, at their initial arrival, prior to the siege, their anticipated threat had not been there, so they drilled as did the 18th and within the very beginning of their military adventure they lost 125 men to illness. It's important to remember more deaths occurred by illness than injury or battle during the Civil War. The 6th had been in General Rain's Brigade of D.H. Hill's Division by the Siege of Yorktown and after the Battle of Williamsburg began to see the suffering of war. They arrived at Richmond according, to Captain James Lofton,

> "broken down and exhausted,"

but after some rest

> "ready and anxious to drive back the invaders."

of September 17, 1862. Meanwhile, the awful massacre in the Cornfield was starting, which some historians believe was underestimated in casualty count to this day. At approximately, 6:30 AM, General D.H. Hill brought his men in to support Hood's assault, and this included the 6th Georgia and Colquitt's Brigade from the Sunken Road up by the Mumma farm. Here they could see the desperate assault on the Confederate Army in the Cornfield. They slowly moved closer filling lines and locations as the next brigade marched into the Cornfield of death. The 6th moved toward where Ripley's command had vacated, north of the buildings being burned down at the Mumma farm. (The Confederates burned down these buildings in fear the Union may use the buildings to strengthen their position.) They knew by this point, the imminence of them joining in the brutality of the fight. They watched Ripley's Brigade have confusion when Ripley was

Cornfield at Antietam, 2022

wounded and Georgia's 4th, Colonel Doles had to take command. Then they watched as the Union from the East Woods halted Ripley's Brigade advance. Ripley's Brigade began to control the Cornfield with firefight and Dole's command stalled the 128th Pennsylvania. The 6th inched closer behind Ripley in an advance led by the 13th Alabama and fellow Georgians from the 23rd, 28th, and 27th in front of them, with the 6th at the rear giving them the false hope that they may be spared. Ripley's weakened formation was protected briefly by those marching into the lead before they left the Cornfield. Colquitt's Brigade and 6th Georgia came forward to try and take control of the Cornfield. The back and forth continued relentless and frightening for both sides. It is believed that the Cornfield changes hands no less than six times between armies during the battle. When the 6th and Colquitt's men entered the field, they were facing the same force that just drove back Ripley's Brigade in tatters under Union General Gordon including the 2nd Massachusetts on the right flank as well as the 3rd Wisconsin and 27th Indiana. New York and New Jersey forces were strong in their reserves and Gordon had thousands of men.

Colonel Colquitt moved forward with his men and Georgia's 6th deep into the Cornfield and described the scene as follows,

> "over wounded men strewn across the ground like chaff after the harvest."

One soldier from Wisconsin recollected their charge at the Cornfield,

> "The Confederate infantry moved steadily across the corn-field, while the decimated brigade in its path fell back step-by-step. The enemy were handicapped by the fact that they were moving diagonally across our front, instead of directly toward us, and our fire was terribly severe…"

Colquitt's attempt to be swift and quick was an attempt to secure command of the Cornfield. Sure enough, there was no swiftness that would prevent Gordon's artillery fire as the Georgians were in the very center of the field. The Union troops began to fill in on all sides of the fence at Miller's Orchard. The Pennsylvania men stopped at the north end of the Cornfield and the men from Massachusetts filled the front when they had space. The 6th Georgia was near to the Northern end of Colquitt's Right flank facing off against this toughness. Gordon was in their front and center, and more Union lay camouflaged in the East Woods.

As Union soldiers came running from the East Woods and the rebels were assaulted on multiple sides, it must have seemed as if they all had to prepare to join the men on the ground and meet God. I cannot imagine the fear and adrenaline simultaneously rushing. In fact, I doubt any of us can. They waited on reinforcements for Colonel Colquitt's brigade. But the reinforcements had gotten disoriented, didn't want to cause friendly fire and were pushing off Union attacks enroute to the Cornfield. Ultimately, in facing a large body of Union troops near the south end of the East Woods, the 6th Georgia's reinforcements of Garland's brigade panicked and fled as did so many on both sides that day – regiments of young men, scared and not able to comprehend the violence in front of them.

The 6th Georgia found themselves in dire straits with exposed front and flank and as they dealt with that Union General Hooker changed his strategy. Rather than having the Union lines march forward, he was going to send the second full corps at his disposal to attack all at once through the Cornfield with one division and East Woods with another. Historians describe this set up as a "vice" that was going to "squeeze the regiment to death."

Suddenly the Ohio regiment advancing to their right unleashed a volley on the Georgia's right front whilst they were unprepared and while Company B's Captain had been looking for Lt. Colonel Newton to report that they were flanked. But before he could make the report the regiment's Major Tracy was struck down and command passed over. A man from the 66th Ohio, recollects the 6th Georgia being stuck at that moment and said,

> "a line of the enemy [was] drawn up along a fence, in the edge of a corn-field. We immediately opened fire upon the enemy, who soon broke."

To their credit, staying any longer would have been suicide for anyone who remained – so the 6th Georgia line broke – they continued in their fight at Antietam. The Ohio soldier went on to state that they followed the Georgia men, engaging in hand-to-hand combat, "using clubbed guns,"

and

"severely punishing"

the Georgia men. Georgia men recollected trying to bring their injured to the Dunker Church for care and walking through bloody corn rows trying to dodge blue-clad lines that kept appearing. As they went through the East Woods, the vice upon them did not let up and turned

"rapidly into a noose"

causing more to try and flee. The officers tried to later explain their men's flight by saying that General D.H. Hill had ordered retreat to Dunker Ridge Church. Colquitt tried to boost their morale while Stonewall Jackson, D.H. Hill and Hood tried to give order at the Cornfield but as the depleted rebels crossed Hagerstown Pike, the field fell to the Union again. Union men ran into the 6th Georgia's injured Lt. Colonel Newton begging for morphine and crying,

"I am shot through, Oh God, I Must die,"

and then rolling over to die in front of them. Ultimately, there were 165 casualties for the 6th Georgia, with at least 52 killed outright. They lost their Lt. Colonel, their major, the Captain of Company B and fifteen other officers. In total their regiment had 63 percent casualties. Later that winter they camped in Virginia outside Fredericksburg where their fame came as they also fought and then rallied to support Stonewall Jackson's flanking maneuver the following spring in Chancellorsville before valiantly fighting in so many more battles. At the conclusion of the war the 6th Georgia surrendered in Greensboro, NC to Sherman's men – but they would never forget the blood bath at Antietam that forever changed them and so many Georgians.

Completely Silenced! Dead Confederate artillery men, as they lay around their battery after the Battle of Antietam by Alexander Gardner, 1862 (Library of Congress)

Also suffering in the hauntingly deadly Cornfield and facing terrible casualty counts were the 10th Georgia infantry. The 10th organized in Jonesboro, GA mustered into service in Richmond, Virginia in June of 1861 assigned to Magruder's Peninsula Division and served with Lee's Army of Northern Virginia for the entire war excepting when they served with Longstreet in late 1863 in Georgia and East Tennessee. Part of the Semmes-Bryan-Simms brigade they had Georgia, Colonel Lafayette McLaws as one of their officers and served in at least 26 major battles. By late September 1861, McLaws assumed brigade command and they too experienced their first combat at Yorktown with more experience being handed to them at Mechanicsville, Malvern Hill and Savage's Station where they saw at least 59 casualties. They joined Lee's army after guarding Richmond and fought at South Mountain before Antietam/Sharpsburg as the 6th did. However, South Mountain had brought the 10th Georgia, sixty casualties and they had only 184 reporting toward Sharpsburg.

Around 9:00 AM on September 17, McLaw's division had reached the West Woods and McLaws immediately sent them into fight. The 10th Georgia was on the left with Semmes's Brigade by Dunker Church. They encountered the 15th Mass and 82nd New York before they returned after Semmes, and they encountered "galling fire" too far from the flank. They climbed a fence east into a stubble field where they were falling on the rocky terrain and had to then run to the Poffenberger farm and reform their lines. At this point the 10th Georgia were able to fire on the Union and break a Union brigade. Semmes then pushed the Georgia boys forward to shore up position but due to communication breakdowns it was too late and the Union artillery had been to their front and flank causing terrible casualties.

The 10th Georgia was exposed on the left and took the brunt of the Union artillery fire. Between this and the stubble field the 10th Georgia lost 84 of its 148 men and suffered 56.7% casualties. They lost Colonel Cumming in the Bloody Lane to wounding. The War Department marker for Semmes's Brigade on the battlefield read as followed:

> 'Semmes Brigade reached the western suburbs of Sharpsburg at sunrise of the 17th and halted until nearly 9 A.M., when it advanced across the fields, in support of Stuart's Cavalry, north and west of Hauser's house. In the general advance of McLaws' Division it was on the left of the line, and

encountered the enemy in the northern part of the West Woods, forcing them to retire beyond the Nicodemus house. Near this point its advance was checked by the Federal Artillery east of the Hagerstown Road. After severe losses it was withdrawn and placed as a reserve to Barksdale's Brigade, in the western edge of the West Woods, where it remained until the night of the 18th when it recrossed the Potomac."

A contrast: Federal Buried, Rebel Unburied, where they fell at the Battle of Antietam by Alexander Gardner, 1862 (Library of Congress)

The boys of the 10th and the 6th were considered some of the worst losses of Georgia regiments at Antietam (next to the 18th as well). The war had just begun, and they had their first enormous brush with death and having young lives cut drastically short all around them.

Georgia men were all over the bloody fields of Antietam falling at two other locations in addition to the Cornfield – the locations are known as the Bloody Lane and the Rohrbach Bridge.

It's interesting, as it relates to the Big 3 of Antietam – Cornfield, Bloody Lane, and Burnside Bridge – though I've had encounters at all, it's the Cornfield that grabs me most. Perhaps, it's because I had Georgia ancestors and there sits the only Georgia monument on the Cornfield, the same style that sits at the only Georgia Monument near Longstreet Tower at Gettysburg. I often stand at the monuments that read,

Georgia Monument at Antietam, 2022

> "We sleep here in obedience to law; when duty called,
> we came, when country called, we died."

At the Cornfield, as I stand there, and put my hand on the monument, I always feel compelled to say a moment of prayer for the souls of all those lost and have a private moment with them. I want them to know they are not forgotten and hope they know wherever they are on the other side, that they need not be scared anymore. To be consumed by fear and have such desperation to survive in the face of chaos and death, you can feel that swirling in the air and energy there. I always feel the need to try and still it for the souls who may remain there reliving those gruesome and horrifying moments. I think of the youth of so many of these boys, fresh to the war, having never been in such a position before.

I've read ghost stories, to be sure, of field trips of students found by the Cornfield fences rolled up into balls, shaking from the sight of soldiers running past and hearing the throes of battle surround them, only to find there was no reenactment or event that would be causing such a scene. I have driven by the old Hagerstown Road at night where the fighting clashed back and forth and I have seen the shadows running back and forth on the Cornfield and stepped out of the car, almost feeling the breeze of them running, even a calm night. It is, undoubtedly, the rush of soldiers that are still fighting there in some other time … their time and I have stepped back into it for a moment – is it a slip in time? Is it a ghost?

I don't have the answers as to how the haunts of the Cornfield work, but I can tell you, it takes your breath away and you know that something happened there beyond any of our modern comprehension. So, on your next visit to Antietam, take a moment, step onto the old Hagerstown Road, park your car and look out into the old fields and remember the soldiers who died there … remember all of them.

Suffice to say, the three locations including the Cornfield have been, without surprise, noted to be the most haunted on all of Antietam.

Sunken Road/Bloody Lane

The men of the 23rd Georgia who organized at Camp McDonald on August 31, 1861 moved into Virginia and began the war in Winter of 1862, seeing battle at least 21 times throughout the entirety of the war and following a similar path to other Georgia men entering the Eastern Theater of the war by way of Yorktown/Williamsburg, Seven Pines and Seven Days, Gaines Mill, Malvern Hill and South Mountain before Antietam. Their Colonel Barclay was even mentioned in Colonel Colquitt's report of South Mountain for noble conduct. The 23rd Georgia was part of Colquitt's Brigade and the War Department markers on the battlefield write of their engagement at Antietam, especially at the Bloody Lane /Sunken Road.

> "Colquitt's Brigade formed lines soon after sunrise, southwest of Mumma's house, in support of Trimble and Ripley. The lines followed Ripley across the Smoketown Road and formed on his right. After a severe engagement, involving heavy loss, they retired to the west end of the Bloody Lane and assisted in checking the advance of French's Division of the Second Corps. Later in the day, portions of the Brigade acted with Evans' Brigade in checking the Federal advance on the Boonsboro Pike."

Then there's second marker bringing them back to the Bloody Lane.

> "After the repulse of the Confederate line in the East Woods and Cornfield north of the Smoketown Road in the morning of the 17th, parts of the Brigades of Colquitt and Garland rallied in the Sunken Road at this point, their right connecting with Rodes, their left resting on the Hagerstown Pike. They cooperated with Rodes in repelling the advance of French's Division, Second Corps, and, in cooperation with detachments of McLaws' and Walker's Division, crossed this road and attacked the right flank of French's Division but were repulsed. In the afternoon, parts of the two Brigades were collected at Sharpsburg and moved out on the Boonsboro Pike in support of Evans' Brigade in its resistance to the advance of a portion of the Fifth Army Corps."

Ultimately, the 23rd suffered 78 casualties at Antietam but their presence in the Bloody Lane cannot be overstated – the Sunken Road gained its macabre nickname due to the sheer amount of carnage that took place there. 5,500 were killed in three hours of combat on the Sunken Road in just three hours. The Confederates in the road stood their ground all morning but the Union, able to overwhelm Hill's men, drove them from the position and hit Confederate lines. Still there was no decisive victory that came from the Bloody Lane, the Cornfield or Antietam as a whole, the lives of those lost continues to stain the land of Sharpsburg. As Union troops approached Confederates in the road that day the trips had a powerful volley at less than a hundred yards and the Union could trample on into the Confederates making them both in completely vulnerable positions at the Bloody Lane and the 23rd Georgia a part of that.

Perhaps the biggest story for Georgians at the Bloody Lane is the wounding of the then Colonel John B. Gordon. Gordon had led

Bloody Lane Antietam, 2022

his regiment of Alabama men in the Peninsula Campaign and Seven Days Battle before they were in Antietam. Prior to the Peninsula Campaign he had been injured and almost blinded by an exploding shell close to him in the battles of Malvern Hill and Gaines Mill. But, having recovered and evolving into a proverbial cat with nine lives, Gordon stayed in the defenses at the Peninsula Campaign before resuming his dangerous post in the lines at Sharpsburg.

Gordon, a Georgia native, and arguably one of the most important Georgians in the war, was with his Alabamians in the center of the line on the Sunken Road on September 17, 1862. Lee asked him, if he could hold his ground and Gordon replied that his men could

"Until the sun goes down or victory is won."

Gordon was able to hold the line against repeated attacks as he remained in command through several injuries. The first volley from the Union sent a bullet through Gordon's right calf, and then he was hit higher up in the same leg but with bones not being broken yet he continued firing. Another bullet went through his left arm,

> "Tearing asunder the tendons and mangling the flesh,"

and as blood dripped down his fingers, his men begged him to go the rear. But Gordon wouldn't. He stated that,

> "Surgeons were all busy at the field hospitals in the rear, and there was no way therefore, of stanching the blood, but I had a vigorous constitution, and this was doing me good service."

Then Gordon was hit again in the shoulder, where a fragment and clothing got stuck in his wound. He began to go into shock from the loss of blood but stood on his feet when suddenly a fifth bullet struck him in the face on the left check and passed out his neck missing his jugular vein. He fell forward facing down in his cap. It is said only a bullet hole in his cap prevented him from drowning in his own blood.

> "It would seem that I might have been smothered by the blood running into my cap from this last wound but for the act of some Yankee, who, as if to save my life, had at a previous hour during the battle, shot a hole through the cap, which let the blood out."

Gordon was finally evacuated from the field feeling as if most of his head was gone and sending his wife almost into shock before she nursed him back to health. Gordon's wife was able to save him – and it is to her who he gives full credit for his life being restored before he returns to war in time for Gettysburg and the subsequent battles (with, of course, more life-threatening injuries.) Gordon would go on to live a fascinating and remarkable life. For more on John B. Gordon – please see Part III, Chapter 16 on Men.

The Bloody Lane is the site of many paranormal legends from Union Irish soldiers being heard with their battle cry sound as if a Christmas Carol to people, swearing they hear the melodic chant in the distance. Others see the soldiers in the sunken road reliving that gruesome moment or their bodies stacked upon each other in spectral form splayed out in their decaying form.

One of the most frightening occurrences of the Bloody Lane came from a reenactor who was sleeping there (naturally). He was panic-stricken trying to relay to his friends what had happened to him. He heard whispers and moans in his ears and rustling of grass between the arm and chest. He brushed it off as his imagination until he saw a human arm rise from the earth next to him that looked blood-soaked next to him. The arm twisted and pressed on his chest as if hold him to the ground. He screamed and the arm released him. His reaction was fitting for such a frightening accident but not unique. You can read accounts from visitors from all over the world who feel their ankles grabbed and begin to feel dizzy, disoriented and sick when they visit the Bloody Lane.

On my most recent to Antietam, I was having a particularly bad day and when I was at the Bloody Lane, I took a small little path through the cornstalks on the side of it and watched as on a windless day some cornstalks moved and parted way as if to summon me. And, I heard someone behind me but saw no one. I felt it more of a comfort to know they were there, perhaps protecting me if not just observing what I was doing. Though for a first-time visitor, the Bloody Lane can be overpowering and scary, going with respect in your heart for those who were lost there and empathy for all, can help you to focus on their presence in a less frightening way and to truly feel the spirit at Sharpsburg.

Rohrbach/Burnside Bridge

Over by Antietam Creek men from the 2nd, 20th and 50th Georgia tried to push back Union Control of Burnside Bridge, then known as Rohrbach Bridge and not named for a Union General. The 20th Georgia was on a high wooded bluff opposite one end of the bridge and the 2nd and 5th continued the line. One company of the 20th Georgia was on a narrow-wooded creek near to Sharpsburg Road. The 2nd Georgia was posted on the bluff and in pits overlooking the bridge as well as to the right of the bridge. In the morning of September 17, their commander, Colonel Holmes was killed in action. Theodore Fogle of Company G, described his time with the 2nd Georgia at the bridge and the immense casualties they suffered there as follows,

> "At a bridge on the Antietam Creek our Regiment and the 20th Ga., in all amounting to not over 300 muskets held them in check for four hours and a half and then we fell back only because our ammunition was exhausted, but we suffered badly, eight cannon just 500 yards off were pouring grape shot, shell and cannister into us and our artillery could not silence them. We held our post until Major William Harris ordered us to fall back. Our Col. (Col. Holmes) . . . was killed about half an hour before. . .We went into the fight with only 89 muskets and had eight officers and 35 men killed and wounded. So many of the men were shot down that the officers filled their places and loaded and fired their guns."

The 20th lost 27.2% of their forces and the 50th had casualties nearing 200 in the Antietam Campaign including Sharpsburg's preceding South Mountain and the others at Antietam on the Bridge. It is believed only a small fraction of their forces present at Antietam and suffered dreadfully so in high casualty numbers.

The Rohrbach bridge was crucial as a crossing for the armies and Georgia's time defending the bridge against Union troops from Connecticut and other northern states was not easy, but they were able to repulse attacks again and again and again. Less than 500 men from Georgia manned the bridge in total versus a much larger Ninth Corps under Union General Ambrose Burnside. Confederate General Longstreet praised Georgia efforts on the bridge and wrote,

> "General Toombs held the bridge and defend it most gallantly, driving back repeated attacks, and only yielded it after the force brought against him became overwhelming and threatened his flank and rear."

Their action in delaying the capture of this bridge for hours allowed General A.P.'s Hill's troops to arrive to Antietam safely. The assault around the bridge between Georgia and Connecticut who would oddly face off again in the Wheatfield of Gettysburg the next year was a defining moment for the battle and in the Civil War as a whole. Ultimately, the battle itself was tactically inconclusive, though Union claimed victory and the bridge thus getting the new name Burnside Bridge.

For those who are akin to natural spirit energy, the Sycamore at the bridge is rare example of a witness tree that stood during the battle as a mere sapling and witnessed what happened on that Bridge as men assaulted each other at close range, fell into the creek and died, turning the creek red and leaving bits of their souls upon the earth that feeds the roots of the beautiful tree. As stated, the song "Sticks That Made Thunder," by the Steeldrivers provides a haunting example of a battle witnessed by a tree.

Burnside Bridge (and the Sycamore) by Alexander Gardner, September 1862 (Library of Congress)

The last time I visited the Burnside Bridge, it was at sunset, and it was one of those sunsets that was just immensely colorful with shades of red, purple and pink against the pale blue sky and the sun fading in the distance. I looked upon the bridge from the steps above, no one else there and I could hear muffled talking, footsteps and leaves crunching and branches breaking, but no animals around except for a squirrel chirping by my feet, upset at me that I was in his quiet space so close to his human-free hours. Yet I felt watched, they knew I was there – was I friend or foe? Were they Confederate or Union? Who held the bridge at that moment of the battle reliving itself? I saw a man in gray run across the bridge quickly and confirmed with my husband that he did not see him, and I thought maybe, it's one of the boys from Georgia trying to hold on to that bridge for dear life.

I read later that visitors who go as the sun has set can hear a drum playing in the woods by the bridge and have seen balls of blue light appear around the bridge as if unmarked graves are evidencing the men coming up from the ground to fight the battle again.

Sunset at Burnside Bridge, Antietam, 2022

Conclusion of Antietam

On the battlefield of Antietam there was a casualty every two seconds on average for twelve hours leaving a three-mile-long line of bodies to be buried at its conclusion with most Confederates being reinterred years later in Hagerstown, Maryland, or Shepherdstown, West Virginia. There were more than 23,000 casualties with nearly 11,000 for the Confederacy. Union General Hooker wrote,

> "Every stalk of corn in the northern and greater part of the field weas cut as closely as could have been done with a knife and the slain lay in rows precisely as they had stood in their ranks a few moments before,"

while Confederate General Hood described the scene as,

> "The most terrible clash of arms that occurred during the war."

Many Georgia wounded were brought to nearby hospitals, and it is town legend that the town's St. Paul Episcopal Church served as the hospital for the Georgia men and is something you can still visit today and feel their desperation as they came in there hoping to live more of their life that was being cut so brief, a bunch young boys desperate for their moms to be there with them to heal them. But instead, they found themselves suffering immense pain and often death from what they had incurred on the field. Many state they can still hear the screams of the injured coming from the building and see flickering lights in the church's tower. Other homes that served as hospitals in town are rumored to still have blood-soaked floorboards as well. And the town of Sharpsburg remains forever changed by the battle of 1862, which became a defining moment of the community and its residents forever, taking decades for a semblance of life to return to any sense of normalcy.

Georgia at Gettysburg

> "In great deeds, something abides. On great fields, something stays. Forms change and pass; bodies disappear; but spirits linger, to consecrate ground for the vision-place of souls… generations that know us not and that we know not of, heart-drawn to see where and by whom great things were suffered and done for them, shall come to this deathless field, to ponder and dream; and lo! the shadow of a mighty presence shall wrap them in its bosom, and the power of the vision pass into their souls." – Joshua Chamberlain, 20th Maine.

… the power of the vision pass into their souls – Union or Confederate, the belief, the life, the loss, all of it is felt on these fields of battle and Gettysburg more than most, where this Union hero so eloquently stated the haunting perpetual nature of such a place.

Georgia at Gettysburg, resulted in the 3rd highest casualty count

Georgia Monument at Gettysburg, 2021-2022

of all Confederate states present. Georgia sent over 13,000 men in the Army of Northern Virginia among three corps and the cavalry as well as their native, General Longstreet, again. Over 2,700 Georgia casualties resulted from the deadliest Civil War battle to ever occur on July 1 to July 3, 1863.

The Georgia monument at Gettysburg is identical to the one at Antietam that reads,

> "We sleep here in obedience; when duty called, we came, when country called, we died,"

and at Gettysburg it sits on West Confederate Ave. near the location where General Semmes's Georgia brigade began its march to attack toward the Wheatfield on July 2.

Both Antietam and Gettysburg park memorials were put up on the centennial in 1961. Oddly, the attack at the Wheatfield was in some ways identical to Burnside Bridge in Antietam with the primary soldiers in both being from Georgia and Connecticut as well. Gettysburg was as eerie and haunting for the men of the north and south going in and being there as it is for us haunt seekers to visit it.

What are the most haunting places at Gettysburg? For me it's between two – Pickett's Charge at Cemetery Ridge or The Wheatfield – with my gut oddly leading toward the latter. It's my personal connection to those who were in the Wheatfield. But truthfully, the Wheatfield was in the crosshairs of some of the most violent conflict at Gettysburg for days as the Confederates tried to push for the Union line at Little Round Top. The Wheatfield presents one of the most confusing parts about the Battle of Gettysburg, but let's try to follow those Georgia boys there as best as we can. By the end of July 2, there would be over 4,000 casualties on the Wheatfield that veterans would come to describe as a

> "whirlpool – a stream of eddies and tides that flowed around the 19 acres of wheat owned by farmer George Rose and changed hands six times,"

of great reminiscence of Antietam's Cornfield. The first Confederate brigade under General George Anderson moved forward at about 3:30 PM from the woods to the south and encountered Union regiments stationed behind a stone wall on the south end of the field (some had moved to Devil's Den) and for an hour the Union kept Anderson's Brigade pushed off. Anderson's Brigade included the 7th, 8th, 9th, 11th and 59th Georgia infantries who Anderson skillfully maneuvered in front of the Union troops conserving ammunition.

Cannon at Gettysburg Wheatfield, 2022

The Union began to run out of ammunition and backed through the Wheatfield as Anderson and the Georgians followed closely and swarmed over the wall. Suddenly, the Union men from Maine were ordered to turn around and they led a bayonet charge at the Georgians and pushed them from the field. The Georgians followed suit, turned around and renewed their attack as Union reinforcements came. The fighting turned incredibly violent in the southern end of the Wheatfield as more Union troops filtered in from the east and west and the Confederates from Rose Farm. The fighting raged steadily for at least an hour and the Union began to pull back until the Irish Brigade from the Union came in to the Wheatfield to push the rebels off a knoll. The response from the rebel army? Bring in the Georgia Brigade under Semmes. Semmes's Brigade included the 10th, 50th, 51st and 53rd Georgia infantries. The Georgia boys followed Semmes into the lower part of the Wheatfield and watched as Semmes' was seriously wounded. Confused, scared and angry, they counterattacked another newly arrived Union brigade. At this point it was bayoneted fighting up close and personal and the Georgians were pushed back to Rose Farm, at least those who survived. More Confederate forces came through the Wheatfield and the Union found them relentless and with them more Georgians. General Wofford's brigade including the Georgia 16th, 18th, 24th regiments and the Phillips and Cobb Legions eventually swept the field, and the final Confederate assault took place at 7:30 PM with a close to battle close to 8:00 PM.

The soldiers were surrounded by the bodies of thousands wounded, dying, moaning and crying with no means to help them. There are several accounts from both sides of the fear of death and confusion in Gettysburg but should one ever doubt the heart wrenching nature in which this was to exist for these young men, I want to share with you a tale of what one man believed to be an angel who came in the form of a soldier from Georgia that day. The spirit of empathy and love among a field of death is perhaps one of the most heartwarming things I have ever come to learn from Gettysburg. In 1907, at a reunion, Thomas Oliver of the 24th Georgia was a little saddened not to see a man named Dr. Purman, who he had encountered during the war at the Wheatfield decades before. On July 3, the 24th Georgia had not yet left the Wheatfield with the others. It was then, that Thomas, just about 23-years-old at the time had a startling encounter. It was something that ended up being what he thought was just an act of humanity but would be

Rows of Confederate Dead positioned at edge of Rose Woods by Timothy O'Sullivan, July 1863, Gettysburg, PA (Library of Congress)

later praised as a heroic deed. Oliver recalled,

> "We had been fighting at a pretty rapid rate the day previous, and the dead and dying of both sides lay pretty thick. On the morning of the 3rd, I was browsing around in front of our camps, when someone called to me to come to him. The appeal was from the direction of the Yankee lines and I felt creepy about venturing in that direction, but the poor fellow made the appeal so strong that I could resist and I got down on my hands and knees and crawled to him, taking a canteen of water. He seemed to be the most grateful man I ever saw, drank the water like he was about famished and told me that one of his legs was shattered all to pieces and the other badly

> done for. He begged me to save his life, if possible. I couldn't see him stay there and die, so I managed to get on my back and crawled off through the wheatfield with him. I experienced no little difficulty in getting within our lines, for he was weak from loss of blood and I was forced to assist in keeping him on my back crawling on one hand and my knees. I expected every moment a Yankee bullet would stop the performance but I managed to land my load safely under a big tree. I gave him a blanket, some hardtack, took his name and regiment and bade him good-bye, never for a moment believing that he would live. But he did. Next day he fell into the hands of his own people the 140th Pennsylvania Infantry of which he was Lieutenant. Several years ago, I received a letter at Gainesville, Georgia at which place I was then living from J.J. Purman, Washington DC. asking me if I was not the man who had saved his life at Gettysburg, that he had been trying to locate me ever since the scrap closed and that he wanted me to write him. I looked over the little book which I carried through the war with me and found that the name corresponded with the one I had jotted down at the time I left him under the tree."

Purman too shared his account with the papers and wrote,

> "For the brave and generous act of this 'old reb' – Thomas P. Oliver, adjutant 24th Georgia infantry, I shall ever hold a warm spot in my heart – I love him."

Purman was only about a year or so younger than his savior – a young man of just 21 or 22 at the time of this battle of Gettysburg.

And though Thomas died in 1907, it wasn't before he got to reconnect with the Yank he had saved. After his reunion in Richmond, he went to Washington and was the guest of Dr. Purman, it was reported to be a

> "Most delightful meeting that occurred between these two veterans and Mr. Oliver had many visitors in Washington not the least of which was one he met at the White House – President Theodore Roosevelt who expressed his great appreciation for his act of bravery."

Dr. Purman died some years later in 1915, but I like to think the men who corresponded for years and had that meeting of fate – and Purman who sought so long to find his angel savior, are together on the other side – and this time not as opponents but as the young men they once were – but instead using their heavenly youth not to fight in war but to have an enduring friendship instead.

Sometimes we forget the youth of those involved, who perhaps were new husbands, new fathers or so young they missed the comfort of their siblings and mother who was the only bosom of nurturing they knew. To show strength and love toward one another on the field of battle is to show that that empathy from family and love is indeed stronger than any cause of war that could come between men.

Another incredible tale is that of Henry McDaniel, a young Lieutenant who was injured horribly in the Wheatfield and had recently taken command of the 11th Georgia infantry after two officers were wounded. By all accounts it looked as if he was about to die as well. He had been shot in the abdomen and his friends had gathered to say goodbye to him, but Henry refused to be left behind to die despite certain death on his trip. He demanded they put him on a litter and carry him or he would walk until he died. The doctors agreed to carry him on the litter and watched as life faded from his eyes and body. His friend, Colonel Nesbit, leaned in close to see if he was still … breathing. Suddenly, McDaniel opened his eyes and said,

> "Nesbit, old fellow. Did you ever see such an ungodly pair of ankles as that Dutch woman on that porch has got."

Nesbit laughed – his friend was not ready to die and indeed, he did not die. He went on to become Governor of Georgia and to found Georgia Tech University.

As for Georgia Brigade leader, General Semmes, after the assault on the Wheatfield and his grueling thigh injury, he was carried back to a field hospital the night of July 2, but having lost all his blood the Confederate surgeons were limited.

A field hospital in Gettysburg, 1863 (National Parks Service)

He was then brought by ambulance to West Virginia but an infection had set in and Semmes was in great pain until his death on July 10. His blood-stained coat is in the American Civil War Museum in Richmond, VA. He was buried at home in Columbus, Georgia at Linwood Cemetery. Semmes was just 48 years old at the time of his passing. On July 9, he had written to his wife that he was severely injured during a charge at the Wheatfield but was out of danger and would write soon. But On July 10th, a letter was written by a West Virginia woman names Mary Oden detailing the Generals' last days for his wife and the care with which they gave his funerary arrangements and visitation,

"My Dear Mrs. Semmes,

I need hardly ask you to pardon me for addressing you in this your season of sore anguish and bereavement, it will be enough to state in apology for so doing, that your sainted husband fell asleep among us; it was a privilege to have his example before us, teaching us that the soldier of Christ has nothing to fear when passing through the dark valley. Dr. [Jacob Milton] Hadley, one of his surgeons, remarked to him that he bore his sufferings with great calmness, his reply was, I am endeavouring to bear them like a Christian philosopher; even when suffering severe pain he seemed to take pleasure in conversing and after he became so ill talked constantly of his family.

In a conversation with him, he told me that he thought he would write the dispatch to be sent to you himself as you would feel less uneasy. I suggested that it might be taxing his strength too far, he wrote but little however; you have I suppose received it, but we thought you would like to have the original, we fortunately obtained it from the operator here, you will find it enclosed with several locks of hair in this letter. I know by experience how hard it is to resign a friend from whom we have been separated for a long time, whom he had fondly hoped to see again; that they should die far from home and among strangers adds keenly to our grief, but you my dear friend in affliction, will derive infinite comfort from the knowledge that his brother, your nephew and a friend that loved him tenderly, when he breathed his last were with him; he passed away just as Dr. Pryor a Presbyterian minister had opened the Testament to read to him.

To a minister who was with him earlier in the evening he expressed his willingness to die; his only regret was leaving his wife and children. Much very much sympathy is felt for you all; I have thought so much of your daughters, I too am fatherless, yes even worse than that an orphan indeed, but little more than a year has passed since our dear Mother was numbered with the dead; my dear Father has been dead a number of years and I know what it is to be without that fatherly love and protection which the heart ever yearns for. Excuse me for referring to my own trouble, I only do it in order that you may feel that you have the warmest sympathy of those who know how to sympathize, because they too have trod affliction's path.

I wish you could see the quantities of beautiful flowers brought here this morning; for fear you may not be able again to look upon the deceased, I will tell you the arrangement, for no particular is trifling concerning those we love; a large bouquet of white flowers and evergreens was placed upon his bosom, white jessamine, clematis, and ivy were placed around the sides of the coffin near his head, on the outside two bouquets similar [inserted: to the first] were placed, one at the foot, the other below the glass, in the middle his coat and sword have been laid. His remains are laid in the sitting room according to Captain Cody's request, as it takes some little time to make arrangements, he preferred it to the parlors.

Your husband desired Mr. Cleveland to find out each of our names in order to tell you, our family consists of my Aunt Mrs. Pendleton, Mr. & Mrs. Allen, (my brother in law and sister) my sister Kate, my brother and myself; we have a friend Miss Murphy who was with us during his sickness. His friends now make efficient nurses that we could not do much, Kate prepared herself what little he eat while here; he came on Sunday morning July 7th [5th] about eleven o'clock, he rested better he thought that night than usual; the next morning he seemed better; in the evening my sister took him some raspberries and cream which he seemed to enjoy very much, he talked to her sometime about Virginia and Georgia.

Thursday evening between three and four we thought he was dying, a surgeon and minister were both sent for, once he asked what time it was on being told that it was three, he said "by quarter past three I hope to be with Christ."

We told Mr. Hanson, that he was far away from Christ that he had not come up to His standard, but he was willing to die and ascribed his conversion to your example. I have been this minute in relating as far as possible all that relates to the departed, for fear that you may not hear all, for gentlemen sometimes forget little things that transpire, then perhaps Mr. Cleveland may not be able to go to you, every word I know is treasured up as a precious memorial in the heart's casket and a twice told tale is not unwelcome when it concerns our beloved ones. While I write my heart is saddened by the thought that you are unconscious as yet of your irreparable loss. I wish you could be here, but God has ordered it otherwise, and may He give you grace patiently and resignedly to say, "Thy will be done."

In conclusion my dear Mrs. Semmes allow me to say, that what little we could do to conduce to your husband's comfort has been a great pleasure; we saw him first two weeks before his death passing through with his Brigade, his appearance struck us so forcibly that Captain Cheever, his commissary whom we had known before asked us if we would like to make his acquaintance, we then invited him to tea, his duties prevented his acceptance of the invitation, Captain Cody came with Dr Told & Capt. Cheever and though we had not known the General he seemed very far from a stranger when brought among us. He has passed away but his spirit is now enjoying perfect peace; we mourn not for the dead but the living: for those who will grieve sadly that the privilege of ministering to the departed was denied them accept the love and deep sympathy of each member of our family, praying again that God may strengthen you even as he did him.

I remain with much love your sympathizing friend.

Mary Oden

One little circumstance I have forgotten; a few moments before the General died, he asked for his sword, laying it across his arm, he asked again for his Testament he took it and with it in his hands expired, they would have left it so, but that he had asked that you should have it. Oh! if all our warriors might die as he did, death would be robbed of half its sting.

PS -- You will also find a few evergreens, taken from the bouquets laid upon the coffin my sister thought you would value them."

The final letter regarding Semmes brings that touch of humanity to the losses at Wheatfield. A high-ranking officer would often get detailed accounts of their death delivered home, but it's safe to say this went beyond the bounds of protocol. Semmes was deeply cared for by his family and his men.

Ultimately, the rebels had brought six brigades, all of them filled with Georgians to fight the Union's 13 brigades and there was a 30% casualty rate for all the 20,444 engaged. The Wheatfield's legacy was born as one of the most violent, deadly, and horrible examples of warfare in the Civil War rivaled only by the Cornfield at Antietam and both defined by the amount of Georgia men engaged. Georgia was with Confederate companions in the Wheatfield from Texas and South Carolina but Georgia's role at Gettysburg became most immortalized in the Wheatfield and Devil's Den on that blood-stained ground.

Woods by Gettysburg Wheatfield, 2022

For me, I believe fully that the Wheatfield is the most haunted location at Gettysburg. When I go there, I can hear the moans coming from the earth, and I have felt grabs upon my ankle from someone desperately looking to go home, get help or talk to someone they love one last time. I can hear their cries for their family in the air. It is the location on the battlefield where I hear the cannon's firing from a distant time and where I often play some music for the soldiers that they may recognize as I sit upon what was once a blood-stained field and think of them. Reenactors have tried to spend the night only to leave shellshocked and unable to sleep on the Wheatfield hearing whispers in their ear. The whispers are indeed quite a real supernatural phenomenon as they sound hushed and coming from the wood lines all around the Wheatfield. For some poor soldiers, July 2, 1863's horrors rage on. Interestingly, historian and author, Mark Nesbitt, has documented that if you sit there long enough you may see the famous "Phantom

Regiment," that has had at least half a dozen witnesses so far, marching from the Wheatfield to Little Round Top, perhaps it was Georgia pushing through to the Devil's Den and beyond.

Devil's Den gets a lot of attention for its name – mostly based on its rock formation but it was the site of some severe conflict. Initially held by the Union, the Georgians of Benning's Brigade of the 2nd, 15th, 17th and 20th Georgia regiments. Benning's Brigade arrived around 4 PM on July 2, just hours before the conflict in the Wheatfield in rear of two other brigades to capture the Devils Den and were able to take prisoners and three guns from the 4th New York Battery. As they approached the Devil's Den monstrous rock location, Benning called out,

> "Give them hell boys, give them hell!"

By all accounts they did just that in the capture of the location. The next day they held the Devil's Den until late in the evening when ordered to retire but the 15th Georgia, due to mistake of orders did not retire directly and moved northward into Union forces where they suffered a huge loss. They lost approximately 509 from Benning's Georgia Brigade out of a presence of 1,500. One account states 519 out of 1,420 were lost with a casualty rate of 36%. The 20th Georgia and 1st Texas were credited with a lot of the guns taken from New York, but Benning's after-action report credits his Brigade with doing so not the 1st Texas.

As for the 15th Georgia, a famous photograph, *The Home of a Rebel Sharpshooter*, taken by Alexander Gardner shortly after the battle depicts a deceased Confederate soldier laid out between the rocks. After careful study of the battle, the uniform and more, many at Gettysburg believe this to be a photograph of a man from the 15th Georgia, whose death agony was immortalized on film. Old beliefs believe that photographs capture a bit of your soul – but what about photographs of those already dead? This

The Home of A Rebel Sharpshooter, Gettysburg, 1863 by Alexander Gardner

photograph does seem to do just that.

Devil's Den is said to be haunted by a Confederate who may help to shield visitors from incoming Yankee attack or even help to give them directions. The phantom is usually described as looking like a hippie, or ragged in tatters with long hair and bare feet. Some have assumed he is a Texan and perhaps he is the 1st Texas who joined the Georgia Boys at Devil's Den but maybe yet he's one of the men of the 15th who conquered the location only to be mercilessly slaughtered after.

Speaking of merciless slaughter, we have to finish up the battle of Gettysburg by discussing the March to Cemetery Ridge, better known as Pickett's Charge.

Pickett's Charge, more or less, became a death march for the Confederate Soldiers as they walked a mile-long wide in perfect formation across an open stretch of field toward a fully prepared Union line organized by General Mead. Whether Lee had faulty intelligence provided or was not thinking clearly due to the recent loss of his beloved General Stonewall Jackson, or tactically was very sure this would work, based on movements from Wright's Brigade on July 2 remains the subject of much debate.

Georgia native, Colonel E.P Alexander who had been an artillery instructor expressed his discomfort before Pickett's Charge and concern to Georgia General James Longstreet. He said,

> "Even if this is attack is successful it can only be so at a very cost,"

to which Longstreet agreed but Lee was firm in his stance that day. Again, something in Lee's mind convinced him otherwise and it changed the Confederacy for the rest of the war. Just after 1:00 PM in the blazing sun on July 3, Pickett's Charge took place resulting in a decision still discussed by historians and military strategists. Robert E. Lee was known for his tactical insight and intelligence but Pickett's Charge changes everything. The charge happened on the third day of battle and as Lee sent his men to what he believed was a weakened center they met the full artillery, battery and infantry of the Union army. Some soldiers were said to have thought of running back to shelter as the shells flew, but instead walked backwards knowing they'd die but at least it would be honorable if they weren't shot in the back. They couldn't see in front of them as they approached the "Dead Angle," anyhow. Instead, they heard if they were to be shot as the bullets whizzed by their head and the cannon obliterated people in front of them with volleys. Lee was said to have heard yelling as he watched the lines from the rear and thought for a moment,

> "Did our men make it?"

Only to find out that it was their yells of death and suffering amidst the Union cheers of success in battle. The Confederates fought for less than an hour and suffered 6,555 casualties in Pickett's Charge of the 12,000 who went forward.

General Ambrose Wright's Brigade of Georgians from the 3rd, 22nd and 48th Regiments as well as the 2nd Battalion Georgia infantry were sent forward, the day prior, on a sort of reconnaissance mission. It was on July 2 in the early evening from their lines toward the Cemetery Ridge when Lee tried to make his plans for the next day and they went forward. They were able to dislodge Union troops, capture several guns and prisoners and break the Union line south of the Bloody Angle. Soon the flanks, however, were not able to keep up and they were both assailed violently which forced survivors of Wright's Brigade to leave. There were approximately 1,450 present that day and many of them died in large number on July 2 during that mission. In fact, as the Union fell into line the next day on the same ground, it was said from war historian Eric Nideorost that there was a

> "Gagging, nauseating smell coming from the unburied bodies of Confederate dead, Georgians from Brig. Gen. A.R. Wright's brigade. Scores of bodies lay just beyond the regiment's position, corpses with blacked faces and rapidly swelling torsos decomposing in the torrid heat. Dead artillery horses, their legs splayed in grotesque postures, added to the noisome stench."

In fact, most casualties on the Cemetery Ridge for Wright's Brigade occurred on July 2 and involved Georgians, those unable to capture guns. They estimate they had a casualty count of at least 873 out of 1,450 by the end of July 3. Despite this cutting of troops, Wright reported in his after-action report on the 2nd, before Pickett's Charge was decided, that he was able to make it to the crest could describe Union troop placements having made it to the "high-water" mark despite their losses on the left flank. Wright then personally reported to Lee that they had been able to charge up the hill easily enough. As such, Lee felt with reinforcements from Pickett's Units, he could reattempt the next day. Lee planned to use his artillery to cause enough of a gap in a line that he assumed would not be as fleshed out as it was. Wright's Brigade often gets the credit as making it the furthest in Pickett's Charge but that is often debated as their charge was on July 2. On July 3, they did participate in the Pickett's Charge as cover for retreating troops where they did have to advance 600 yards before being moved. Their marker sits on West Confederate Ave. near Cemetery Ridge.

Little Round Top from Devil's Den, 2022

The rebel men of Pickett's Charge claimed to have seen deceased General Stonewall Jackson, almost urging them to retreat as they marched forward, trying to save their lives, dressed in Union uniform as if to warn them what they were walking into. Was the spirit of Stonewall trying to get Robert E. Lee's attention? The Union men had seen the specter of General George Washington guiding them to Little Round Top upon their arrival. It stands to reason that the Confederates would see their late fallen hero and he would come to them in this desperate hour.

I often feel like the Ghost of Stonewall Jackson has a large part to play in the Civil War after his death, the absence of him in the flesh and the soul of the man trying to aid from the other side and reckon with the ongoing war and his part in it. But for those who visit Gettysburg and Cemetery Ridge and Pickett's Charge, know that it is overwhelming for the senses. People capture images of specters running across the road and through the field, they feel overcome by nausea and sadness, not even able to step foot near the ground. If you go to the Robert E. Lee Virginia monument and look across to General Mead's horse in the distance marking Union Lines just past the Angle later known as the Bloody Angle, you can feel a pit in your stomach and begin to see the line march forward. When you are on the Union side at the angle and walk out in the area where the clash occurred most violently, and begin to walk backwards as they did, time stops and stands stills. I have walked it and felt them march in time next to me, the earth vibrate with cannonade, heard the screams, and felt as if someone was falling in front of me or I just next to them. It's terrifying and you almost feel as if you are going to be pulled back into another time, in the heat of battle but you will never return. There's not a sense that the spirits see the visitor as vividly as we do them, but rather that that the battle is still occurring. It seems that in Gettysburg there is some sort of vortex where we are all just one breath away from being pulled back to 1863, into an imprint in time that will forever cycle in that small, rural Pennsylvania time.

Gettysburg's reputation as one of the most haunted is well-deserved. The deadliest combat in the Civil War caused 51,000 casualties in three days. The Georgians were also fighting at Culp's Hill and in Iverson's Charge on the first day of battle at Seminary Ridge, as well as the fight at Barlow's Knoll led by future Governor of Georgia, John B. Gordon against young Barlow and his New Yorkers. And no matter what ancestor or soldier you care to visit from Georgia at Gettysburg, if they were lost there, you'll feel their soul guide you.

Of note, Georgia native, Alfred Iverson's Charge of North Carolinians was an incredibly deadly event for the Georgia General and his men. Early on July 1, they were formed into lines and ordered to march toward a line of trees about 300 yards away in a move to outflank the Union First Corps at Oak Hill on Seminary Ridge. Historians can't sort out why Iverson did not deploy an advance line of skirmishers to prevent ambush and instead sent his men all at once – ignorance? Overconfidence? Iverson was quickly overcome with regret from which he would never recover as the whole event turned into a prophetic glimpse of what would be the totality of Pickett's Charge. A line of Union troops from behind a stone wall rose up and poured volleys of fire into the rebels at point-blank range. The North Carolinians were shot down in the lines they had marched and within just a few minutes there were at least 500 of them were dead in the grass from the first volley alone.

> 'They nobly fought and died without a man running to the rear. No greater gallantry and heroism has been displayed during this war,"

wrote Iverson. A few straggled to leave and survive. Iverson was not wounded but after this event he suffered a nervous breakdown and was relieved of his command and instead assisted with the Georgia Militias in protecting their home in 1864. The North

Carolinians were buried in trenches quickly dug in the spots they fell and people could see the trenches where the graves were for years to come and labeled them "Iverson's Pits." The farmer who owned the land claimed wheat grew tallest in that part of the field but that he would always hear the gunfire, the yells and see the ghostly specters of the men forever after.

Many bodies in Gettysburg were exhumed for burial in the 1870s but the farmhands continued to see the ghosts of the Iverson's Pits. In fact, Iverson's pits are considered the oldest reputedly haunted site of the battlefield (excluding, of course, the stories of George Washington and Stonewall Jackson). The guides of Gettysburg say that at dusk if you look out from the eternal flame toward the pits you can see the men begin to line up and then begin to see them all fall one by one in formation – reliving the ghostly event. Others report hundreds of white handkerchiefs fluttering above the ground in mist or spots that disappear.

I visited Iverson's Pits just after sunset and stood near the eternal flame. When my husband was separated from me taking photographs of the flame and I stood near where Iverson's charge began and looked back, I saw a man with dark hair, dark eyes and a fearful look. Was it me he saw? Was it past me? He began to move forward, and I called out for my husband; all of this captured on an audio recorder. I felt uncomfortable, though not threatened. The vision was so vivid I got into the car and explained what had happened to my husband who raced over when he heard my panic. As began to pull away in the car my husband asked me if the man was still there. I didn't see him as vividly; I could sense the man by the car window to the passenger seat, so I replied that he was. Suddenly, the indicator light that something was within close range of the vehicle began to beep though nothing else was there. Was it Iverson stuck in that moment or one of his men wandering looking for aid not knowing what happened so quickly? I think of that moment often and of the Georgia man who could never move past that moment in his life, and the 900 who christened Gettysburg opening day with their sacrificial blood on the land of above the Mason-Dixon line.

As for Barlow's Knoll, Officer and future Georgia Governor John Gordon was worried about Union General Barlow in so much as it looked like he would succumb to his battle injuries from July 1st. Gordon kindly made arrangements for Barlow's wife, a Union nurse to pass through the lines for her husband's final moments and left the scene to find out later that Barlow survived. Gordon would have his own near-death experience more than once and Barlow too thought he had died later in the war only to find out he had not. It made for a peculiar post-war legend. For more on Alfred Iverson and John Gordon – Please see Part III on Men.

Georgia at Gettysburg: tales of hope, tales of courage, tales of death, tales of fear. When you visit Gettysburg, try to take everything in, all the feelings and stories in and allow the presence of the men of the Peach State to surround you in their embrace as they share with you, their story.

Notable Regiments of Fighting Georgia Spirit

With so many thousands of Georgia men and dozens and dozens or regiments, hand-picking battles and regiments is no easy task as the spirit of them all can be felt throughout the country. The aforementioned regiments and battle highlights seemingly only touch the surface of depth. However, before we close out this section, I wanted to give a shout out to some other fascinating regiments and people from the Goober State.

27th Georgia

125% Casualty Rate

The 27th Georgia, of which my own 3x Great-Grandfather was a Private and died at the young age of 20 – 21-years-old in Orange, Virginia early in the war from disease, is a favorite of regiment mine for several reasons, personal and historical. Suffice to say, the 27th is a particularly hearty regiment. The little regiment that mustered out on Halloween 1861 into Virginia had arrived without any arms and as such were assigned to build a bridge over the Occoquan River near Manassas. They had suffered losses early in the war from disease and during their time in Williamsburg, Yorktown, Seven Pines, etcetera. And then, like many of their Georgia brethren they met the Bloodiest Day in American History in Sharpsburg and suffered 60% casualties having served much of their time in Cornfield. They were lightly engaged in Fredericksburg and then gallantly took part in Stonewall Jackson's flank attack in May of 1863. The regiment moved to Charleston Harbor for the end of 1863 into early 1864 when they were assigned to Colquitt's Brigade and fought in the Battle of Olustee on February 20, 1864, where they suffered seventy-four casualties before their involvement just months later in the battle at Drewry's Bluff and Cold Harbor. Ultimately, they joined the Siege of

Petersburg in June 1864 losing more officers and participated in the Battle of The Crater on July 30 and in early 1865 jumped right into combat with the second battle of Fort Fisher, Battle of Bentonville and Battle of Durham Station. Coming in with nothing in the way weaponry, it didn't take long for the bridge builders to become fighters. They put in more than their fair share of battle time and suffered a mind-blowing casualty rate of 125% due to some men being wounded more than four times.

According to descendant, Vernon House, the Redwine United Methodist Church in Gainesville still stands and honors the 27th Georgia Company D. A monument to the 27th stands there. Mr. House stated that his family still has reunions there at the church and that the tradition started as the 27th had their reunions there for years after the war. At one point in the 1930's there was a totem pole commemorating the end of the war and showing Grant and Lee shaking hands but some did not like it and it was later burned down. For the Civil War enthusiast and Georgia soldier soul searcher (try to say that three times past), the church should be added to any list for visits through Georgia.

Sketch of Redwine Methodist Church, Home of Company D of 27th GA, Date Unknown (Provided by Vernon House)

44th Georgia

Stonewall Jackson's Flank, Spotsylvania and Highest Casualty Rate for the South

The 44th Georgia mustered out 1,115 men and suffered 900 casualties in the war – 350 killed and 450 wounded, a terrible casualty rate to be sure. They mustered out of Camp Stephens in Griffin, Georgia in March of 1862 and were quickly engaged in the Seven Days Battle and then Battle of Beaver Dam Creek where they lost 335 casualties out of 524 men brought there with their Colonel being mortally wounded and their Lt. Colonel being wounded. They then went to Gaines' Mill and Malvern Hill where they had 65 men out of 142 registered as casualties by the end. For the summer there was movement around into Maryland where they fought at South Mountain and then in Sharpsburg where they were posted at the Mumma Farm and Dunker Church, losing 17 men to death, 65 wounded and four missing. Just months later they fought at Fredericksburg with minimal casualties. In May of 1864, the 44th Georgia were at the Battle of Chancellorsville, which in many ways but them in Civil War fame and infamy. Post – Chancellorsville, just two months later they fought at Gettysburg with 364 men, losing 77 casualties.

But, circling back, what happened in Chancellorsville in May of 1863? And what happened to the 44th when they returned a year later to the same spot for the Battle of Wilderness and Spotsylvania

Battle of Chancellorsville by Kurz & Allison, 1889 (Library of Congress)

Courthouse? In early 1863 the Georgia Brigade including the 44th moved to Rodes Division of Stonewall Jackson's Corps and on May 1, 1863, they led the flanking on the Orange Plank Road near Chancellorsville, assaulting the Union near Chancellor House and driving the Union away. They suffered thirteen killed and sixty-four wounded. It was the next day on May 2, that the 44th Georgia participated in Jackson's famous flank March and the smashing charge in the afternoon where they captured several prisoners and pieces of artillery. Jackson's flanking maneuver went down in military history, and it involved quite a gamble. Jackson, with 30,000 troops, and the 44th Georgia being in the center front of this plan followed a series of country roads and wood paths to reach the Union right and Lee remained with 14,000 in infantry over their miles long trek to divert attention. Then, used his strength to "smash" forward and fracture the Union into pieces. Jackson did just that, and at first, Union troops did notice Jackson trying to get the right flank but because of the maneuvers and long pathway to get there, the Union began to believe Lee and Jackson were withdrawing and began to worry less about an attack on their forces. Jackson stayed steady and true, as the Union grew to feel less in peril, his commitment to the plan his worked. On the afternoon of May 2, the Confederates under Stonewall arrived at long last. They sounded a bugle from the woods and the soldiers having marched miles and miles let out their guttural Rebel Yell as they erupted from the trees to scared Union soldiers. A Massachusetts man recalled,

> "Along the road it was pandemonium, and on the side of the road it was chaos."

Stonewall Jackson Print ,1871 (Library of Congress)

The 44th suffered 121 casualties at Chancellorsville.

Chancellorsville was an enormous victory for the Confederacy, but it came at great cost including the loss of their beloved General and military genius, Thomas "Stonewall' Jackson. The mastermind behind the flanking maneuver was shot by friendly fire when some men from North Carolina mistook him as Union cavalry in the wooded darkness that night. His wounds worsened as he was carried miles to be cared for and was dropped several times. Despite amputation, infection and pneumonia set in and Stonewall was lost. The burial of his arm can be found not far from the Chancellorsville site and the exact spot of his mortal wounding can be visited on the battlefield. You can also travel to the place where he died. The Ghost of Stonewall Jackson hangs heavy over the Chancellorsville Battlefield and over the Confederacy with many believing that the loss of this General was the beginning of the end of the Confederacy and of Robert E. Lee's genius as well. They were something of a dream team.

It was just a year after Chancellorsville that the 44th Georgia composed of men from the East and South of Atlanta found themselves walking among the dead they lost a year before in the area where they lost their beloved General Jackson. In May of 1864 at Spotsylvania, the brigade was at the center of a bulge known as the "Mule Shoe." The 44th Georgia was once again in the center and had entrenchments just 200 yards from disorienting pine forests that did not allow them to see what the Union was doing. On May 10, the Union, now with Grant on their side, launched an overwhelming attack and the 44th Georgia under Doles sector suffered an outnumbered attack of five-to-one with bayonets fixed against them. After heavy losses, the Georgia boys were forced to yield and then later Georgia native, Gordon was able to restore the Confederate line. However, at this point the 44th realized they had suffered 26 killed, 28 wounded and 182 captured. One company lost thirty-eight out sixty-three men. (At Spotsylvania, the Confederates also suffered the near fatal wounding of General Longstreet oddly also by friendly fire in the same spot as General Jackson.) Never fully able to truly regain their strength, in the Confederacy after this engagement especially in the 44th Georgia, they bravely persevered in the battle and the war.

They suffered a

"steady hemorrhage of casualties,"

in the Shenandoah Valley Campaign and were present with just 62 men for the final assault and truce at Appomattox Courthouse. The 62 men, two days later out of the original 1,115 when it was declared that they suffered more casualty in action than any other regiment on the Southern side.

Those who visit Chancellorsville, say they often feel the spirits there and at Spotsylvania in their deathly spots especially the Mule Shoe and often leave offerings of tobacco and jerky for the spirits there who may rest there, in no sense of peace.

Confederate dead of General Ewell's Corp who attacked Union Lines on May 19th, 1864 at Spotsylvania, Lined up for Burial at Alsop Farm (Wikimedia Commons)

23rd Georgia

Capture at Chancellorsville

Georgians at Chancellorsville extended beyond the sacrifices of the 44th and the 23rd Georgia. The 23rd Georgia was at the tail end of the column of the flank march by Jackson and was attacked by Union soldiers from Sickles as they appeared to be leaving the battlefield. They displayed a desperate rear-guard action but ultimately several were captured. They were stuck at Catharine Furnace since the Georgians had fallen back to the protection of a railroad embankment. Yet still being visible inside the woods, the Union sharpshooters outflanked them to capture many of them. There are two markers for the 23rd Georgians at Chancellorsville. They had 275 men captured prior to continuing on in the war with limited fighting power at Drewry's Bluff and Cold Harbor and encountering more loss in the Siege at Petersburg. Prior to Chancellorsville, they had already suffered nearly 100 casualties at Antietam as well.

24th Georgia

"Confederate Irish Brigade" & Irish Jasper Greens - Georgia Militia

Many readers may be familiar with the Irish Brigade of the Union – men from regiments in New York, Massachusetts and Pennsylvania of Irish descent and birth came together and fought together in the war. The "Irish Brigade" of the South is less defined in its size or number of regiment but the nevertheless existed in two regiments – the 10th Tennessee and the 24th Georgia Volunteers – the 24th Georgia being quite famous for their participation in the war, especially in Fredericksburg, when they fought their fellow Irishmen from the Union Irish Brigade.

It is widely debated between war historians and modern culture exactly how Irish the 24th Georgia was. It seems Georgia's 24th was defined a great deal by their bonafide Irish Colonel, Robert McMillan of County Antrim in Northern Ireland. Born in Ireland in 1805, McMillan was a new settler in Georgia in Elbert County and worked as a grocer and dry goods merchant before serving as a State Senator between 1855 – 1854. In 1861, at the beginning of the war, he was appointed Colonel of the 24th and brought with him his son, who was the Unit's Major. After fighting at Fredericksburg, McMillan even unsuccessfully ran for Confederate Congress and then resigned his commission in the following year on January 9, 1864. However, he joined right back in the fray when the war came to Georgia's doorstep as the Colonel

Portrait of Colonel Robert McMillan

(FindAGrave.com)

of the 4th Georgia Militia. He died shortly after the war in 1861 in Clarkesville, Georgia and was buried in the "Old Cemetery."

It was McMillan's account of Fredericksburg that went down in infamy and perhaps led movies like *Gods and Generals* to perpetuate the Irish Brigade as Cobb's Brigade or Legion which was not the case – everything definitive about the Irishness of the 24th came from McMillan. *The Richmond Whig*, just after Christmas in 1862, ran a story about the "*Gallant Irishman at Fredericksburg*," "

"A GALLANT IRISHMAN AT FREDERICKSBURG

The following extract from a private letter will show that Meagher met his match at Fredericksburg in a gallant son of the Emerald Isle, Colonel Robert McMillan, of the 24th Georgia. We should like to see McMillan at the head of the lamented Cobb's brigade, pitted against Meagher or Corcoran in an open field:

"But the rejoicing ceased for a time, and mourning sat on every countenance, as four grief-stricken litter bearers passed down the lines, bearing the heroic Cobb, who had fallen in the first charge of the enemy. Lieutenant Colonel Cook, commanding Phillip's Georgia Legion, was killed at this period of the action. A fixed resolution seemed at once to possess every heart, to avenge the death-wound given to their General, and it devolved upon Col. Robert McMillan, of the 24th Georgia Regiment, to lead them in the effort. An opportunity now offered. A column, stronger and heavier than the first, was seen to advance. Flash after flash was seen upon the opposite river bank. Shell after shell fell around us, which were responded to from the heights in our rear. Colonel McMillan directed the small arms to cease until the enemy should come within musket range. The artillery continued its thunder, the musketry remaining silent, till the enemy came within fire of our shortest range guns. Soon leaden hail commenced pouring from the clouds of smoke before us. The Colonel passed along the lines surveying the movements of the enemy, when suddenly, at his command, the brigade rose and sent a volley into the ranks of the foe, which carried ruin in its way. Again and again was the assault renewed, and again and again was it repulsed, with tremendous slaughter. For the troops, the position chosen was an admirable one, but on the part of the officer who did his duty, there was required the utmost coolness and courage. This, Colonel McMillan certainly manifested. While he was passing along the line, waving his sword, and encouraging his men, they seemed to catch the spirit of their leader, and redouble their efforts, while his own regiment turned, in the thickest of the fight, and gave him three hearty cheers. He possesses the confidence of his troops. They love him, and, if need be, will follow him to the death. In the battle of Fredericksburg, he won a laurel wreath, to which fresh leaves will doubtless be added, when the tocsin shall again summon him to the field."

There's no doubt of McMillan's Irish homeland and his affection for North Georgia. The 24th Georgia, made mostly of mountain residents were arguably mostly American though many were of Irish descent more than Irish birth like McMillan. But McMillan's legacy so large, it was defining for the regiment. And it was he inspired the cinematic reference in *Gods and Generals* and in legend where it was "recorded" that the Confederates said when they saw the Irish Brigade attacking at Marye's Heights in Fredericksburg,

"Oh God, what a pity! Here come Meagher's fellows."

That implied of course the pity of killing one's fellow countrymen. The South had no shortage of Scots-Irish immigrants. In fact, that is most of my familial descent and I even hail from the Clan McMillan. Maybe Robert is a long-lost cousin. But again, please remember it is still disputed how Irish the 24th was.

What's my opinion? They were Irish in heart, in stubbornness and fearlessness. So, whether they had Irish DNA or not simply mattered not. They served in battles throughout the war suffering great casualties so much so that only sixty survivors surrendered at Appomattox in 1865. There were at least thirty-six casualties at Fredericksburg for the regiment and 875 at Chancellorsville. They had fought at Gettysburg before moving to Georgia with Longstreet and luckily avoided the engagement Chickamauga. They had forty-five casualties at Antietam prior to that. These men were seasoned in battle and in respect for one another. Of famed Irish loyalty, there was no shortage.

So, whether the Irish Brigade's aka the 24th Georgia's heritage began and ended at McMillan or was truly in the bloodlines of those who enlisted remains to be proven, their heart and their impact on history and the modern narrative is timeless and meaningful.

There were also the Irish Jasper Greens part of the Georgia Militia many of whom were Irish of birth. They were young, Irish immigrants who had arrived to Savannah in search of work and formed their own military unit in 1842. When the war took off, they were at Fort Pulaski until it was captured and then the young Catholics move station to Fort Jackson until they were needed to fight in the Atlanta Campaign where they fought at Kennesaw Mountain and other battles to great casualties. Many are buried in Catholic cemeteries in and around Savannah.

Black Georgians in the Civil War

Georgia had a large enslaved population, to say the least, and many of these enslaved peoples had to await their freedom at the war's end unless they made it to free territory after the Emancipation Proclamation and that journey was hairy and treacherous. There were believed to be about 3,500 Black Georgians who served in the Union Army and Navy during the course of the war. These men primarily served in South Carolinian regiments as their enlistment took place on the Union occupied Sea Islands of Georgia and in North Carolina (later territory for 40 acres and a mule policy.) As the war waged on and Sherman marched through Georgia in the Atlanta Campaign and beyond, they were able to enlist in northwestern Georgia and southern Tennessee by the middle of 1864. These efforts were led by Colonel Ruben Mussey of Nashville. And in July to September of 1864, the 44th U.S. Colored Infantry was stationed in Rome, Georgia to recruit. Approximately 800 were enlisted and commanded under the white Colonel, Lewis Johnson at that time.

Earlier in the war, when the Confederates surrendered Fort Pulaski in Savannah in 1862, the enslaved Georgians began to make their way to the Union lines if they could do so. And, a man named Abraham Murchison, a Savannah preacher who had

At Port Royal, South Carolina, the 1st South Carolina Colored Infantry receives its regimental color (Civil War Research Engine at Dickinson College)

escaped slavery, recruited 150 formerly enslaved men for a black regiment organized in Hilton Head, South Carolina. Though it was disbanded, a company of thirty-eight men was sent to St. Simons Island in Georgia where they helped other enslaved who had runaway defend themselves against attack. Later in 1862, Union authorities authorized black enlistment and the St. Simons men along with thirty to forty other recruits joined in Company A of the First South Carolina Volunteers. They were also the bulk of Company E and were in smaller regiments throughout the Union. By June of 1863, there was special draft for the 3rd South Carolina Volunteers, part of which was in Fort Pulaski, Georgia and also just off the Georgia border in Florida where more black men were recruited and then consolidated with the Fourth and Fifth South Carolina Volunteers in the 21st Colored Infantry. It was estimated to be more than 300 men, when the ranks were filled by Sherman's arrival in December of 1864.

Despite being an aggressive Union commander, General

Sherman was hardly a great emancipator or equality advocate. In fact, many accounts state that he was just the opposite and his presence in Georgia wasn't particularly helpful in any way for the blacks who were enlisting or endeavoring to be free. Of course, there were the events at Ebenezer Creek but moreover, Sherman, a described

> "reluctant liberator,"

wrote in derogatory terms about black people in his personal letters and was determined that black workers be laborers not soldiers and that his command remain exclusively white. He actually issued a field order on June 3, 1864, forbidding officers to recruit black soldiers who were employed by the army in any capacity.

Of course, the 44th recruitment efforts were underway despite Sherman's feelings and in Dalton, there were Black soldiers on garrison duty on October 13, when Confederate General Hood's 40,000-man army ended up converging on the village and cutting off avenues of retreat. Skirmishing between the newly enlisted Black Union and the seasoned Confederates left many casualties, but Hood did not restrict any of his men who acted with extra aggression. So, Johnson, withdrew his Black troops despite their

> "greatest anxiety to fight,"

and surrendered the garrison. Sadly, this sent the 600 enlisted black Americans back into slavery or laboring on fortifications in Alabama and Mississippi. Others became war prisoners in Columbus and Griffin, Georgia not released until May of 1865 and released in deplorable conditions. Many Black veterans never spoke of their time in service after this, as they did not want reprisal from their Confederate sympathizer neighbors.

At the conclusion of the war, more black enlistment did take place in Savannah and surrounding areas where black Georgians were able to go into service in the Navy and serve on Union vessels.

Did any black Georgians fight FOR the Confederacy, one may wonder? The short answer is, yes. The long answer is, yes, but we don't know how many. We know that somewhere between 3,000 and 10,000 black men fought for the Confederacy and that there were 20,000 to 50,000 black laborers in addition to this. This information has not been broken down state-by-state according to a Harvard study. Some Southerners have even made the assertion that the South knew slavery was wrong and was working toward the end of it by the time the war broke out and one man even was quoted to say.

"The greatest danger to slavery was the Southern Heart."

This particular sentiment, if at all true, backs the much-disputed belief and/or theory that the Confederates were fighting more for state's rights and economic reasons than the perpetuation of this terrible institution of slavery. Frederick Douglass even spoke with a fugitive slave who had witnessed black units formed in Georgia, South Carolina and Virginia for the Confederacy and made an interesting discovery. It seemed that these black units were more light-skinned men who had been freed and were trying to identify and fit in with white culture. Others account for a conflict of interest, fighting for the Confederacy and working for them, some with choice, some without, while hoping the Union won. The issue, ironically is not black and white when it comes to blacks serving in the Confederate Army. But we can say for certain, that Black Georgians fought on both sides of the American Civil War.

Children & Siblings of the Confederacy (The Freeman Brothers)

It's no strange thing to hear about young soldiers. The average fighting age of most soldiers was late teens to early 20's and teenage soldiers fought on both sides of the war. Remarkably, from Georgia, however, was the proclaimed youngest Confederate and his name was David Bailey Freeman, born May 1, 1851 in Ellijay, Georgia. He was one of ten children his parents had, eight of whom were boys and his older brother, Madison, raised a cavalry company in their home county, Gilmer County. When Madison mustered out, he was worried as he was crippled with "white swelling," that affected his joints. As such, David accompanied him in the Fulton Blues. Madison was just a young man of 20 years old and was elected Lieutenant. They organized into Smith's Legion. David accompanied him as an aide with permission from his mother and brother. His father had passed away. David later described his duties and said,

> "I went in at ten, entering in April 1862, as a marker for the 6th Georgia Cavalry; but as there was practically no drilling to do, in a month or two I was in the regular ranks, and did all the duties of a soldier…unless legitimately on some detachment or

other mission, never missed an engagement…which was nearly three years…I was armed with a short saber and two saddle pistols."

David Bailey Freeman, Youngest Confederate (Georgia Civil War Commission)

David served in Company D of the 6th Georgia and did survive the war.

Others of his elder Freeman brothers also enlisted in the war. 29-years-old at the start of the war, his brother, Wesley, was a Captain of the 25th North Carolina Infantry Regiment, Company C. Wesley survived the war and lived until 1891. His elder brother Jasper, just 23 years old at the start of the war was a Sergeant in the First Georgia Regulars and was killed early on in the conflict at The Battle of Second Manassas in August 1862, just 24 years old at the time of his death. David's foster brother Oscar, 25 years old at the start of the war and a 2nd Lieutenant in the 36th Georgia went missing after the war in 1876. Sadly, Madison, who David accompanied to war died in 1869 from the "white swelling" or yellow fever, not even yet 30 years old.

After the war, David was a newspaper publisher, editor and writer as well as a mayor of Calhoun, Cedartown and Cartersville! David's first election to Mayor was in 1876 at the young age of 25-years-old, and his first son was born that year. He continued his military service and became General of the Northern Brigade, Georgia Division, UCV. David lived to be 78 years old and passed on June 18, 1929. He was then buried in Cartersville at Oak Hill Cemetery.

As it turns out David truly was the youngest soldier of the entire Civil War as the youngest Union soldier was being reported at age twelve and no other soldier on the Confederacy claimed to be younger than David Freeman.

David's story doesn't just tell of brave children and brave mothers who sent their sons off to war at all ages knowing they may never return but the tale of brothers in war. Throughout Georgia and the Confederacy, throughout the Union as well, brothers in arms enlisted together. They had grown up together, played together, did chores and learned to be young adults together – if they got that far and then they went off to fight for their home together, to fight for their moms, their sisters, their fathers…and some if they were old enough their own wives and children. But their brotherhood would be what helped them to feel safe, to feel secure and to know they weren't alone. Brothers died together and survived together, some watched their brothers die or heard about it later if they weren't together. It's a horror to think of, and something that I, as a sister cannot even imagine. But I know this to be true as well, there is no one in this world that I feel more secure with than my siblings and no one I would rather go through a life-changing experience with than them. And, in that, I imagine these young boys felt the very same about their brothers and I take heart that at least they had each other in what was likely some of the worst years of their lives.

END VOLUME I

Continue in
Civil War Ghosts of Georgia
Part II

In the following book, we will look through a closer lens at some of soldiers and officers of Georgia whose stories left an impact not just physically but spiritually. We will also explore the museums, train tracks, fortifications, prisons and mountains where specters of the Civil War have become known and where legends were forever carved into infinitude. The heartbeats of history continue to echo in story and name in Volume Two.

BIBLIOGRAPHY

(Full Bibliography can be found in Part II)

ABOUT THE AUTHOR

Courtney McInvale is the founder of Seaside Shadows Haunted History Tours LLC, with locations throughout the East Coast and is a licensed tour guide, historian and published author. Courtney lost many ancestors to the Civil War and researching and writing about War between the States seems to be her destiny. She is is a New England native with Southern roots in the heart of Georgia. She spent 5 years in DC after completing her studies at Catholic University of America and the University College Dublin where she studied abroad, majoring in International Relations. After earning her degree, she worked for the FBI as an analyst, having been influenced by her time interning at NCIS for the Cold Case Homicide Unit. Then Courtney spent 2 years in Vermont working for the Department of Homeland Security and honing her investigative skills.

McInvale avidly studies histories of early American cultures and Celtic cultures specializing in rebellions/times of war. Her love for rebellion history dates to the studies of the American Civil War that began in childhood. Her father, a history major at the University of Georgia, had Courtney memorize the names of Civil War Generals by photograph before she turned seven. Courtney is also a practicing spirit medium able to communicate with spirits. She has frequently had experiences involving the supernatural. In Courtney's childhood home in central Connecticut, the inexplicable events were so extreme that the Warren family came to investigate and cleanse the house during her teenage years there.

Due to her haunting past and spirit communication, Courtney has always taken an interest in the unknown and has now put her sensitivities, investigative skills, love of history, and writing aspirations to work.

Courtney is also a realist amongst all things and believes no tour or book can be complete without corroborating information. Each book and tour she creates is inundated with historical facts to validate all the haunting occurrences surrounding the topic and to give deeper meaning to what a spiritual experience means. The truth is history can be haunting all on it's own and McInvale embraces this.

This is Courtney's second book for Haunted Road Media and second for the *Bury my Bones* series. Courtney is also the author of *Haunted Mystic* (2014) and *Revolutionary War Ghosts of Connecticut* (2016) published with the History Press/Arcadia Publishing. Courtney has been featured as a historian and medium on Travel Channel's *Portals to Hell* and as a medium on Travel Channel's *Ghost Adventures*. She hosts paranormal investigations and historical site fundraisers annually. Courtney loves spending time with her husband, Marty, her loving pets, her sisters and nieces and nephews. When she is not writing about Civil War Ghosts or hosting tours, you can find her traveling to Whiskey Myers and other Southern Rock concerts and festivals across the country.

Made in the USA
Columbia, SC
15 September 2024